Negotiation

Additional Praise for
NEGOTIATION

"Brilliantly, Max Bazerman highlights the need to adapt proven concepts of effective negotiation to new contexts involving culture, politics, relationships, economic strengths, and communication modes. Brilliantly, again, he doesn't just show us the need for this tailoring process; he also shows us how to do it optimally. The result is a tour de force presentation of the ways to apply negotiating wisdom wisely."

—ROBERT CIALDINI, *New York Times* bestselling author of *Influence*

"*Negotiation* is essential reading for anyone navigating today's complex negotiation landscape. Max Bazerman, one of the foremost authorities on negotiation, provides a new playbook for dealing with the economic, political, and cultural shifts reshaping the art of dealmaking. He blends timeless wisdom with innovative strategies, equipping readers to negotiate effectively in any context. Whether you're a seasoned professional or new to the negotiating table, *Negotiation* will revolutionize how you create and claim value in our rapidly changing world."

—MICHELE GELFAND, Stanford Graduate School of Business

"Max Bazerman is a giant in the study of negotiation and has written some of the most important and influential books on the subject. In this one, he has surpassed his own genius to address the most frequent question people have when they learn the principles of negotiation: but how does this apply to my situation? With memorable examples and wonderful anecdotes, Bazerman shows how. This book should be required reading for anyone who wants better collaborations and outcomes in their professional and personal relationships."

—DON A. MOORE, author of *Perfectly Confident: How to Calibrate Your Decisions Wisely*

"Max Bazerman is the apex negotiator among the world's most renowned negotiation experts—and his new book is a revelation. With his groundbreaking insights and meticulously researched strategies, he offers a masterclass in the art of negotiation in the post-pandemic landscape. This book is essential for anyone who aims to negotiate not just for advantage but to create value and achieve mutual success."

—LEIGH THOMPSON, author of *Negotiating the Sweet Spot:*
The Art of Leaving Nothing on the Table

Negotiation

The Game Has Changed

Max H. Bazerman

PRINCETON UNIVERSITY PRESS

PRINCETON & OXFORD

Published by Princeton University Press
41 William Street, Princeton, New Jersey 08540
99 Banbury Road, Oxford OX2 6JX

press.princeton.edu

All Rights Reserved

Library of Congress Cataloging-in-Publication Data

Names: Bazerman, Max H., author.
Title: Negotiation : the game has changed / Max H. Bazerman.
Description: Princeton : Princeton University Press, [2025] |
    Includes bibliographical references and index.
Identifiers: LCCN 2024035095 | ISBN 9780691249445 (hardback) |
    ISBN 9780691250311 (ebook)
Subjects: LCSH: Negotiation in business. | Negotiation. | BISAC: BUSINESS &
    ECONOMICS / Negotiating | BUSINESS & ECONOMICS /
    Decision-Making & Problem Solving
Classification: LCC HD58.6 .B39 2025 | DDC 658.4/052—dc23/eng/20240809
LC record available at https://lccn.loc.gov/2024035095

British Library Cataloging-in-Publication Data is available

Editorial: Joe Jackson and Emma Wagh
Production Editorial: Nathan Carr
Text Design: Karl Spurzem
Jacket / Cover Design: Karl Spurzem
Production: Danielle Amatucci
Publicity: James Schneider and Kate Farquhar-Thomson

Illustrations on pages 28, 54, 55, and 152 © 2023 by Robert C. Shonk,
all rights reserved.

This book has been composed in Arno Pro with Neue Haas Grotesk Text

Printed in the United States of America

10 9 8 7 6 5 4 3 2 1

Contents

Preface

When Professor Jeanne Brett and I were first thinking about creating an executive negotiation program at the Kellogg School of Management at Northwestern University, we were fortunate to have Phil Kotler as a colleague. Kotler is often described as the "father of modern marketing." So, we asked him to meet with us to help us think about how to market the new program. It was a very useful discussion, but we didn't follow one of his suggestions—namely, to tailor the training to participants' context. According to Kotler, it would be easier to sell a program with a focus on a select group of executives facing a common negotiation challenge—business development, procurement, sales, and so forth. He argued that people want training that appreciates the uniqueness of their specific challenge. Yet, obsessed with the notion that all professionals need to improve their negotiation skills, Jeanne and I created a broader program. Still, I found it fascinating that a great marketing mind argued that potential participants would want a program focused on their specific context rather than one useful to all.

While my negotiation teaching heavily leans in the direction of general messages, I enjoy hearing about specific contexts. After all, I already know much of the broad material on negotiation and have much to learn from the contexts in which executives negotiate. And, to be honest, I've never had a permanent real-world job—I have been an academic all of my life. But I am an academic who loves real problems. Friends seek out my negotiation advice when they are buying houses and cars and applying for jobs. I have also been fortunate to have had consulting assignments where I help executives negotiate more effectively. These opportunities have taken me to thirty-two different countries, crossing sectors and industries along the way. My consulting experiences have allowed me to learn a great deal about some industries, like pharmaceuticals and insurance. In these cases, I understand the context well. I enjoy learning about new contexts, listening very carefully, and figuring out the connections between my general expertise in negotiation and the specific cultures, opportunities, challenges, personalities, and talents involved. I learn about the context, and the executives I'm working for hopefully learn about how to negotiate more effectively in their context.

When I am consulting in an industry that I do not know well, people sometimes respond to my advice with comments like, "That isn't the way we do things in our industry." This usually means one of two things, both of them good: either I'm about to learn something very interesting about negotiating in their industry or my advice may help them rethink typical negotiation processes in their industry for the better. To figure out which story will develop, I need to better understand their context.

I have now taught tens of thousands of MBA and executive students how to negotiate more effectively. When I was a professor at Kellogg, Jeanne and I created the first executive negotiation program at a business school. After I moved to Harvard in 2000, I started a program called "Changing the Game," an intensive weeklong course on negotiation that has been offered over sixty times to more than 4,500 students. I have also been a member of the executive committee and the faculty of the executive programs for the Program on Negotiation at the Harvard Law School. By my count, I have taught over thirty thousand students to negotiate more effectively. I have also mentored doctoral students who now teach negotiation as professors at Harvard, Stanford, Wharton, Cornell, Columbia, NYU, Berkeley, Carnegie Mellon, the University of Chicago, Northwestern, and many other excellent schools. I love to teach people to negotiate more effectively and am delighted to be involved in training the next generation of professors of negotiation.

What do we teach? Most of us offer a set of core ideas, derived from research, that can help executives and other leaders make more effective decisions in negotiation. These ideas have proliferated in business schools, where negotiation is often the most popular course. We teach people how to think about and improve their alternatives to reaching agreement with the other party. We teach people how to create value—for example, by making trades across issues that the parties care about differently, so that both parties get more of what they want. We teach people about the importance of thinking about the perspective of the other side. We teach people to identify the cognitive barriers that prevent them from thinking optimally about the negotiation. And we teach people how to think about the complexities of negotiating with multiple parties, negotiating with parties who represent the interests of others, and the differences between negotiation and dispute resolution. Some would describe these topics, even the more complex ones, as generic, since our advice is intended to be relevant for most class participants, regardless of their industry, country of origin, current home base, and customs that govern how they conduct deals. While generic negotiation programs have thrived at Kellogg, the Harvard Business School, and many other business schools, it is true that executives love to get negotiation advice specific to their culture, company, or function. This book is my integrated response to their concerns about their context.

Negotiation

Chapter 1

The Game Has Changed

One of the pleasant aspects of my job is that most students thoroughly enjoy negotiation courses, which are highly interactive: students practice negotiating in simulations and receive feedback on how to improve in a low-risk setting. Negotiation also turns out to be fun to teach. While we cover many useful and practical ideas, there are always course participants who ask about topics that I failed to cover, whether by speaking to me directly or sharing this information in a course evaluation. This feedback is helpful to me. It generally starts with a compliment, then quickly continues to the substance: "This was a fine course, but . . ."

- it doesn't account for the cultural norms of negotiating in my country.
- it doesn't deal with negotiating with people from China [or pick any other country].
- you didn't cover the supply crisis that we are currently facing.
- do your ideas apply when dealing with liars or irrational opponents?
- negotiating over Zoom is different than negotiating in person.
- how does the course apply to negotiating with my romantic partner?
- how does it apply to getting my patients to take their medicine?
- what if my negotiation counterpart doesn't have the power to commit to an agreement?

This list, based on the many batches of feedback I have received, could easily be far longer. While each comment seems unique, the critiques more broadly highlight the fact that the course was not focused on the student's particular *context*—the circumstances and conditions that surround a negotiation.

All of these criticisms are valid. In addition, research evidence supports the difficulties in transferring knowledge across domains, or what academics call analogical reasoning.[1] I wrote this book to respond to such questions—specifically, to explain how to adapt systematic frameworks for negotiating more effectively to your context. I will address many of these questions directly in the book. More importantly, I will show you how to adapt the central ideas of negotiation to your own questions and to the particular contexts you face.

Generic Ideas versus Context in Negotiation

My core strength as a scholar has been to develop novel ideas about how people think in negotiations. My research explores the systematic and predictable ways in which even experienced negotiators act that are not fully rational—that is, as they would with greater reflection. Paralleling research in the field now known as behavioral economics, my work offers a critique of traditional game-theoretic models of negotiation, which assume all parties engage in perfectly rational thinking throughout the process.[2] In fact, our actual behavior departs significantly from this assumption of rationality.[3] To take one example, I found that most negotiators do not adequately think about the perspective of the other side, though understanding the other side is often critical to creating a wise negotiation strategy. I have also provided negotiators with a framework for better understanding the likely decisions of their counterparts. I have shared these ideas in my writing and draw on them regularly when advising my consulting clients.

I believe my research has made valuable contributions to the theoretical and practical literatures on negotiation. My work has been broadly accepted by behavioral economists and scholars who focus on the psychology of negotiation. But I certainly have had my critics, and they tend to focus on my failure to think about context. These scholars often study the uniqueness of specific negotiations, whether due to culture, economics, politics, relationships, modes of communication, the behavior and identity of the other side, or many other important factors.

For simplicity's sake, it is easiest to plead guilty to having done my core research while controlling for, or ignoring, many of these contextual variables. Most of the formal research I published in academic journals was done in sterile laboratory contexts, devoid of much of the real-world context that surrounds any specific negotiation. The research is meant to identify basic aspects about how humans think in negotiation and to be generalizable across negotiation contexts. Similarly, negotiation professors like myself often organize our courses around the key analytic ideas about negotiation, and participants later criticize us for excluding certain factors. That is, the instructor presents analytic concepts (like reservation price, which we will soon cover in chapter 2), and practitioners want to know if and how those concepts apply to a very specific context, such as their home culture or industry. The executive programs that I teach at Harvard Business School (HBS) often have executives from many dozens of countries and a similar number of different industries. It would be impossible to be fully responsive to all of their contexts, including their nationalities, industries, and particular challenges. During breaks and over meals, I am always happy to hear about their specific contexts, and I try to tailor the course to their specific application as well as I can. But even if I could address all their contexts directly in class, I don't think doing so would provide the best negotiation education.

I can explain this view more clearly by describing interactions I often have with potential clients who are thinking about hiring me to teach negotiation to their executives. When discussing the possible assignment, the potential client asks whether I will be using simulations that focus on the group's function (such as procurement, sales, or business development) and/or their industry (pharmaceuticals, energy, tech, etc.). Even when I have access to simulations that match their function and/or industry, I discourage the use of such simulations. My goal, I explain, is to provide compelling evidence that even seasoned executives do not intuitively think about negotiations optimally. I want the executives to understand this independent of their unique context so they can determine how to analyze and plan for a variety of negotiations. For example, many negotiations assume the pie of value is fixed in size, when in fact it can be enlarged. I want students to learn this lesson in an environment that will clearly reveal where they are missing opportunities to create profit based on their faulty intuition. And I want them to learn how they can create value and improve their approach to negotiation.

If the simulation is too close to home, executives will try to connect it to their most recent or most salient negotiation. Rather than focusing on the lessons at hand, they will focus on how the simulation differs from the real-world negotiation most on their mind. In contrast, after the class develops some frameworks based on simulations far from their turf, participants are often extremely effective at applying the concepts to their own actual contexts and provide strong answers to the question, "What could you do more effectively in your real-world negotiations?" Generic knowledge is powerful and useful for figuring out how to improve the context-rich worlds we all inhabit. Thus, for custom negotiation programs, I usually recommend more general training on the front end and application sessions on the back end, where executives bring their own negotiation stories to the class for analysis.

One of my most memorable external teaching assignments was with a well-known publishing firm. My job was to teach these publishers and editors how to negotiate more effectively with people like me: authors. In fact, this particular company had published one of my books many years prior to this teaching engagement. A senior vice president, my main contact, informed me ahead of time that many of the other senior executives were skeptical about whether a professor had much to teach them. The president and my main contact pushed me to start with a publishing simulation to get their attention. I argued against this but ultimately agreed to their demand, since I wanted the assignment. What better way to understand the other side of these negotiations that were an integral part of my life? I didn't have a publishing simulation, so I wrote one. It was based on one of my real-life book contract negotiations.[4]

I had a blast writing the simulation. Teaching it was fun, too. But when the session ended, two of the most senior people in the room (famous names in the publishing world) made a point of informing me that all of my facts (which were actually facts) were inconceivable in the publishing industry. When I pushed for clarification, they shared anecdotes about very different book negotiations, anecdotes that I am sure are true. Not surprisingly, publishing negotiations can be very different from each other. I didn't tell them that they were accusing an actual publishing story of being inconceivable.

Despite their claim that my story could not possibly be true, listening to them helped me understand the importance of negotiating contexts. Rather than focusing on the lessons I thought they would need to learn to improve their negotiating skill, like thinking about alternatives and reservation price, setting the most effective anchor, and considering the other side's perspective, these publishers were fixated on the specifics of their most recent or vivid negotiation. General learning was lost in the details of comparing different publishing negotiations. In contrast, had the simulation been over buying a parcel of land or securing syndication rights to a TV show, I am confident the publishers would have focused on the more abstract concepts that would have helped them negotiate book contracts more effectively and train others to do so.

The challenge for any real-world negotiator is to figure out how ideas that you might learn about in a class or a book generalize to your negotiation context. In this book, we will examine when the research literature offers useful advice for your real-world negotiations as well as how to apply negotiation advice to specific contexts. Most of the time, the answer will be that the ideas presented in classrooms and books will be useful across contexts, with some tailoring. This book is all about good tailoring.

A Tool Kit for Contextualizing Negotiations

I hope that this book is useful to those who have never read a book on negotiation or taken a negotiation class. I would like it to serve as a great introduction to negotiation that recognizes many contextual changes that have occurred in society in recent decades. But I also hope the book will provide lots of new insights to those who have had some exposure to the key concepts in negotiation theory, like BATNA (best alternative to a negotiated agreement), reservation value, zone of possible agreement, value creation, and even Pareto-efficient frontier. When these concepts come up, I will typically explain what they mean but also highlight ideas for thinking about how a particular context affects how you might use these concepts. Rather than concluding that reservation values, say, matter in some negotiations but not others, I will focus on how the context we're discussing affects how you assess your reservation value. Readers with extensive knowledge of prior books on negotiation should feel free to skim over the material that introduces the core concepts they already know well.

When the talented students and experienced executives I'm teaching raise contextual challenges surrounding negotiation, I try to remember that their challenge is unique—different in some way from the other stories I've heard about before. At the same time, these challenges often share commonalities. Organizing negotiation contexts into different types enables me to offer useful advice in particular situations. Any categorization of contexts will be imperfect. But, based on the thousands of unique negotiation stories and challenges I have heard, I have found this particular categorization to be helpful—to me and to my students.

The categories that follow—culture, economics, politics, relationships, modes of communication, and the behavior of the other side—provide important contextual information that we can use to assess the core concepts that go into all important negotiation analyses. These contextual variables are not a list of the chapter topics that follow. Rather, they are an overview of contextual categories I will refer to throughout the book to describe how social context can be used to develop effective strategies that incorporate our best general models of negotiation. The book's chapters will focus on different conceptual challenges where the analysis is informed by the consideration of the contextual information that I now overview.

Culture. The most common contextual factor that comes up in teaching executives from around the globe is the role of culture.[5] "Changing the Game," the executive program that I lead, highlights the importance of understanding the other side—what they value, their

BATNA, their reservation price, and so on. Gaining this understanding can be harder when we negotiate with people from other cultures. Cultural rules and norms that are very different from ours can seem strange, and negotiating with members of cultures that we don't understand feels difficult as a result. Rather than focusing on our own limited ability to understand a very different culture, we sometimes end up viewing other cultures negatively or even pejoratively.

A few decades ago, when the Japanese economy was peaking, and Japan seemed like the main economic threat to the United States, people would ask me for tips on negotiating with the Japanese. Today, people more often ask me for help negotiating with the Chinese. Similarly, I have found that people from cultures around the world find negotiating with Americans to be difficult and are eager to hear my advice. Interestingly, the cultures I'm asked about most tend to be those that are thriving. This leads me to believe that cultural differences aren't the main barrier for these negotiators. Instead, the real issue may be the other party's economic strength. If someone seems to have many more options than we do, we might develop the impression that they are difficult negotiators. Rather than recognizing the weakness of our own negotiating position, we view their behavior as strange and as caused by their unique culture.

If I ask a group of executives to think about a culture that they find difficult to negotiate with in the real world, they tend to assume I am asking about someone from another country. But industries, companies, religions, and municipalities also have cultures. New York and Texas are both in the United States, yet norms of behavior are very different in these two states. Similarly, I can think of numerous large cities outside the United States where I feel more comfortable than I do in small towns in the American South and Midwest.

Generally, when someone tells me about the difficulty they're having negotiating with a group from another culture, I try to better understand the other party's behavior by determining what is unique about them. Do they have better options? Are they simply more patient? Do they value the relationship differently? Are the other party's negotiators authorized to commit to an agreement? Are there behaviors that the other side might find rude or offensive? Each of these questions may well be connected to culture. But these more specific attributes provide additional insight into the other side in ways that are meaningful for developing an appropriate negotiation strategy. Most of us better understand people from our own culture than those from other cultures. Yet, more and more, we find ourselves negotiating with people from different cultures. These circumstances highlight the value of understanding culture and diversifying our teams.

Economics. No executive has ever called me to say, "We have a negotiation that is going really well, but we thought that with your help, it might go even better." Rather, when I get calls for help, it is typically because something has gone wrong. Most commonly, the executive seeking my advice lacks economic power in comparison to the other side.

I find it just as interesting to make the best of a bad situation as to make marginal improvements on a great situation. I used to be a very good card player, and like any good card player, I had fun when I was dealt a great hand. Yet I knew that the decisions I made when I was dealt a lousy hand were also very important. The same is true in our negotiations. In negotiation training, we typically advise negotiators to think about their alternatives to an agreement, as well as their counterpart's likely alternatives. To do this, we need to think about the economic conditions affecting both sides. Economic conditions include basic financial considerations but also market conditions more broadly.

Economic conditions help us understand why the other side might seem unusually tough and assess whether they really will walk away from the deal on the table. Economic conditions help us understand our alternatives to an agreement and the opposing party's alternatives. And economic conditions can help us identify creative solutions to difficult negotiations.

Politics. The political environment is another factor that affects the context of negotiations. Sometimes governments pass laws that change the dynamics between negotiation parties. A law that makes it harder for employees to unionize, for example, might give management more power in a particular employment negotiation. Sometimes one party in

a negotiation has better information about future political develop-
ments than their counterpart. For example, in a simulation case that I
often teach, "Hamilton Real Estate" by Deepak Malhotra, the potential
buyer of a parcel of land is politically connected and has learned that
upcoming zoning changes will dramatically affect the value of the land.[6]
Part of the challenge for the seller is to discover this aspect of the
political context in which they find themselves.

In both governmental and corporate contexts, our perceptions of the
political environment surrounding our negotiations are predictably
asymmetric. When the political context favors our side, we tend to view
that environment as normal or fair. In contrast, when the other side has
the advantage, we tend to see the politics as "political," or unfair. From
a negotiation perspective, we need to gather as much knowledge as we
can about the political environment and how it affects the options of all
the parties at the table and develop a wise negotiation strategy based on
that reality—rather than on the world as we wish it was.

Relationships. In negotiation, relationships matter a great deal.
Negotiating with a close friend will be a very different experience than
negotiating with a supplier you have never met before. You can trust
your friend to be honest and transparent, but you can't yet rely on your
new supplier to be honest and transparent. Your friend will want to treat
you fairly in the negotiation, while the new supplier may or may not care
about your long-term outcomes. At the same time, you might push for
a better deal in your negotiation with the new supplier and be less as-
sertive when negotiating with your friend. Similarly, when you are negotiating with others in your organization, the organization has a right
to expect you to negotiate in a manner that is in its best interest and
improves its overall value. As a result, such internal negotiations are
likely to foster more positive relationships than external negotiations
with suppliers and customers.

Modes of communication. At the start of the Covid-19 pandemic,
we all learned new ways to work, socialize, and try to stay healthy. I
learned to teach on Zoom, which wasn't on my radar screen in 2019.
Many salespeople who lived their lives on airplanes suddenly found
themselves spending their days on Zoom and other similar platforms.

Developing relationships with customers over meals was no longer possible, and "reading" people became more challenging.

When I was forced into Zoom teaching in March 2020, I didn't like it at first. But I adapted and eventually learned to enjoy it. This was especially true when, in 2021, I started teaching some classes in person, with everyone wearing face masks. I found it more comfortable to teach on Zoom, where at least I could see the students' faces. Before the pandemic, I didn't appreciate the degree to which I relied on facial expressions when teaching. I imagine people who negotiate all day long and made similar transitions experienced similar patterns and preferences.

Most of us prefer dealing with people in a way that allows for comfortable communication. Yet we often find ourselves negotiating in contexts where we can't choose the mode of communication. This contextual factor affects our negotiation strategy. The more the social context deviates from a comfortable mode of communication, the more we need to think about the social context and plan our negotiation strategy accordingly.

The people on the other side of the table. In psychology, there have been decades of debate about whether the person (the parties in a negotiation) or the environment (the specifics that define the negotiation) is the most important determinant of behavior. Those unfamiliar with the empirical literature are often surprised to learn that most research psychologists agree that the environment explains far more of the variance in individual behavior. However, that doesn't mean that individual differences are unimportant in negotiation. When we approach a negotiation, characteristics of our counterpart are indeed an important part of the context.

In particular, the other party's gender, race, ethnicity, personality, intelligence, negotiation skills, and other individual differences all matter, and they affect the deal that is negotiated. Yet too many negotiators are overconfident in their ability to assess the personality of the other side and predict their behavior. Too many negotiators are overconfident that they can predict their counterpart's behavior based on gender, racial, and other stereotypes.

Social psychologists have documented that most of us view the demographic groups to which we belong as heterogeneous but assume that members of other demographic groups, those to which we do not belong, are more homogeneous. For example, Americans tend to use stereotypes to anticipate the behavior of Chinese counterparts but accept a wider range of behavior from American counterparts. When we run into problems in negotiation, we are too quick to rely on stereotypical descriptions of people who share the demographics of the party we are facing. It would be a mistake to assume that the other party's behavior will be consistent with the stereotypes available from quick Google searches. We give too much weight to demographic stereotypes and would be better off observing our counterparts' actual behavior, research shows.

Similarly, we shouldn't assume we have the clinical skills required to quickly assess others' personalities. A great deal of research sheds doubt on our ability to accurately and swiftly size up someone we've just met. Individual personality differences are important in negotiation, but most of us lack the ability to understand how these differences will affect people's behavior. When we try to do so, we often rely on stereotypes of categories of people. What should we do instead? Respond to people's behavior, not their demographics or our intuitive assessments of them. Demographic information can help us appreciate what we might not fully understand about the other side, but we should develop our negotiation strategy based on their actions—a very important part of the social context.

The World Has Changed

My students often ask whether the material in my negotiation classes has changed over the last couple of decades. The honest answer to this reasonable question depends on what a participant means by "the material." The core negotiation concepts have remained intact: you should still think about your best alternative to reaching an agreement with your current counterpart, as well as the other side's perspective. But during these decades, the negotiation context has altered dramatically—along with the world.

Consider some of the changes we have witnessed in the United States during the current millennium (it would be easy to create an overlapping list for many other countries):

- As the most massive attack the United States has ever experienced, 9/11 changed the country's perceived power, our alliances with other countries, and the culture of the largest U.S. city. It also made many Americans feel much more vulnerable.
- The Great Recession, dating from late 2007 through mid-2009, burdened most Americans financially. It also shaped our understanding of the real estate economy and the nature of negotiations for mortgages. And it affected the job market, including candidates' bargaining power in salary negotiations.
- Over the last twenty-plus years, Americans have become much more bifurcated, a process that sped up during the Trump era. Political polarization has affected relationships. Some feel a stronger bond with their negotiating counterparts due to shared political preferences. Others find they must negotiate with people they now view as enemies. At the political level, it has become much more difficult for elected officials to reach bipartisan agreements that would improve the welfare of most citizens.
- The online economy has shaped how parties reach agreement. You can now rent another person's home without talking to them or to their agent. You can set up an e-auction to buy or sell goods for your company without talking to the other side.
- The phenomenal growth of the Chinese economy has given the Chinese government and Chinese companies more power while taking away power from the U.S. government and U.S. companies. It has also dramatically altered which parties belong to the trading networks of corporations all over the world.
- Our work life is much more diverse than it used to be. The globalization of the economy and societal shifts that bring more

diversity to the workplace mean that we interact with people who differ from us more than in the past. Obviously, this is wonderful. It also requires us to confront our own biases and to try to understand counterparts who have different norms than people who are more similar to us.

- No change has surprised us and altered the way we negotiate more than the Covid-19 pandemic. We have different trading partners and interact with our negotiation opponents in different ways. Supply chains have been disrupted in ways that no one ever expected. Negotiations over retail and office space have changed dramatically as demand for that space shrunk significantly. And the social aspects of our interactions have transformed as we moved many of our negotiations online.

While these changes are enormous, none of the core concepts we taught a couple of decades ago have become irrelevant or obsolete. Rather, what has changed dramatically in many negotiations is the context. The title of the executive program that I direct at HBS, "Changing the Game," highlights the importance of defining the negotiation game rather than simply implementing moves in a fixed game. Fundamental transformations in our world have changed the game we are playing. We need to understand the context created by these changes and adapt core negotiation concepts to take account of our new context. That is what this book is all about.

Contextualizing the Simple and Complex

The early chapters that follow explore basic challenges that negotiators have faced for a very long time. In chapter 2, we consider the conventional wisdom of making extreme offers, and in chapter 3, we assess how to think about dividing the pie. Many readers will be for or against these negotiation strategies. You will not be surprised to learn that I think context matters. As the book continues, we will move on to contextualizing some of the challenges created by changes in contemporary society, seeing how our core negotiation frameworks apply and how we can use our conceptual tool kit to handle these challenges more effectively.

Each chapter starts with a thought-provoking question that I have received from a student. The chapters will present information relevant to the challenge and related ones, then close with direct responses to the question. The goal will be to show how the chapter content helps us understand context-specific questions.

Chapter 2

Extreme Anchors

"Some very important people in my company have stressed that a key to getting the best possible price from suppliers is to start with a very low offer, leaving plenty of room to negotiate if needed. At company events, my colleagues have been praised for their aggressive negotiation style. I am currently in a situation, post-Covid, where we need a large quantity of a product where there is very little supply available. The supplier I am about to negotiate with has their choice of buyers. Should I still make a very low offer to anchor the discussion effectively?"

. . .

How extreme should your initial offer be? This is a remarkably common question facing negotiators, and both naive and experienced negotiators often have strong opinions about the answer. I've heard many stories about the impressive results people obtained by making extreme offers. However, these storytellers seldom mention the deals they screwed up with their tough stance. Recall Donald Trump's demand that Mexico pay for a wall separating Mexico from the United States. This extreme demand led Enrique Peña Nieto, then the Mexican president, to cancel a planned meeting with Trump soon after he took office and reduce cooperation on border issues. Mexico paid none of the costs associated with Trump's wall-building activities.[1]

An academic literature suggests that anchoring—putting a number on the table as a starting point to "anchor" the outcome in your preferred direction—is a powerful negotiation tactic and that extreme anchoring—starting with an extreme offer—is also effective. But do extreme anchors scale to the real world? Not surprisingly, my answer is that it depends on the context.

In their book *Friend or Foe: When to Cooperate, When to Compete, and How to Succeed at Both*, Adam Galinsky of Columbia University and Maurice Schweitzer of the University of Pennsylvania argue that an extreme anchor explains why the Chicago Bulls paid Michael Jordan $30 million for the 1996–97 basketball season—$10 million more than the previous highest NBA salary—and $33 million the following year.[2] Their account attributes Jordan's success to his opening with an extreme offer of $52 million for the 1996–97 season. Based on a number of empirical studies by Galinsky and colleagues, Galinsky and Schweitzer write, "Your first offer should be just *this* side of crazy, as opposed to *that* side of crazy."[3]

Friend or Foe may be right in attributing Jordan's record-breaking deal, at least in part, to his extreme first offer. However, plenty of other explanations are available, including Jordan being the greatest basketball player who ever lived and his ambiguous interest in returning to basketball. We will return to a contextual analysis of Jordan's negotiation later in the chapter.

I solidly agree with Galinsky, Schweitzer, and others that anchors are important in negotiation and worthy of careful deliberation. But this deliberation requires that we understand how to contextualize anchors. For now, I encourage you to start thinking about whether extreme offers make sense in the negotiation contexts most important to you. How might the other party respond when your offer is too extreme?

The Basic Effect

Please pause and answer this question before reading further: Between the start of the Covid-19 pandemic on March 11, 2020, and February 19, 2023, according to the World Health Organization, was the number of people who contracted Covid-19 worldwide higher or lower than 10 million? Now, what do you think a more reasonable estimate of Covid cases worldwide would be?

Notice that I didn't make any claim that 10 million was a reasonable estimate. In fact, it was not. But did asking you about whether the actual number was higher or lower than 10 million affect your estimate? Most people think they are able to ignore this clearly low anchor when faced with this question, but they turn out to be wrong. Consistent with hundreds of other demonstrations of the anchoring effect, when people are asked whether the number of Covid-19 cases during this time was higher or lower than 10 million, and then asked for their estimates, their estimates are dramatically lower than those of others who were first asked whether the number of Covid cases was higher or lower than 3 billion during this time period and then asked for their estimate. (The actual number of Covid-19 cases as of February 19, 2023, was around 775 million.)[4]

If people know that 10 million is a low estimate and 3 billion is a high one, why would they be affected by such irrelevant "anchors"? Research suggests at least two answers. First, we naturally form our estimates by starting with an initial anchor based on whatever information is available to us. For example, we might start with someone else's claim or demand and adjust from that anchor to come up with our estimate. Our adjustments from anchors tend to be insufficient.[5] In addition, anchors lead us to think of information consistent with that anchor.[6] For example, a low estimate of Covid cases leads us to think about the reduction in cases created by vaccines, while the high anchor prompts us to think about cities and countries with the very worst Covid rates.

Many people have heard of Amos Tversky and Daniel Kahneman's initial demonstration of anchoring.[7] Study participants observed the spin of a roulette wheel. One group saw the wheel land on the number "10" and then were asked whether the percentage of countries represented in the United Nations that were African was higher or lower than 10 percent. A second group saw the wheel land on "65" and were asked whether the percentage of African nations in the United Nations was higher or lower than 65 percent. Those who saw "10" gave an average estimate of 25 percent, while those who saw "65" gave an average estimate of 45 percent. Although the participants saw that the initial estimate was random and unrelated to the judgment task, the anchor had a dramatic effect on their judgment. This is a remarkably strong and generalizable effect found across most contexts.[8] Thus, we can see how Jordan's $52 million demand could have influenced the Bulls' estimation of what his final salary should be.

Over the last decade, there have been numerous cases of outrageous fraud in the start-up world, such as Theranos's fake blood-testing innovation and FTX's use of customer funds in the cybercurrency world.[9] Many have asked why so many watchdogs didn't bark, including these companies' boards of directors, auditors, investors, and others. One possibility is that these parties anchored on the assumption that the companies they oversaw were acting with integrity—"innocent until proven guilty."

In one study, researchers presented a group of professional auditors of major accounting firms, selected at random from a larger pool, with the following problem (which I have adapted from the original to keep it current):[10]

> It is well known that many cases of management fraud go undetected even when competent annual audits are performed. The reason, of course, is that Generally Accepted Auditing Standards are not designed specifically to detect executive-level management fraud. We are interested in obtaining an estimate from practicing auditors of the prevalence of executive-level management fraud as a first step in ascertaining the scope of the problem.
>
> Based on your audit experience, is the incidence of significant executive-level management fraud more than 10 in each 1,000 firms (that is, 1 percent) audited by Big Four accounting firms?

> a. Yes, more than 10 in each 1,000 Big Four clients have significant executive-level management fraud.
> b. No, fewer than 10 in each 1,000 Big Four clients have significant executive-level management fraud.

What is your estimate of the number of Big Four clients per 1,000 that have significant executive-level management fraud? (Fill in the blank below with the appropriate number.)

_____ in each 1,000 Big Four clients have significant executive-level management fraud.

Other auditors were randomly selected to see the same problem, except they were asked whether the fraud incidence was more or less than 200 per 1,000 firms audited rather than 10 per 1,000 firms audited. Auditors in the first condition estimated 16.52 per 1,000 on average, while those in the second condition estimated 43.11 per 1,000.

Anchors matter in decision making, and they matter more than most of us expect. We make worse decisions when influenced by misleading anchors, and others may be able to manipulate our decisions by using anchors in our negotiations with them. We can use anchoring to our advantage in our own negotiations, though there may be societal and ethical concerns to consider.

It is well known that women (on average) are paid less than men, even after controlling for differences in their jobs. Explicit and implicit sexism play a role in these differences. Two decades ago, in their book *Women Don't Ask: Negotiation and the Gender Divide,* Linda Babcock and Sara Laschever argued that women were less likely than men to negotiate a higher salary after receiving an initial offer.[11] While that has changed in the last two decades, and women now ask at least as frequently as men, they are less likely to get a positive response to their requests.[12]

Unfortunately, differences in pay continue throughout women's careers. "What's your current salary?" is a question that employees, especially women, often hear when seeking and negotiating wages for a new job. This question exacerbates discrimination by anchoring on past discrimination. In August 2016, the state of Massachusetts banned employers from asking this question,[13] precisely to reduce gender-based discrimination caused by employers anchoring on the past when negotiating with potential new employees. As of 2022, twenty other states have followed Massachusetts's lead.[14]

Empirical Evidence That Anchors Matter
in Negotiation

In a 1987 study, researchers Greg Northcraft and Margaret Neale asked real estate brokers in Tucson, Arizona, how accurately they could appraise the value of a house. On average, the brokers said they could assess the value of a property to within 5 percent of its true value.[15] The brokers were then given one of four different information packets about a house for sale in the area. The packets were ten pages long and full of data about the house and comparable properties in the area, including their sales prices. The four information packets were the same, with one exception: the house's listing price was presented as 11 percent higher, 4 percent higher, 4 percent lower, or 11 percent lower than the actual appraised value of the property. After reading the material, all the brokers toured the house and the surrounding neighborhood. Next, all the brokers were asked to estimate the house's true value. Their estimates suggested they were significantly and strongly affected by the listing price (the anchor); those given higher prices made higher estimates, and those given lower prices made lower estimates. Despite this evidence, the brokers denied being influenced by the listing price they were given.

This and other controlled laboratory experiments have found that anchors matter a great deal in negotiation.[16] They matter even more when the party being anchored has less information than the party anchoring about what a fair price would be.[17] Adam Galinsky is the scholar who has published the most studies on anchoring in negotiations, and in much of this research, he and his colleagues recommend making the first offer in most negotiations.[18] For example, in the buyer-seller context, they argue that if you're the buyer, you should open with a very low number, and if you're the seller, you should open with a very high number. You can then expect to benefit from your counterpart's insufficient adjustment away from the anchor. They also argue that by starting with your preferred anchor, you prompt the other side to think about justifications for that number. We will examine this conclusion by considering the context.

Galinsky argues for making extreme first offers on the basis of anecdotes, like the one about Michael Jordan, carefully controlled laboratory experiments, and analyses of class simulations. Indeed, lots of evidence supports his position that extreme first offers can serve as effective anchors. "More extreme first offers produce a more extreme anchoring effect and give you a better outcome," Galinsky and Schweitzer conclude.[19]

Despite the argument that you generally should put your number on the table first, you will undoubtedly face situations where the other party puts a number on the table first—a number you really don't like. How should you respond? First, don't expect to get accurate information about what a fair agreement would be from the other side's opening offer. Rather, do your own research in advance so that you know what a viable range would be. You should also enter important negotiations knowing your best alternative to reaching an agreement (more on that later in the chapter). In addition, avoid the temptation to respond to an extreme offer with your own extreme offer, as this may simply validate to the other side that their offer was a reasonable starting point. Instead, be ready to firmly reject the other party's extreme offer as not being a viable starting point and figure out how to reset the negotiation—perhaps on a different day.

The Downsides of Extreme Anchors

While anchors undoubtedly matter in negotiation, I do have doubts about the wisdom of making extreme offers. I also question the advice to make the first offer in negotiation as a general rule. One of my concerns is that extreme offers risk destroying the possibility of reaching agreement by making you appear to be an unreasonable counterpart. If you make an offer that is far worse than what your counterpart could get elsewhere, they might be offended and walk away.

So, why does the research data point to the benefits of extreme offers? To understand why, we need to understand the context of the research evidence. The bulk of it comes from laboratory experiments and classroom simulations. I like both of these contexts. I have published many laboratory experiments, and I love teaching using negotiation simulations. But when interpreting data, the context matters. My own experience leads me to believe that in both contexts, participants are more motivated to reach an agreement than negotiators typically are in the real world. As a result, I predict that agreement rates are much higher in both laboratory experiments and classroom simulations than they are in their real-world parallels.[20]

To see why, consider a typical classroom simulation, in which a buyer and seller are negotiating the possible sale of a pharmaceutical plant. Imagine that the buyer would never pay more than $20 million. What happens if the seller asks for $100 million? In the real world, the buyer would most typically end the discussion and look for a different plant to buy. But when the two parties are taking my class at Harvard Business School, and I give them forty-five minutes to negotiate, the common response to extreme offers is different. When the buyer is asked to pay $100 million in the first five minutes, the negotiation often continues. I have seen many negotiation pairs reach agreement in classroom simulations, often at the last minute, because they don't want to come back to class without a deal. When I asked the less effective party whether they would have accepted the final agreement in the real world, they tell me they would have walked away much earlier. The same is likely to be true for two participants in a research study who have been assigned to play roles in a negotiation simulation. While real-world negotiators want to close deals as well, the social demands of experiments may lead people to have a higher tolerance for staying at the negotiating table when presented with an unreasonable offer. The context matters: the classroom and experimental contexts let the seller escape the downside of making a ridiculous opening offer.

Many of us have also heard fascinating negotiation stories, like that of Michael Jordan, where an extreme opening offer is part of the storyteller's success. I rarely hear stories about the times that same storyteller made an unreasonable offer and the other party simply ended the negotiation—that is, where the extreme opening offer destroyed the potential for a mutually beneficial agreement. Such cases are uneventful, not favorable to the storyteller, and cost their firm a great deal by blowing a viable agreement.

If you are a baseball fan, you might recall the amazing career of Matthew Harrington. More likely, you won't, since his career actually wasn't so amazing—in part due to an extreme offer made in a negotiation. In 2000, at age eighteen, Harrington was profiled on the covers of *USA Today* and *Baseball America*.[21] These and other media outlets described him glowingly as a hardworking, modest teenager who was arguably the best pitcher available in the Major League Baseball (MLB) draft. Harrington and his family selected Tommy Tanzer, a well-known players' agent, to represent him in negotiations with teams. To scare away teams that lacked the budgets needed to pay a high signing bonus and salary, Tanzer announced before the draft that the team that selected Harrington would need to offer at least a $4.95 million first-year bonus to sign him— an extreme offer at the time. The high figure scared away some of the teams with early picks, but the Colorado Rockies chose Harrington as the seventh pick in the draft. The Rockies made it clear that they would not pay what Tanzer was demanding. But by that point, the Harrington family had begun to believe that Tanzer's high anchor was appropriate.

The Rockies made a number of lucrative offers, including $5.3 million over eight years or a $3.7 million signing bonus without a long-term commitment. Tanzer made it clear that Harrington was insulted by the Rockies' reasonable offers and rejected all of them, and no agreement was reached. Harrington's unreasonable expectations created a gulf between the parties. When Harrington reached an impasse with the team that drafted him, he was prohibited from signing that year with another MLB team or with any of the highest-level minor-league teams. He settled for signing with the lower-level independent-league St. Paul Saints, hoping to cement his skills in preparation for the MLB draft the next year. However, he had a disappointing season with the Saints.

For the 2001 MLB draft, Harrington switched to another famous players' agent, Scott Boras. The San Diego Padres chose him as the 58th overall selection. With his previous year's extreme offer and the Rockies' counteroffers in mind, Harrington turned down the Padres' final offer of $1.25 million over four years with a $300,000 signing bonus.

This again kept him out of the MLB. In 2002, Harrington was chosen as the 374th pick and was offered less than $100,000 from the Tampa Bay Devil Rays. Once again, he passed. In 2003, the Cincinnati Reds drafted him as the 711th pick, and no deal was reached. Harrington had become the longest holdout in the history of MLB. In 2009, he was working in the tire department of the local Costco, earning $11.50 per hour. Looked down on as greedy and foolish, Harrington's parents became pariahs in their community of Palmdale, California, and moved away. Harrington sued Tanzer for mishandling the negotiations; the parties settled out of court for an undisclosed sum. "I'm not without blame here," Tanzer told ESPN.com. "I think the story is a tragedy for [Harrington] and for everybody involved."[22]

Harrington remained a likable person throughout this extended story. In fact, he told ESPN he has put the past behind him and appreciates his low-key family life.[23] Notably, not only did Harrington have enormous potential as a pitcher, but his personable nature suggests he could have had a career in coaching, scouting, or broadcasting—the kinds of activities that can follow a successful MLB career. So, why did he end up working a low-wage job at Costco? At least part of the answer is that his side of the negotiation made an extreme offer.

Notice that this story includes an agent. The agent set the extreme anchor of $4.95 million, which appears to have been part of his pitch to the Harringtons. "I was told, 'They'll never not sign you. They'll *never* not sign you,'" Harrington said of the advice Tanzer gave him and his family about the Rockies. "Well, obviously that wasn't true."[24] If you have ever sold your house, you may have noticed that prospective agents often mention extreme listing prices when trying to convince you to choose them to represent you. What if you start to believe the agent's extreme anchor is a fair price? Your home could sit unsold for a significant amount of time. Something similar appears to have happened with Harrington and his family.

The context of Harrington's negotiations differed from the context of Michael Jordan's negotiations with the Bulls, as well as from the many extreme offers made in laboratory and classroom demonstrations. Experimental participants, students, and the Chicago Bulls were all under extreme pressure to stay at the table, despite their counterparts' extreme opening offers. The Bulls knew they could win the championship with Jordan, that they would be a mediocre team without him, and that Bulls fans would have been furious if they didn't close a deal. Harrington was a very good pitcher, but he wasn't good enough to force the Rockies to negotiate well outside their range of reasonable agreements. Extreme offers can dramatically lower the chance of finding a mutually beneficial agreement, especially when the other side doesn't feel an overwhelming need to close a deal.

A key focus of later chapters will be the power negotiators have to create value, such that they come up with innovative solutions they wouldn't have thought about on their own. I'll explain how negotiators can learn about each other and make trade-offs across issues, a process often called logrolling. This type of value creation (making the pie bigger) takes place in a context where negotiators are also trying to claim value (getting more of the pie for their side) at the same time. One problem with extreme offers is they lead both sides to focus on claiming value. As a result, the important process of creating value can suffer.

Additionally, negotiating with someone you trust is fundamentally different than negotiating with someone you do not know. Relationships are critically important in negotiation. Not only will the quality of your relationship affect the negotiation, but your negotiating behavior will also affect your relationship. What happens when you make an extreme offer? Not only will you increase the likelihood of impasse and destroy opportunities to create value, but you will harm the relationship, both in your current negotiation and in the future. Making extreme offers is simply not how people who want to build or maintain a positive relationship should behave. Relatedly, most negotiators care about their reputation in their industry and beyond. Having a reputation for being tough but reasonable is better than having a reputation for being unreasonable. A habit of making extreme offers will lead you to be perceived as less credible and will harm your reputation. While relationships and reputation may be less important in some contexts (for example, when buying a car), it's important to consider the context when you are deciding how extreme your opening offer should be.

Effective Anchors

Given my criticisms of some of the advice provided by other leading scholars about extreme offers and my argument that the context matters, it would only be fair for me to provide an alternative structure for assessing how extreme a first offer should be. My framework for thinking about how to make an effective opening offer depends on the context, including the alternatives available to both parties.

Before I elaborate, I need to quickly review some ideas that I expect you have run into before. Before you start any important negotiation, for example, you should consider what you will do if no agreement is reached. What is your best alternative to a negotiated agreement, or BATNA?[25] Your BATNA provides guidance on what you expect to get if you don't reach a deal and allows you to compare any proposed deal to that alternative. In a simple price negotiation, your BATNA allows you to logically set your reservation price—the lowest price you would be willing to accept or the highest price you would be willing to pay. You should also think about the other side's BATNA, which will help you estimate their reservation price. This, in turn, will help you contextualize what an effective anchor would be.

Consider the following example:

You are a potential investor in a start-up alternative protein (protein from sources other than animals) company. The start-up makes a great product but needs funds to hire a sales team to get the product on shelves at places like Whole Foods, Trader Joe's, and so on, and to build its manufacturing capacity. You and the start-up have jointly agreed that it needs $2 million in funding to grow the firm and to prepare for a larger round of fundraising in eighteen months— hopefully, raising the value of the firm during this time. You have the $2 million available, so the question is, what percent of the company would you own in return for the $2 million? You are hoping to get the start-up's founders to agree to a $5 million post-investment ("post-money") valuation, which would mean that $2 million would provide you with a 40 percent ownership stake of the firm. How should you think about whether to make a first offer? If you do decide to make one, what should that first offer be?

Any prior negotiation book you may have read or negotiation class you may have attended would have encouraged you to think about your BATNA, such as other investment options you would pursue with the available funds, when answering these questions. After identifying an alternative investment, you conclude that a post-money valuation of $10 million for the alternative protein company (giving you only a 20 percent stake for your $2 million) would make you indifferent between reaching a deal with the company versus pursuing the alternative investment. This $10 million is your reservation value—that is, the highest valuation you would accept to make your $2 million investment. (From your perspective, a lower valuation allows you to obtain a larger percent of the company for your $2 million investment.)

In an early conversation, the start-up founders said they were looking for a $2 million investment, with a post-money valuation of the firm at about $12 million (giving the $2 million investor a one-sixth stake in the company). After talking to other venture capital (VC) firms and asking more probing questions of the founders, your best estimate is that their BATNA would be to get the $2 million from another VC firm at an $8 million valuation, which would give that investment firm a 25 percent stake for their $2 million. Notice that negotiating the valuation and the percentage ownership for the $2 million are objectively the same, as $2 million equals the post-money valuation multiplied by the ownership percentage.

Before continuing the analysis, I want to highlight that too many negotiators only think about their own information and miss the strategic benefits available from learning about and thinking about the other side's interests and alternatives. In this example, once we have thought about both sides, we can create a graphic depiction of the zone of possible agreement (ZOPA) for the ownership percentage (and implied valuation) being received for the $2 million investment, as shown in figure 2.1. The ZOPA is the set of valuations that are more attractive for both the start-up and the VC firm than their alternatives. The

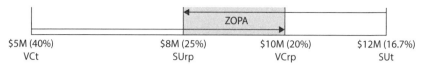

$5M (40%) $8M (25%) $10M (20%) $12M (16.7%)
VCt   SUrp   VCrp   SUt

VCt = venture capital firm's target
SUrp = start-up's reservation price
VCrp = venture capital firm's reservation price
SUt = start-up's target

FIGURE 2.1. Zone of Possible Agreement.

reservation prices of the two parties establish the ZOPA, in this case $8–10 million, or a 20–25 ownership percentage.

The idea of a ZOPA can feel counterintuitive, since we do not typically envision a zone when we negotiate. Rather, negotiators make offers tilted toward their preferred side of the ZOPA, or perhaps even more extreme offers than that; if they reach an agreement, they simply meet at a particular point. But even at the point of agreement, both sides often would have been willing to make a further concession, if required, to get a deal done. Thus, a typical real-world agreement represents just one point within the viable ZOPA.

Returning to our venture capital deal, we can see that a broad ZOPA exists—$8–10 million—rather than a single figure. If this assessment of the ZOPA is accurate, and you made an offer of $8.2 million and convinced the start-up that this was your final offer, we would expect the start-up to accept the offer, since it would beat what they should expect to get elsewhere. Notice that if the start-up had the negotiation insights and knowledge needed to come to the same assessment of the ZOPA as you, they might try to convince you that $9.9 million is the lowest valuation they would accept before pursuing an alternative course of action—going with another VC firm, delaying the raise, or moving more slowly with existing resources. The parties' BATNAs provide the context needed to assess each side's reservation price and the ZOPA, and thus to see if agreement is possible and how to effectively anchor the negotiation.

Now, as the venture capitalist, it is time for you to try to set an effective anchor. You could focus your arguments on features that would imply a very low valuation (like the fact that the start-up currently has hardly any revenue) and propose a $3–4 million valuation; this range feels justifiable and marginally extreme. But if you did your preparation and investigation well, and are confident that the start-up founders can get a valuation of about $8 million from another high-quality VC firm, I question why you would even mention numbers in the $3–4 million range. In fact, these numbers might simply serve to get the other side to focus on their best alternative to working with you. Your goal instead should be to make a first offer that grabs their attention and creates a pathway to an agreement at your preferred end of the ZOPA, such that you end up around $8.2 million. So, if you think that the start-up anticipates a negotiation dance, you might start with a $7.8 million valuation, move to $8.0 million in response to their counteroffer, and then make a final offer of $8.2 million, clarifying that this is where you expect to end up unless they can provide compelling information for you to move further—such as information they haven't shared with you yet, a written offer from another VC firm, and so on.

Why start with $7.8 million rather than $3 million, given the information I presented earlier that more extreme offers lead to more extreme outcomes? Because $3 million will not register as an anchor when the other side is considering $8 million elsewhere. In fact, it is likely to end the conversation. In addition, consider which of the following patterns of offers from you would better convince the other side that you know the market well:

$$\$3M \rightarrow 5.6M \rightarrow \$8.2M, \text{ or}$$

$$\$7.8M \rightarrow \$8M \rightarrow \$8.2M$$

I argue that the latter will be more effective at setting an anchor, capturing the high end of the ZOPA, and reaching agreement. Similarly, I think Michael Jordan would have been better served by an opening offer in the $35–40 million range rather than the $52 million number he chose. Jordan moving from $37 million to $33 million would have been more convincing to the Bulls than moving from $52 million to $33 million.

As noted earlier, one reason to avoid making an extreme anchor is that it could harm your relationship with the other side, and that relationship could affect your long-term outcomes. Einav Hart and Maurice Schweitzer (the same author linked to the *"this* side of crazy" advice regarding anchors) insightfully point out that deal terms in negotiated agreements often affect the actions of the parties after agreement is reached.[26] For example, if you drive a hard bargain with a contractor on price, the quality of their work after the contract is signed might not be ideal. Similarly, the VC firm will benefit from its investment if the entrepreneur succeeds, and the entrepreneur will be more motivated to succeed if they have the prospect of earning wealth for themselves. Thus, making an extreme offer could backfire on you financially if it leads to an agreement that doesn't create a strong financial incentive for the entrepreneur to succeed.

Now that you have settled on an opening offer of $7.8 million, the question becomes, should you try to present it first or wait for the other side to make their opening offer? In this context, I agree with Galinsky's assessment that you want your number on the table first. Better to start with $7.8 million and adjust up than to hear them offer $12 million and have to work down. Anchors matter, and we insufficiently adjust from them.

Here again, though, context matters. Imagine the same story with a couple of changes. In this version, the start-up founders haven't been very responsive to your questions, and you have no idea whether they have received interest from other VC firms. More broadly, you have very little idea about their BATNA. Should you still make the first offer? If so, should it still be $7.8 million? When you lack information about the other side's BATNA and reservation value, your priority should be to learn as much as possible from them at the negotiating table, even if that means risking that they will put the first number on the table. That would be a better situation than putting the wrong number on the table. Notice that if you offer $7.8 million, you are never going to get a lower valuation, even if they would have been happy with a number closer to your initial target of $5 million. On the other hand,

$3 million could still offend them by suggesting you don't understand their business model.

Now imagine instead that you have credible information that the founder has another offer for a $2 million VC investment, which puts the valuation precisely at $8 million. In this case, you shouldn't bother making an offer based on a $7.8 million valuation. Instead, I would recommend starting with an offer based on a $8.2 million valuation and noting that your analysis suggests that this is a couple of hundreds of thousands of dollars above what you expect they have heard elsewhere. You are now anchoring, while increasing your credibility and providing a justification for why they should accept this offer.

Galinsky and Schweitzer offer an intriguing strategy for dealing with a lack of information about the other party in a negotiation: "Make the first offer later." In this case, they would propose that you clarify to the founder that you hope to make an attractive offer but first need to learn more from them. This should open a discussion that encourages both sides to share information while at the same time discouraging your counterpart from putting a number on the table. When you have learned much of what you need to know, you should be able to confidently anchor near your preferred end of the ZOPA. Being able to justify your offer with strong logic will make the anchor even more effective.

As this analysis suggests, the context matters a great deal when you are deciding whether to make the first offer and, if so, how extreme it should be. We have discussed the financials of the two parties and the information they have available, which could be affected by factors such as the relationship between the parties and cultural norms regarding information exchange. Your relationship with your negotiating counterpart could also affect your preference for where you want to fall in the ZOPA.

Now let's assume again that you have excellent information about the start-up, but the founder is your sister, rather than a near-stranger, and one of your favorite people in the world. You both simply want a fair outcome, one that allows you to work together toward creating value.

Would you still aim for your preferred end of the ZOPA? Most of us would say no. If pressed for where the deal should end up, many would suggest the middle of the ZOPA—an equal sharing of the surplus created by the deal. "Let's just split things equally" is a proposal we all have heard, and that is where we are headed next.

· · ·

"Some very important people in my company have stressed that a key to getting the best possible price from suppliers is to start with a very low offer, leaving plenty of room to negotiate if needed. At company events, my colleagues have been praised for their aggressive negotiation style. I am currently in a situation, post-Covid, where we need a large quantity of a product where there is very little supply available. The supplier I am about to negotiate with has their choice of buyers. Should I still make a very low offer to anchor the discussion effectively?"

"You should not make an extreme offer in the economic context that you're facing. Try to learn as much as possible, before and during the negotiation, about the other side's actual alternative to reaching an agreement with you. If you are confident they have a great alternative, put an offer on the table that is slightly better for them than their alternative. Making an extreme offer, one well outside the zone of possible agreement, could easily lead them to walk away and pursue their alternative. If they do stay, they will not accept your extreme offer. When you start making concessions, they will have little reason to believe you are done conceding when your offers finally become reasonable. It is far better to anchor aggressively within the zone of possible agreement, which allows you to convey that you understand it would be in their best interest to accept your offer."

Chapter 3

50-50 Splits

"I was just at the car dealer, and after an hour and a half of haggling, the salesperson said, 'We're only $600 apart, and we're both reasonable people, so why don't we just split the difference?' Did it make sense for me to agree to this intuitively reasonable compromise?"

■ ■ ■

- "Here are two credit cards," your dinner companion says to the restaurant server. "Can you split the bill in half?"
- "When I die, my two children should each get 50 percent of my assets."
- "The dog needs two more walks today. How about I do the 4 p.m., and you do the 8 p.m.?"

We have all heard people propose equal divisions such as these, and most of us have suggested such 50-50 splits. Do they make sense? Are they fair? Should you make and accept such proposals? Negotiation experts offer very different answers to these questions. Not surprisingly, I will argue that it depends on the context. But, first, let's learn about some different views on the question.

"Never Split the Difference"

Chris Voss, a former FBI hostage negotiator turned corporate negotiation advisor, feels so strongly that you should "never split the difference" that he gave his book that title.[1] The book is filled with interesting stories about high-stakes hostage negotiations and offers many useful insights on managing the emotional side of tough negotiations. Voss also underscores the importance of listening to the other side—particularly when they are holding your relative hostage. And he highlights the lack of logic in splitting the difference between two arbitrary positions. Unfortunately, the title of his book is what too many people remember as its number-one takeaway. And when an author puts a title like this on his book cover, he becomes responsible for that takeaway.

Never Split the Difference points out the illogic of compromising when your partner wants you to wear black shoes when you want to wear brown shoes: the compromise solution of one black shoe and one brown shoe doesn't seem like the wisest choice. And Voss argues that if the bad guys are holding two hostages, getting just one released is not a good outcome. Voss provides convincing examples that splitting things 50-50 doesn't work in all situations.

Voss further blames the mantra "win-win," found throughout the negotiation literature, for so many people making the mistake of splitting the difference. As I will discuss later, I am not a big fan of the term "win-win" either, but that is because I like more precise terms, like enlarging the pie of value or, in economics lingo, reaching the Pareto-efficient frontier (the range of options such that there is no option that is better for one or more parties without making another party worse off). However, Voss provides little insight into why he pairs the concept of win-win with splitting the difference.

I also agree with Voss that it is a bad idea to open an important negotiation by simply trying to compromise, which he seems to equate with splitting things 50-50. Again, as we will cover later in the book, compromising too quickly can eliminate the possibility of coming up with creative ideas that would allow you to enlarge the pie being divided between the parties involved. But the fact that splitting the difference doesn't make sense for a pair of shoes or hostages, and that compromising can eliminate the search for even better solutions, doesn't demonstrate that we should *never* split the difference. Here again, context helps guide us toward knowing when splitting the difference may make a great deal of sense.

Consider the dog at the beginning of the chapter who needs to be walked twice more today. Walking the dog has some benefits for the walker: exercise and time spent with a fine companion. But the walk also comes with some small costs: the walker may need to interrupt their work or leisure time, bundle up, perhaps risk being rained on, and pick up poop. To resolve the issue, the two human partners could evaluate the situation in more detail by figuring out who would get more benefit from the walks and who would incur more costs, and assign the dog-walking task to the partner who gets more benefit and suffers less. They could also add more issues to the negotiation, such as figuring out who will make dinner, who will clean up after dinner, and so on. Or, they could simply split the difference on the two remaining dog walks and not have to spend time analyzing the issue further. The simplicity of the 50-50 solution, coupled with the limited importance of the negotiation, makes splitting the difference a reasonable solution in this context. Thus, I would never argue that you should "never split the difference."

"Split the Pie"

As is also clear from the title of *his* book, *Split the Pie*, Yale School of Management professor Barry Nalebuff has a very different view of 50-50 splits than Voss does.[2] In *Split the Pie*, Nalebuff argues that two negotiators should *always* split the pie 50-50, as long as they understand what constitutes the pie. After all, many numbers typically are mentioned in a negotiation, so which numbers you choose to split from can matter a great deal. In Nalebuff's view, the parties should split the additional value they create from working together, over and above the sum of what each could obtain from their BATNA. Nalebuff isn't recommending choosing one brown shoe and one black shoe, since that would not create value for either party over the wiser strategies of two black shoes or two brown shoes.

In a *Harvard Business Review* adaptation of his book, Nalebuff teams up with his prior coauthor Adam Brandenburger to argue in favor of always splitting the pie using an example adapted from an actual merger discussion between two companies in the same industry.[3] Company A is worth $240 billion on its own, and Company B is worth $160 billion on its own. The best estimate of the combined value of the two companies is $430 billion. Thus, the merger will create $30 billion in value if Company A buys Company B. How should the $30 million be divided? They argue that proportionality commonly affects the division in such large-scale business discussions, which would lead to $18 billion of the surplus being allocated to Company A and $12 billion to Company B, based on their stand-alone values. Nalebuff and Brandenburger argue that this division is not fair, since the parties each need each other equally to achieve the $30 billion of synergy. Thus, the authors argue that splitting the synergy evenly—$15 billion for each party—is most fair. I agree with them.

This example provides clarity on why, at least sometimes, we should split the value created in negotiation 50-50. In this case, doing so allows the parties to move forward and create $30 billion in synergy. And the argument that they both need each other to create the synergy provides a logic for why they should evenly share the surplus. I also like the clarity of Nalebuff and Brandenburger's argument about what is being shared—the additional value over and above what they could each obtain on their own. If another company, Company C, suddenly offered to buy Company B for $180 billion, that would change Company B's BATNA and reservation price in its negotiation with Company A. Now Company B would demand at least $180 billion to be bought by Company A, which would change the surplus to $10 billion ($240 billion + $180 billion = $420 billion, $10 billion less than their combined value). In this case, Company A and Company B would each get $5 billion. The outcome would change, but not the logic for dividing the synergy.

In *Split the Pie*, Nalebuff argues that if negotiators can agree to split the pie equally and then agree on how to assess the pie, they can then focus on value creation—making that pie as big as possible. As we'll see later in the book, most negotiators have much larger opportunities to expand the pie than they realize. Nalebuff highlights that if all parties can agree on how to split the surplus created, they will want the surplus to be as large as possible.

One of the simulations I use when teaching executives to negotiate more effectively involves a negotiation between two divisions of the same corporation. The salaries of the employees are affected by the profitability of their division. The negotiation involves the transfer of technology within the firm, from one division to the other, but there are issues beyond the price of the transfer, and the structure of the deal can affect how much joint profitability the technology creates. Even when teaching experienced negotiators, I am continually struck by the degree to which they fail to find an agreement that maximizes joint, or total, profitability. They essentially throw corporate cash in the garbage can and burn it.

Why? First, many negotiators assume that what the other side gains comes at their expense—they believe in a mythical fixed pie. This assumption is simply wrong in most complex negotiations, where value can be created through wise deal structures. Thus, negotiators need training in value creation—and, indeed, value creation is a focus of virtually all negotiation courses at leading schools of business. Second, negotiators are thinking about how to claim value when they should also be thinking about creating value. Negotiators fear that if they focus on negotiating deals that create more value, they will lose on the claiming side—the other side will get more of the larger pie created. If they were to agree in advance to split any surplus they created equally, they would be less distracted by claiming value and more focused on creating value. This strategy would also be advantageous to the firm. The goal of its CEO is for the two divisions to create an agreement that maximizes joint profitability so that the collective corporation is made better off. Nalebuff would argue that if the parties can agree to split the pie equally and agree on how to define the pie, they could then focus on what the corporation wants: finding an agreement that will create the biggest pie. In chapter 4, we will discuss other strategies that can help employees maximize value within their organizations.

Nalebuff is insistent that splitting the pie equally is a wise strategy anytime two negotiators are dividing a known pie and have full information. I am not convinced. When it is time to buy a new car, I can estimate my own BATNA and reservation price, as well as the dealer's, and then aim for a price precisely in the middle. Yet this will not be my strategy on my next visit to a car dealership. Why? I doubt my ability to get the car salesperson to buy into this logic. And I don't want to waste my time trying to negotiate a deal that is fair to both sides with a party that will be focused on extracting a maximum price from me. So, I think I will continue my past strategy of doing my research before going to the dealership and anchoring the discussion at the low end of the ZOPA, knowing that an impasse will lead to my attractive BATNA of going to another dealer.

In their *Harvard Business Review* article, Nalebuff and Brandenburger offer a fun hypothetical example of splitting an actual pie—specifically, a pizza from Pepe's, Barry's favorite pizza shop in New Haven, Connecticut.[4] I have been to Pepe's with Barry and enjoy his enthusiasm for their pizza but personally prefer a doughier, New York–style pizza. But, back to Pepe's. Imagine that Pepe offers Alice and Bob a twelve-slice pizza if they can decide how to divide it. If they can't, he will give them only half the pie, with four slices going to Alice and two to Bob. Nalebuff and Brandenburger argue against using a proportional rule that would give Alice eight slices and Bob four, based on her seemingly greater power in the negotiation—the fact that she will get more pizza if they don't reach agreement. They also argue against dividing the pie 50-50— six slices apiece. Instead, they argue that Alice and Bob should divide the six slices over and above their BATNA. This would leave Alice with seven (four from her BATNA plus three from sharing the surplus) slices and Bob with five (two from his BATNA plus three from sharing the surplus) slices.

Without dwelling on the peculiarity of Pepe's offers, let's imagine a slightly more straightforward negotiation dilemma, the kind most of us have probably faced at one point or another: How should you divide up the twelve slices of a pizza you are sharing with a friend? I think most of us would go with the "eat until you are full" rule or, if you were both hungry enough to jointly eat the whole thing, six pieces each would be the obvious solution. I'm trying to imagine being in Alice's position, with Marla (my spouse) in Bob's. Even if I could draw on all of Barry and Adam's excellent analytic insights, arguing for seven slices for myself and five for my spouse, it probably would not go over well and would be far from the marital-maximizing solution. As I will argue in the next section, we often split items 50-50 in negotiations not because doing so is fair but because doing so allows us to move forward with a decision where the costs of active negotiation exceed the value of what we are negotiating about.

More broadly, in negotiation contexts far beyond pizza, the Nalebuff solution of attempting to explain the concept of BATNA and how to assess a 50-50 split of the surplus above each party's BATNA would be a tough sell. Educating the other party about the strategy could be too time-consuming and difficult. In many cases, proposing the Nalebuff solution would violate social norms of fairness. Lack of trust and limits on information would also make it hard to implement the "split the pie" solution. While aiming for a 50-50 split of the pie as Nalebuff defines the pie may be helpful, wise, and fair in many situations, pursuing the Nalebuff solution with an opponent who ruthlessly pursues a more aggressive path may have its limits. In sum, context matters.

At the same time, I appreciate the logical elegance of Nalebuff's solution and can imagine using it in many situations, particularly important ones. Next, we'll consider why this solution is consistent with so many contexts where we simply split the difference.

Why Do People Split the Difference?

Like Voss and Nalebuff, my former colleague at Northwestern University's Kellogg School of Management, David Messick, studied the issue of whether to split the difference in negotiation.[5] Rather than advocating for or against this proposal, Messick focused on the psychology of *why* we tend to split things 50-50. His work can help us understand whether and when it's the right strategy to split the difference.

Messick argued that negotiators often split resources 50-50 not because doing so is the fairest or best option but because they have learned that such "social heuristics" help them get along better with others. Messick used the term "social heuristics" to refer to the rules of thumb, or cognitive shortcuts, people use to make snap decisions in interpersonal interactions. Decisions based on heuristics are biased and not fully rational, but they enable us to make choices quickly.

Negotiators often compromise not because it is the fairest solution in that specific context but because doing so helps us avoid conflict. In particular, Messick noted that splitting the difference reduces conflict. Thus, when two couples go out to dinner, they often split the bill 50-50 rather than carefully itemizing who ate what; trying to fairly allocate the bill might not be great for one's social life. Messick's view provides both a compelling rebuttal to Voss's "never split the difference" rule and a simple reason why we don't bother to think about the parties' BATNAs as needed to implement Nalebuff's "always split the pie" (where the pie is different than simply splitting the bill equally) rule. As Messick observed, violating social heuristics can cause you to lose things far more important than the specific resources at stake in a negotiation.

Splitting the difference can be a useful device for resolving minor negotiations with people with whom you have ongoing relationships. But negotiators often split the difference when a more creative solution would have allowed them both to get more than half of what is at stake. When people have a very close relationship, their concern for that relationship can lead them to make the socially comfortable choice of compromising rather than searching for creative gains through trade-offs, researchers Kathleen McGinn, Margaret Neale, and Elizabeth Mannix have found.[6]

Messick highlighted that people have a strong tendency to think of 50-50 as a fair negotiated solution even if a different division would clearly be justifiable and beneficial. Consider the following example:

You have a civil relationship with your next-door neighbor but are not close friends. You and the neighbor receive an email from the city informing you that $10,000 was found near the boundary of your two lots. The owner has not been found, and the city technically owns the money. But they have decided that if the two of you can decide how to divide the $10,000 in the next 72 hours, they will turn the money over to you. However, if you are unable to agree on the division in the next 72 hours, the $10,000 will go into a general fund. You are delighted to learn of this windfall but less pleased when you receive the following email from Arti, your neighbor: "Glad to receive notice of the windfall. Our lot is four times as large as yours, making it more likely that the money was on our land. We propose that we get $8,000 and you get $2,000. We are leaving town and will not have a chance to review counterproposals. So, this is our final, 'take it or leave it' offer. If you accept it, you get $2,000. If you reject the proposal, we both get nothing. Please let the city know your decision and cc: us on your email."

Many readers of this book are likely to reject this split while fully understanding that doing so leaves them with zero extra dollars rather than $2,000. People will reject this offer for a variety of reasons. They might object to the way the neighbor dealt with the situation. They might not like the phrase "take it or leave it." They might believe the neighbor isn't entitled to any of the funds, for various reasons. In addition to these viable explanations for rejecting the offer, perhaps the most common reason people will decline the offer is that they do not want to accept an unfair allocation and do not want Arti to benefit from their acceptance of it. Some might also argue that they are doing society a favor by punishing Arti for proposing an unfair offer. A common reaction is that Arti has violated the social norm of splitting the money 50-50.

A great deal of research has explored how we react when people violate the expectation of dividing resources 50-50.[7] In the "ultimatum game," a classic in the field of behavioral economics, Player 1 is asked to divide a known sum of money (commonly $10) any way she chooses by filling out a form stating, "I demand X." Player 2 then can either accept the offer and receive his portion of the money, as allocated by Player 1, or reject the offer, leaving both parties with nothing. Traditional economic models assumed that players would behave in their rational self-interest in the ultimatum game: thus, economists predicted Player 1 would offer Player 2 only slightly more than zero dollars, and Player 2 would accept any offer greater than zero. Yet research studies have found that participants in the role of Player 1 most commonly offer an even split of the money and that those in the role of Player 2 often reject offers lower than half the total money being allocated. Research using the ultimatum game shows the power of the 50-50 norm, despite many people's ability to see that rejecting a positive amount less than 50 percent fails to maximize their own outcome.

In the ultimatum game and the $10,000 neighbor problem, it's clear what is being split. But in many negotiations, what is being split is less clear. In the teaching simulation I mentioned earlier involving two divisions of the same corporation negotiating a technology transfer, negotiation pairs often end up with 50-50 splits and walk away with the idea that their outcome was a fair one. During the class discussion of the case, though, they then find out that other groups with 50-50 splits ended up with very different results due to their differing ideas about what pie is being split. Some negotiation pairs divided the total profit from the technology being transferred between divisions equally. Others split the profit equally and also allocated the investment costs of creating the technology equally. Others split the difference between their "final positions." And some did what Nalebuff would recommend: they agreed to divide all profits above their BATNAs equally, then worked together to make sure they created the biggest pie possible. I like the Nalebuff solution in this instance, but most groups that agree to a 50-50 split (of whatever they are splitting) think they found the only fair solution (at least until the class debriefs all of the possible 50-50 splits).

Context Matters

We've seen arguments for and against 50-50 splits in negotiation. When should you propose a 50-50 split, and when should you accept or reject one? It depends on the context.

Culture matters. People from collectivist cultures, including many countries in Asia, Africa, and South America, tend to emphasize the interests of the group over the needs and desires of each individual.[8] Collectivist cultures place a high value on social harmony, respectfulness, relationships, and the interests of weaker parties. By contrast, members of individualist cultures, including Western nations like the United States, England, and Australia, tend to focus on independence, competition, and personal achievement. Notably, however, within any particular country, some sectors, industries, and communities are more collectivistic or individualistic than others.

Collectivists tend to favor equality more than individualists do, and they often do not use value above their BATNA as a benchmark for creating equal divisions.[9] As a result, members of collectivistic cultures are more likely to propose and accept 50-50 splits in negotiation than members of individualistic collectivist cultures are. However, a collectivistic logic in negotiation can also be self-motivated. When the party with a weaker BATNA in a negotiation proposes a 50-50 split of shared profit to a stronger party, and the stronger party rejects the proposal as unfair, you are likely witnessing a clash that can be interpreted based on negotiation power or culture.[10]

Economics matter. Economic factors affect parties' BATNAs, and splitting the synergy created above parties' BATNAs, as Nalebuff proposes, incorporates the economics of the situation. Thus, Nalebuff helps us understand the logic for a party in a strong negotiating position rejecting a proposal to split the difference between the last proposals on the table. Take the case of a supplier that has a limited amount of goods that are in high demand and a potential buyer who needs those goods to manufacture their main product. The parties trade offers, and eventually the buyer proposes splitting the difference between the two offers on the table. The supplier can be predicted to reject the offer if they can get far more for their goods from another party.

Relationships matter. When I was a teenager in the early 1970s, earning about $800 a year (a bit less than $6,000 in today's money) as a ballpark vendor at Pittsburgh Pirates and Pittsburgh Steelers games, my parents and I didn't split the bill when we went to a restaurant for dinner—they paid. Once I was an adult, earning more than my parents ever had, I picked up the check, and that became our new family norm. I do not recall us ever dividing the check equally. But when my spouse and I go out to dinner with another couple we're friendly with, it is common for us to split the check evenly. And when I go to the Spangler Center at the Harvard Business School for lunch with my colleagues, we each pay for our own lunch separately.

When parents die without leaving a will, their adult children sometimes get into financial disputes. Typically, the wealthier sibling(s) would prefer to split the assets equally, while the poorer sibling(s) are more likely to think about a needs-based distribution. In addition, the sibling who spent the most time caring for the parents may think that their inputs should affect the outputs. The quality of the relationships among the siblings may also affect their ability to resolve the dispute.

When my mother died, some years after my father, my sister had been living in my parents' home. The will specified a 50-50 split of my mother's modest assets, which included some money and the house. I was wealthier than my sister. On our mother's passing, my sister, with whom I had a close relationship, implied that she would be moving out of the family home, since she could not afford to live in it with her half of our inheritance. In contrast, I had no need for our mother's assets and didn't desire a 50-50 split. My sister and I agreed to keep the house and other assets in both of our names and for her to live in the house and use the assets as she saw fit. We had the fortunate opportunity to negotiate the use of my mother's assets with the party who would benefit most from a 50-50 split (me) having no desire to do very well in the negotiation, and my sister having no expectation beyond the 50-50 split that she was legally entitled to receive. I attribute this positive process to our strong relationship.

Many siblings encounter such situations without starting from a positive relationship. In such cases, it is helpful to understand your sibling's perspective. A wealthier sibling will honestly see a 50-50 split as fair, while the less well-off sibling might consider a needs-based view to be more appropriate. Unfortunately, many people have self-serving views of what is fair. It is helpful to try to understand their perspective even if you do not agree with their views. As these examples show, the decision of whether to split the pie often hinges on the nature of our relationship with the other party.

The Final Word on 50-50 Splits

As we've seen, the answer to the question of whether to split things 50-50 is that it depends on the context. I hope I have clarified some of the contextual factors that will help you think through this issue in your own negotiations. As noted earlier, it is also important to keep in mind that your negotiating counterparts may have different notions than you about whether and how to split the pie. Understanding the contextual environment surrounding the negotiation will help you plan your strategy.

■ ■ ■

"I was just at the car dealer, and after an hour and a half of haggling, the salesperson said, 'We're only $600 apart, and we're both reasonable people, so why don't we just split the difference?' Did it make sense for me to agree to this intuitively reasonable compromise?"

"In your negotiation with the car dealer, you should have assessed the attractiveness of the price that would result from a 50-50 split and responded to that price. That fact that you were splitting the difference between two arbitrary points (where you were in the negotiation) does not automatically make that price reasonable or a reason to say 'yes.' If you were buying the car from your brother, this would have been a fine way to avoid further haggling with a family member with whom your ongoing relationship may be more important than small differences in the negotiation outcome. In the one-shot negotiation you described, you should not be manipulated into paying too much simply for the sake of dividing the pie."

Chapter 4

Value Creation as a Way of Life

"I appreciate the value of helping the other side achieve their goals, and I see the benefit of trading off what is more important for me with what is more important for them. I think I am pretty good at following this advice with people I know well and who have similar communication styles. But my most important negotiations involve people from different cultures who have very different communication styles and do not share information easily. How do you create value with people from cultures that are more reserved and less communicative?"

. . .

In our discussion of strategies for effective anchoring in chapter 2, all the negotiation stories had just one issue at stake. In the case of Michael Jordan's salary and the price of a house in Tucson, Arizona, the issue was how much money one party paid to another. Similarly, most negotiation stories that people tell at cocktail parties center on price. By contrast, most important real-world negotiations involve multiple issues, with price being just one of them.

Consider the negotiation between the start-up and the venture capital (VC) firm described in chapter 2. My description focused on just one issue, namely what percent of the company the VC firm would receive for its $2 million investment. I skipped over lots of other issues that are important in any negotiation between founders and investors. In addition to the obvious question of what percentage of the firm the venture capitalist will get for their defined amount of dollars, other issues are bound to be involved in such a dialogue. These issues might include whether the VC firm will have a seat on the start-up's board, the degree to which the VC firm will control the next round of funding, founder compensation and termination, potential paid or unpaid advice the VC firm might provide to the founder, and voting rules on important strategic decisions, including possible future control of the firm.

Some may see these as side issues, in comparison to price. But great negotiators recognize that negotiating multiple issues enables favorable trades that increase the overall value created by the deal. These added issues can be enormously important. By creatively packaging a deal across all issues, finding mutually beneficial options, and making wise trade-offs, parties create value, and both sides achieve better outcomes. Value creators are more effective negotiators, develop stronger relationships, have better reputations, and contribute to making the world a better place. This chapter provides a concrete set of strategies that will help you become a skilled value creator. I will cover value-creation strategies that are addressed in other negotiation books, including my own. In addition, I will provide guidance on how the context helps define the most effective value-creation strategy in any specific negotiation.

Back to the Venture Capital Deal

Chapter 2 presented the investment negotiation as a fairly simple one in which the parties were haggling over what percentage of a start-up a VC firm was buying for $2 million. The investment amount was fixed, and there was no mention of potentially bringing in other investors, what the VC firm could provide other than money, control of the company, board seats, or a host of other relevant issues. In actual VC negotiations, these other issues are important. They also allow the parties to create value. So it is time to tell a more complete version of the story from chapter 2.

In this fuller version, the leaders of the start-up and the VC firm met when they attended the same negotiation seminar and struck up a conversation. The VC firm is a well-funded investment group focused on the food industry and has critical knowledge that could be useful to many start-ups. Specifically, the VC firm has expertise in two critical areas facing start-ups: co-manufacturing and distribution. Co-manufacturers are organizations that make products for new companies as they grow. As an example, many food companies start off making their products in the founder's kitchen, then move to a small industrial facility or perhaps a restaurant kitchen. As demand for the product grows, and before they can build their own manufacturing facility to meet the greater demand, start-ups might address their need to rapidly increase production by reaching an agreement with a co-manufacturing facility to produce the product. The other critical challenge facing food start-ups is how to get their products on the shelves of major retailers. For plant-based products, retailers like Whole Foods and Trader Joe's might be key targets. One feature that differentiates the VC firm in this transaction from other potential investors is that it offers to accompany its investments with expertise on co-manufacturing and product placement. While the firm charges a fee for its consulting (or takes an additional small equity ownership percentage of the start-up), it also presents these sources of expertise as a key benefit relative to other VC firms. As the negotiation approached, the VC firm sought to make its integrated approach visible to other founders that it might partner with in the future.

On the other side, the start-up was very anxious about getting its product in front of customers. It was interested in the expertise the VC firm claimed on manufacturing and distribution but was concerned the firm might be overselling that expertise. The start-up's founders were also nervous about giving up a large percentage of their company. But they needed funds and had no in-house expertise about the start-up fundraising process.

Let's return to the simple version of the negotiation that I presented in chapter 2, where the two parties were haggling over a zone of possible agreement (ZOPA) for what the VC firm would get for its $2 million investment. As you'll recall, the possible outcomes lay between an $8 million post-investment valuation (providing the VC firm with 25 percent of the start-up) and a $10 million post-investment valuation (providing the VC firm with 20 percent of the start-up). It is easy to imagine the parties reaching a final agreement in the middle of the range, a $9 million post-investment valuation, which would give the VC firm a 22.22 percent stake in the start-up.

But because they applied the skills they had just learned at the negotiation seminar, that was not the final agreement. Rather, they reached the following terms:

- VC firm provides start-up with a $2 million investment.
- VC firm receives just 18 percent of the start-up up front.
- Start-up receives consulting services from the VC firm on co-manufacturing and product placement up front.
- Start-up agrees to provide the VC firm an additional 8 percent of the firm from the founder for no additional cash if the start-up: (1) obtains a viable co-manufacturing agreement within 18 months, (2) gets its products on the shelves of at least 2,000 retail locations within 24 months, and (3) succeeds in generating its next round of funding for at least $2 million within 30 months (these are outcomes that the founder does not expect to achieve without significant help from the VC).
- VC firm gets a right of first refusal as the lead investor in the next round of funding.
- VC firm is allowed to publicly announce the agreement to promote its business model.
- VC firm gets a seat on the start-up's board.

Later in the chapter, I will explore the value-creation strategies they used to reach this specific agreement.

The start-up was delighted to reach an agreement that gave away less of the firm on the front end than it had anticipated and to be receiving the VC firm's focused attention to help solve its manufacturing and distribution challenges. The VC firm was also pleased with this agreement, despite being guaranteed less than the lower end of the ZOPA described in chapter 2. What the VC firm lost on the dimension of guaranteed percentage up front it more than made up for on other pieces of the agreement. The start-up was hesitant about paying for advice from the VC firm or giving away more of the firm if the advice didn't lead to effective solutions to their challenges. In contrast, the VC firm was optimistic that it would help the start-up achieve its goals, put its own business model on the map, and develop a successful relationship with the start-up's founders. The parties were able to bet on their differing expectations with a contingent contract that would reward the VC firm with an additional 8 percent if it met the negotiated goals. Both sides viewed this agreement as far preferable to the simpler agreement of the VC firm getting 22.22 percent of the firm for $2 million.

The parties created value by exploring what each party cared about and developing a very creative agreement. Many negotiators fail to find this type of mutually beneficial agreement—one that is better for both sides than what they would get if they only focused on price—because of their fixed-pie mindset. Assuming anything that would benefit the other side would be bad for them (a topic I discuss in detail in chapter 11), they obsess about who will get the best deal. They also lack the skills needed to find more creative deals. Most important negotiations require us to work to create more value (a bigger pie) and claim a good portion of the larger pie for ourselves. But when negotiators are obsessed with claiming value, value creation can get lost in the process. That is what happened at Uber.

The Battle for Uber

Uber changed the way hundreds of millions of people arrange their local transportation. Today, many of us far prefer getting rides from Lyft and Uber over taxis. And drivers enjoy many of the features of the Lyft/Uber environment, including their independence and flexibility.

While Uber created a true revolution in transportation and tremendous value, one of the company's founders, Travis Kalanick, who led the firm from 2009 to 2017, was famously difficult in many ways. Media accounts presented Kalanick as arrogant, as having ignored and arguably contributed to sexual harassment within the firm, as needlessly adversarial to government regulators, and as abusive to Uber employees who disagreed with him. Uber also faced many allegations of stealing data from competitors and using legally questionable software to compete with rivals and confuse regulators. Kalanick was also not very good at creating value.

Uber got off the ground around 2010 with significant VC funding, most notably from Bill Gurley and his firm Benchmark. Gurley was a respected advisor in the VC world, having successfully invested in Grubhub, OpenTable, and Zillow, all of which went public and created enormous profits for Benchmark. The frequent negotiations between Kalanick and Gurley form the centerpiece of the 2022 miniseries *Super Pumped*, based on the 2019 nonfiction book of the same name.[1] Benchmark invested $12 million in Uber in 2011 for an approximate 20 percent interest. By 2017, Benchmark's stake was worth billions.

In most negotiations between start-up founders and venture capitalists, a tension exists over how much advice the founder will accept from the funders. Kalanick clearly wanted Benchmark's money and had little interest in having Gurley monitor his leadership. Gurley often defended Kalanick to other investors while trying to coach him to do better. Kalanick was self-centered, trusted his intuition, had little idea of what was legal and viable, and had an enormous dislike of bad news. He wanted to count Uber's "gross bookings" as revenue, though most of that money went to Uber's drivers. "We can't do that," Gurley argued; Kalanick eventually backed down.[2] Gurley advocated for more professional management at Uber, while Kalanick resisted. Gurley saw Kalanick's lack of professionalism as a barrier to maximizing Uber's value. More broadly, Gurley wanted to add qualified financial and legal talent to the firm, which Kalanick continued to resist.

By 2017, Uber was embroiled in ruthless competition with Lyft. Rather than focusing on building a company that would make a profit, Kalanick was obsessed with dominating the market and destroying Uber's rivals.[3] In Kalanick's view, growing revenue, rather than profit, was the key to fundraising as he worked to obtain additional venture capital. The media also saw him as obsessed with the destruction of rivals and avoiding normal corporate controls.

Gurley questioned Kalanick's plans to rapidly expand Uber into new countries, launch a food delivery business, enter the self-driving car business, and build its market in China. Hoping to instill discipline in the company, in 2015 Gurley pushed for Uber to move toward an initial public offering (IPO). Kalanick didn't want the constraints that would come along with an IPO process. Going public would crush Uber's ability to move quickly, he argued. Once again, he ignored Gurley's advice.[4]

Evidence of both Kalanick's brilliance and Gurley's wisdom is indisputable. Combining the best of what each had to offer would have been a powerful combination. And while Kalanick and Gurley reached accommodations on many issues, Kalanick was often dismissive of Gurley and the rest of Uber's board during internal discussions at Uber. In fact, he saw himself as "playing chess" against the board, with himself many moves ahead of them.[5] Notably, chess is a zero-sum game: one player loses if the other player wins. In chess, the goal is to beat the other side. That should not be true of negotiations between founders and VC firms, between founders and their board, or in most negotiations involving many issues. Rather, when negotiation counterparts work together, they can find wiser strategies that make all better off. That is not what happened at Uber, and the infighting dramatically reduced the firm's value as it moved toward becoming a publicly traded company. Gurley played a key role in forcing out Kalanick in mid-2017, with billions of dollars destroyed as the parties focused on their internal conflict rather than developing wise strategies for the business.

Kalanick's approach to negotiation with his board limited the degree to which Uber seized the value it created by its amazing innovation. His approach also worsened his personal outcomes and destroyed his reputation. Very different negotiation strategies could have allowed him to obtain better outcomes for himself and for Uber, not to mention for the Uber employees he claimed to care about.

The Tension between Creating and Claiming Value

Why did Kalanick miss so many value-creating options? Why did he pick a strategy that ultimately forced his board to take his firm away from him? Like Kalanick, many negotiators view negotiation as a chess match in which the goal is to win by beating the other side. By comparison, great negotiators do more than just claim as much value as possible. In most complex real-world negotiations, creating value and increasing the size of the pie is a much more important part of the process. Yet, overly focused on claiming value, or simply beating the other side, many negotiators leave lots of money and other resources on the table.

The culture of venture capital can work against value creation. Founders are often focused on maintaining control of their company, while VC firms want to know that the founder will listen to their advice. Discussions about VC investments tend to focus on valuation and less on synergies that are being created. Yet, mutual beneficial deals are much easier to develop when a true partnership is created.

Would you prefer 60 percent of a $10,000 pie or 60 percent of a $20,000 pie? This seems like a silly question. Yet, lots of negotiators opt for the former option. They haggle over a small pie rather than seeking ways to make the pie larger. And even if you ended up with 50 percent of $20,000, rather than 60 percent of $10,000, you would be better off. I am not arguing (here) for altruism; rather, I am arguing for following strategies that will be of more value to your side. And if you happen to care about the other party, your reputation, and your relationship with the other party, that's even more reason to exercise the genius of value creation.

Returning to the limited view of the negotiation between the start-up and the VC firm in chapter 2, you will recall figure 2.1, where we described the claiming battle between the two parties on one dimension—namely, how much of the start-up the VC firm would get for their $2 million. We can easily convert that one-dimensional depiction to two dimensions, as seen in figure 4.1.

In figure 4.1, the same ZOPA exists between points A and B as in figure 2.1. Point A would be an agreement giving the VC firm 20 percent

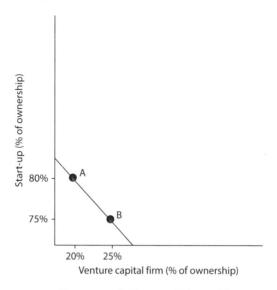

FIGURE 4.1. Creating and Claiming Value in Negotiation.

of the start-up for their $2 million, while Point B would be an agreement giving the VC firm 25 percent of the start-up for their $2 million. What the start-up gives up, the VC firm receives. A high percentage is better for the VC firm and worse for the start-up. All points on the line between Points A and B are possible and within the ZOPA.

Now let's convert the axes on the chart from percent ownership to a broader notion of value to the parties. This account will be affected by the ownership percentage negotiated as well as by other negotiated issues, including the overall value of the start-up. So, if the start-up succeeds in solving its manufacturing and distribution challenges, the overall value of the firm will be greater. If the VC firm can leverage this negotiation to help create and market its unique model, more value will be created.

Figure 4.2 converts the prior figure from percent ownership to value. Points A and B remain the same, but each side views Agreement C (outlined earlier in the chapter) as better than both Points A and B for both sides. By identifying a creative package, more value has been created. Notice that Point C is just one of many points on the most northeasterly

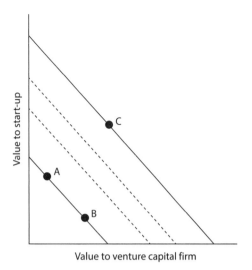

FIGURE 4.2. Creating More Value in Negotiation.

line. Thus, simply creating value does not eliminate the need to claim the larger pie of resources available. It is also possible, or even likely, that instead of a line, the points to the northeast would end up as a curve. Economists use the term "Pareto-efficient frontier" to define the set of possible agreements that exist where there would be no agreement to the northeast of that point—that is, you could not move from that point to improve the outcome of one of the parties without reducing the value to the other party. This chart highlights what I see as an appropriate objective of negotiation, which is to create the biggest pie possible while simultaneously claiming the biggest chunk of that pie that you can, subject to concerns for fairness and the ongoing relationship.

Preparing for Value-Creating Negotiations

When learning negotiation skills through simulations, experienced executives are often struck by the importance of preparation. They become aware that they have underemphasized preparation in their past negotiations. Negotiators should think through all the issues they care about in their relationship with their counterpart. In addition to thinking about what percentage of the start-up the VC firm will receive for its $2 million investment, parties preparing for that negotiation—both the seller and the VC firm—should think about the other factors that affect the attractiveness of the deal. These might include the value/cost of a board seat, the worth/cost of consulting advice from the VC firm, the option for additional equity being earned by the VC firm in the future, and so on. Notice, some of these issues are easily quantified, while others are more difficult to quantify. Yet, when we negotiate multiple issues, we are explicitly or implicitly making trade-offs across these issues. The parties should be thinking about *all* the things each side values. The goal is not to create unneeded complexity but to create the conditions for finding a wiser agreement, one that is better for both parties than if they simply haggled over one issue.

Once you have identified a broad list of issues, the next step is to think through their relative importance. If you are the VC firm, how much are you willing to give up on equity percentage to secure a consulting contract with the seller? How much equity would you give up for a board seat? Such calculations can sound difficult, and they are. Some might even argue that you are comparing apples to oranges. In fact, you are! You are trying to figure out how to integrate the value of multiple issues so you can compare different overall packages. Why would you try to compare apples to oranges? Because if you don't think about how many oranges you would give up for ten apples, you are unlikely to make wise trade-offs at the negotiating table—and any multi-issue negotiation requires you to explicitly or implicitly make such trade-offs. If you trust your intuition to make these trade-offs on the spot, you will do far worse than if you think systematically across issues as part of your preparation.

When teaching negotiation simulations to MBA and executive students, I often provide participants with a verbal description of the case and then summarize it with a scoring system that organizes the multiple issues and prioritizes them so that participants have an overall metric for any agreement they might reach. These scoring systems list each issue and weight it according to its importance. The metric might be in dollars or points. Scoring systems help participants evaluate package offers from the other party and structure offers strategically.

Many executives note that in their actual negotiations, no one gives them such an integrated scoresheet. I respond that this is my experience as well. Then I ask them whether such a scoresheet might be helpful in the real world. They quickly realize that it would be extremely helpful. They then leave the class realizing that their job requires them to prepare to think systematically across issues in important negotiations, perhaps by creating an integrated scoresheet.

In the realm of creating value, it becomes even more important to think systematically about the other side so that you can identify value-creating trade-offs. In negotiation, there often will be issues that you do not care about or that are of minor concern to you—but that the other side cares about very much. It's critical to identify these issues. For example, you may be indifferent between starting your new job in June or July. But if your potential employer strongly prefers that you start as soon as possible, this is a valuable piece of information. Now you are positioned to give them something they value (at no cost to you) and get something of value in return (such as a preferred initial project). Or imagine you are buying a house, and your mortgage is secured. A contractor friend looks the place over before you submit an offer and confirms that the house doesn't have any major problems. With these pieces in place, you may well be positioned to make your offer on the house without any contingencies, such as an inspection. This concession costs you little but might be of significant value to a seller who wants to make sure the sale will go through. This concession might also make your offer more competitive and attractive in a seller's market.

Strategies for Value Creation at the Table

I have asked many experienced executives whether they think they should negotiate the easy or tough issues first in complex, multi-issue negotiations. Many negotiators respond that it's best to start with the easy ones. They argue that beginning with the easy issues allows negotiators to build trust and gather momentum. If you start with a difficult issue, they say, you might derail the negotiation from the start. Other executives argue it is better to begin with the tough issues. If you can't reach agreement on those, they claim, there's no point in wasting time on less important issues, and you can move on to find an alternative buyer or supplier. A third group argues "it depends," and then mentions a variety of issues on which it depends.

All three responses are wrong answers to my trick question. I don't think *any* issue should be resolved first. While negotiators often negotiate with an issue-by-issue agenda, any process that separates the issues from each other is a barrier to finding the trades across issues that allow for value creation. This does not mean that you need to talk about every issue at the same time. But it does mean that you should avoid finalizing an agreement on any one issue before you have had the opportunity to discuss every issue. A more productive path is to discuss both sides' perspectives and preferred outcomes on each issue. With a better idea of the totality of issues on the table, you can begin exploring relative preferences across issues, finding trades, and creating value. And, rather than starting with a tough or easy issue, I recommend creating a wise process that will allow the parties to create value.

We can get clues about how best to create value from the context of the negotiation. Culture, the economic environment, and the relationship between parties affect where value-creation opportunities lie and which negotiation strategies can best develop these opportunities. Too often, negotiators fail to share information needed to create value. Fearful they will be exploited if the other side knows what they value, they keep all their information hidden and assume this is essential to being a tough negotiator.

The following four strategies can help you elicit the information necessary to create value, resolve conflicts, and reach efficient agreements. My experience is that executives often search for the strategy they like best, but that's not what I recommend. Rather, you should have all of these strategies available in your toolbox, as the right strategy for a particular situation depends on the context. Culture, norms, industry standards, and other contextual features will affect how much trust exists between the parties, and the level of trust will affect the right strategy for the context. Generally, the more the parties trust each other, the more appropriate the earlier strategies will be.

Strategy 1: Build trust and share information. Imagine that you are the CEO of a company with two divisions that are about to negotiate a complex multi-issue agreement. While the divisions are individually rewarded for their profitability, you and the company's shareholders are affected by the combined profitability across the entire organization. How do you want these two divisions to negotiate? If I were the CEO, I would want them to share all their information openly and honestly so they would have everything they need to find a creative deal that maximizes joint profit across the two divisions. Yes, they might care about how well their division does at claiming the overall value created, but I want them to negotiate over the biggest pie possible—and I don't want their concerns about value claiming to keep them from creating a bigger pie.

Complicating this goal, managers of many organizations have told me it is tougher to negotiate with others in their company than with outside suppliers and customers. My reaction is that there is something wrong with this story. A main responsibility of leaders is to create an organizational culture where people focus on value creation over value claiming. This means being trusting, trustworthy, and open about how much they value the various issues on the table.

Beyond corporations, we all negotiate with people we care about in our personal lives, and in these contexts, value creation clearly should be more important than value claiming. If you and your partner have different ideas about where to eat dinner and what movie to see, you hopefully would prefer to find a trade-off (your preferred restaurant, their preferred movie) than to simply get your way and annoy your partner. We also have key customers, suppliers, and strategic partners with whom more benefit comes from creating value through information sharing than from simply value claiming. Across all these contexts, we need to recognize the importance of creating trusting relationships and engaging in the information sharing needed to find all the value that can be created. Context is of central importance.

In many negotiations, of course, trust between parties is low or nonexistent. How do we find value-creating trades in less trusting environments? The next two strategies offer guidance.

Strategy 2: Ask questions. Thinking about what the other side cares about before negotiating will help you recognize what you do not know—specifically, which issues are important to the other side and how important those issues are to them. When you recognize what you don't know, you can enter the negotiation with an openness to learning.

Part of your job in negotiation is to let the party on the other side of the table know what information you need from them so that you can make the most attractive offer possible. Many people note that the other party doesn't always answer their questions. But, clearly, they are more likely to answer your questions if you ask them than if you do not. And, as it turns out, many negotiators like to talk.

Of course, part of the trick is to know how to pose the right question. How can you phrase your questions so that the other side is more likely to provide useful information? "Can you just tell me what you really want?" is less likely to lead to useful information than "Can you help me better understand how important various issues are to you, so that we can put an offer on the table that is most likely to be attractive to you?" or "It would be extremely helpful to know of all of the issues you mention, which is most critical to your team?"

Asking questions is especially important when the other party makes an offer that surprises you or that you are skeptical about. For example, when the VC firm's representatives keep focusing on the services they can provide, rather than viewing this as a distraction as you seek funding, ask questions to better understand their perspective. When they make a demand that is unreasonable or that simply doesn't make sense, probe deeper to find out why they are making a demand that seems so unreasonable to you. Perhaps there is a creative way to help them accomplish their actual goals.

Strategy 3: Give away some information. What should you do in a negotiation when trust remains low and the other side is clearly not answering your questions? Consider leveraging the *norm of reciprocity* by giving away some information. Humans tend to reciprocate behavior. When you yell at people, they are more likely to yell back. When you apologize, you often get an apology in return. And when you provide useful and honest information to the other side, they often become more willing to share information with you. That's the norm of reciprocity in action. You can then continue to share information incrementally.

Of course, it is critical to share the right kinds of information. Rarely should you start by sharing your reservation value, as this would only help the other side claim value from you. By contrast, it is generally beneficial to share information regarding your relative priorities across issues. This strategy provides two important benefits. First, if the other side is a wise negotiator, they will work with you to identify trades that will create value. But even if the other party lacks such negotiation skills, they are still likely to reciprocate, and the flow of information may begin.

Strategy 4: Make multiple offers simultaneously. I believe Strategies 1–3 have the potential to help you create the biggest pie possible in most of your complex real-world negotiations. But if I stopped here, many readers would complain that in their most difficult negotiations, these three strategies would fail to persuade their counterpart to provide useful information. While I often find that people have not actually tested this assumption, I certainly believe there are difficult opponents who will resist sharing information. Thus, we need a tactic that elicits information without the other party directly providing it.

This brings us to our fourth strategy: instead of making just one offer at a time, make several offers at once. These multiple offers should be of equal value to you but differ from one another on the issues at stake.

Returning to the start-up negotiation, imagine that instead of simply asking for a 27 percent stake in the start-up for its $2 million, the VC firm instead makes the following three offers, each of which it perceives to be of equal value, at the same time:

1) a 27 percent stake in the start-up for $2 million;
2) a 24 percent stake in the start-up for $2 million and a consulting contract for advice on manufacturing and distribution for a fee of $400,000; or
3) a 20 percent stake in the start-up for $2 million, free consulting on manufacturing and distribution, and an additional 8 percent of the firm for the VC firm if the start-up (1) obtains a viable co-manufacturing agreement within 18 months, (2) gets its

products in at least 2,000 retail locations within 24 months, and (3) secures at least $2 million in its the next round of funding within 30 months.

Now imagine the start-up responds that none of the three offers is entirely acceptable but that the third one is the best starting point for further discussions. This response provides important information. Since the three proposals were crafted to be of equal value to the VC firm, the start-up's response reveals where more value can be created. In the process, the VC firm receives information it might not have gained by asking direct questions.

Note that the other party does not have to *accept* one of your offers to signal their relative priorities. The start-up's desire to negotiate the third offer puts the VC firm on the path to a value-creating deal, even if they shave a couple of percentage points off the up-front stake in the start-up. From there, you can adjust other issues that can allow you to continue to grow the pie.

Making multiple offers simultaneously provides a number of advantages. In addition to enabling you to discover the interests of reticent negotiators, it also allows you to come across as flexible. By providing several options, you signal your willingness to be accommodating and your interest in understanding the other party's preferences and needs. Making multiple offers allows you to find wise trades, grow the pie, appear more flexible, and increase your likelihood of getting a deal done, even with an opponent with whom the earlier strategies were not viable.

Choosing which strategies to use. Which of the four strategies should you start with to create more value? It depends on the context. When your relationship with your counterpart is already strong, the earlier strategies on the list should work well. If you have a great relationship, there is little reason not to share information, turn the negotiation into a problem-solving session, and find the Pareto-efficient frontier. If the relationship is good, but not good enough for Strategy 1, then Strategies 2 and 3 can help you create value. Strategy 4 is available for those extreme occasions where trust is too low for any of the first three strategies to be viable. In general, try out the earlier strategies if you think they might work, but don't give up on negotiating over a bigger pie just because the relationship isn't strong.

It's Not Over Just Because It's Over

This section provides a fifth strategy for value creation, but it's one to use *after* you've reached an agreement. Many of us have reached agreements we weren't fully satisfied with, and perhaps the other side was not either. In such cases, you may have failed to create as much value as possible. So, why stop after you have an agreement? Instead, try creating value after the deal is done via a *post-settlement settlement (PSS)*, an idea first suggested by decision theorist Howard Raiffa.[6]

Imagine you have just reached an agreement with a tough counterpart and want nothing more than to put this long and difficult negotiation process behind you. Instead, consider telling them that you plan to implement the agreement and hope they do as well, but you have one more idea: perhaps you could meet one more time to take another look at your deal to see if there are terms that would be better for both sides. Be sure to clarify that the PSS is not an attempt to renege on the deal or to obtain any additional concessions. Rather, it offers a chance to make further trades that both parties would value. Both parties must benefit, or the initial agreement will remain in place.

A PSS can offer a last chance to create value when you missed opportunities in the initial negotiation. After the tough initial negotiation, neither side wants to simply make an additional concession to the other side. But, perhaps a value-creating trade is possible. The initial agreement confirms that the deal will move forward if you fail to agree on new terms. Once you shake hands on the deal or sign the agreement, the parties may feel less adversarial and be more open to sharing information. Essentially, the initial agreement becomes the new BATNA for *both* parties.

Like making multiple offers simultaneously, PSSs are an underused tool. In fact, most executives have never heard of a PSS. Some are wary of the risks associated with renegotiating, while others think it just sounds strange. But as many have found, a PSS process can be an excellent final opportunity to create value for both parties. Notably, you don't even have to negotiate a PSS immediately upon signing the initial deal. You might want to wait a day, week, or month. The main argument is that when the deal is signed, you may still have room to create value with the other party.

Value Creation as a Way of Life

Probably like you, I negotiate with lots of people. I negotiate with my unit head over my teaching assignments. I negotiate with colleagues on who will do what work on a project. I negotiate with consulting clients about the scope of projects and my fees. As a small-stakes investor, I negotiate with start-ups. I also negotiate with my spouse a great deal. None of the people I negotiate with would describe me as a pushover. But across all these contexts, I hope, and expect, that they would describe me as a good partner, creative at finding mutually beneficial agreements, and focused on how our agreements affect both of us rather than on whether I "won" or "lost" the negotiation. I do care about claiming a reasonable percent of the value created for myself. But I find it far easier and more valuable to spend more of my efforts on growing the pie than on claiming it.

Value creation goes well beyond negotiation, but the concept remains the same. Economists talk about maximizing social welfare, or the sum of the welfare of all members of society. An honest politician should work to maximize the collective welfare of a broader group than just one individual, family, or organization. Maximizing social welfare is synonymous with creating as much value as possible. In philosophy, an ethical perspective called utilitarianism argues for maximizing aggregate benefit for all and applies this concept to assess the ethicality of people's behavior. To a utilitarian, value creation for all is a moral requirement. And just as you shouldn't lie in negotiations for ethical reasons (unless you can save the world by doing so), you also shouldn't destroy value. Whether from a welfare-maximizing perspective or a utilitarian perspective, when you move toward the Pareto-efficient frontier, not only are you likely to get a better outcome for yourself, but you are making the world a slightly better place.

Relatedly, I really don't like waste. I don't like to waste time, and I don't like uneaten food ending up in the trash. In negotiation, we waste value when we fail to find mutually beneficial trades. We *can* do better. I hope this overview of value creation refocuses your efforts on how to understand your context to allow you to produce better results for you, your company, and the world in your negotiations.

■ ■ ■

"I appreciate the value of helping the other side achieve their goals, and I see the benefit of trading off what is more important for me with what is more important for them. I think I am pretty good at following this advice with people I know well and who have similar communication styles. But my most important negotiations involve people from different cultures who have very different communication styles and do not share information easily. How do you create value with people from cultures that are more reserved and less communicative?"

"Your observation about the complexity of dealing with people who are different from you is intriguing. There is lots of evidence that we are more comfortable with other people who match our communication style. Yet, in the global economy, we often need to interact with people who are very different from us, including people who speak different languages or have very different norms. As China and India grow as international economies, more executives will have the opportunity to create value through interactions with people from these cultures. In fact, our differences with people from these cultures create opportunities, and we need to figure out how to seize those opportunities. Often we are interacting with people who can contribute something very different to our collaboration or contribute with a very different cost structure. We simply need to figure out how to best put together the deal in the context that confronts us. This chapter has highlighted multiple strategies for creating joint value. Depending on the level of trust you have with the other side, you can pursue the right value-creating strategy. Part of the beauty of the idea of presenting multiple simultaneous offers and suggesting a post-settlement settlement is that they can be used even when the conversation needed to share information about differences is more difficult."

Chapter 5

Negotiating Ethically

"We have been searching for a new home, and a friend of ours is our real estate agent. We have always trusted her, but have noticed that she keeps advising us to make offers that are higher than we believe are reasonable. We are concerned that this serves her interest in getting a quick sale but not our interest in getting as low a price as possible. Should we question her ability to offer us ethical advice? Should we listen to her advice? Should we even remain friends with someone whose advice would benefit her but not necessarily us?"

. . .

When my students ask me about challenging negotiation contexts they are facing, they often describe negotiating against counterparts they perceive to be difficult. These people may seem difficult due to cultural differences. They may seem difficult as a result of the economic environment, such as problems in the supply chain. But in many cases, as in the question above, students cite unethical behavior as a big part of the story. Negotiators often obsess about the ethics of their counterpart, I've noticed, while failing to fully consider their own ethical (or unethical) behavior. In fact, the ethical behavior of the two (or more) parties at the table is often related. In this chapter, we will explore your own ethicality, the ethical norms of others, and how they are intertwined.

Which of the following best describes your view about lying in negotiations?

1) You should never lie.
2) You should very rarely lie.
3) You should avoid lying, but lies are often necessary in negotiation.
4) Lying is simply a part of the negotiation process.

The first and last choices (1 and 4) are popular ones. And if I were faced with only those two options, I would choose never lying over the view that lies are simply part of the negotiation process. But when given all four choices, I would choose #2—you should very rarely lie. Why not the more straightforward statement that you should never lie in negotiations, which many philosophers would endorse? To begin with, let's consider what was quite possibly the most important lie ever told in a negotiation.

The Best Lie Ever Told

In October 1962, the world came closer to nuclear war than at any other point in human history. The U.S. government discovered that the Soviet Union was installing armed nuclear missiles in Cuba, which is less than 100 miles from the southern tip in Florida. The missiles were capable of hitting targets within 1,500 miles (which included Washington, D.C.). The Soviet Union had promised the United States that it would not install missiles in Cuba, but it did so anyway (this wasn't the best lie ever told; that is coming later).

The intuitive response of President John F. Kennedy and virtually all his key advisors was that the government needed to initiate an air strike quickly to take out the missiles before they became operational. We know that deliberation leads to wiser decisions than relying on intuition does, yet many leaders put too much trust in their intuition. Thankfully, Kennedy's executive committee deliberated, and the administration transitioned to a strategy of negotiating the withdrawal of the missiles with the Soviet Union.

A bit of history is useful for understanding the negotiated solution. From 1956 to 1959, Fidel Castro led a guerrilla war in Cuba and succeeded in ousting the nation's U.S.-backed authoritarian leader, General Fulgencio Batista. The revolution took place during the Cold War between the United States and the Soviet Union. Following Castro's rise to power, the U.S. government cut off all purchases of Cuban sugar, the country's leading export, which created an economic crisis in Cuba. To create a market for its sugar, Cuba developed a political alliance with the Soviet Union. Meanwhile, the United States made numerous attempts to remove Castro from power and to assassinate him (an initiative known as Project Mongoose that included the unsuccessful Bay of Pigs invasion in 1961). The U.S. government, which had gained enormous nuclear superiority over the Soviet Union, installed nuclear weapons in Turkey that were capable of reaching the Soviet Union. From the Soviet perspective, positioning nuclear-armed missiles in Cuba would deter the United States from launching a first strike.

After missiles were identified in Cuba on October 13, 1962, the world was on the brink of nuclear war for thirteen days.[1] Eventually, the leadership circle around Kennedy implemented a strategy of quarantining Cuba so that it could not receive further weaponry from the Soviet Union, and a complex negotiation process began between the United States and the Soviet Union. The fact that the quarantine was chosen over the initially intuitive strategy of an air strike (a strategy that the military and the CIA continued to recommend throughout the crisis) ended up being fortunate. In 1992, after the collapse of the Soviet Union, American officials learned in discussions with Russia and Cuba that, in addition to the missiles the United States had identified, other Soviet nuclear missiles and warheads were based in Cuba. Had the United States chosen an air strike, it is likely that the Soviet Union would have launched multiple nuclear weapons, leading to a full-scale nuclear war.

While there were many complexities in the negotiation between the United States and the Soviet Union, a seemingly rigid barrier to agreement existed over the Soviet demand that the United States remove its missiles from Turkey in return for the Soviets removing their missiles from Cuba. In fact, the missiles in Turkey were obsolete; the United

States didn't value them and had previously considered removing them. But Kennedy refused to publicly agree to remove them, for fear of appearing weak to our allies and to the American public in response to the Soviet threat.[2]

In a secret meeting, President Kennedy's brother and most valued advisor, Robert Kennedy (also the U.S. attorney general), and Anatoly Dobrynin, the Soviet ambassador to the United States, reached an agreement that included the withdrawal of Soviet missiles from Cuba, the withdrawal of U.S. missiles from Turkey after a six-month delay, and a promise that neither side would publicly reveal that the removal of the missiles from Turkey was part of the deal to get the missiles out of Cuba. After this agreement was in place, President Kennedy and many other U.S. leaders denied any connection between the missiles in Cuba and the missiles in Turkey. That is, the two parties agreed that the United States would lie about their actual deal.

The secret agreement on U.S. missiles in Turkey and the lies that followed may have protected the world from a nuclear disaster. So, I have trouble condemning these lies. I also don't want to condemn many white lies told to maintain our social and business relationships, such as "We have tremendous respect for your company," "You look very nice today," and "It's not a problem that you took three weeks to reply to our proposal."

At the same time, I side with those who think lying should not be a component of most negotiations. Lies cause great harm, and I advise against lying in the vast majority of circumstances. I do so not because I believe categorically that it is wrong to lie. Rather, I generally recommend against lying because lies more often destroy value than create it. When people lie in negotiation, their goal is typically to claim value from the other side. In doing so, they risk destroying the value that the parties could create together in a more trusting and trustworthy relationship. This chapter is about ethical behavior as a means of creating the most value possible.

As I've noted, I do not condemn lies that create more value than they destroy. Notably, this is very rarely the case. The lie about the missiles in Turkey may have created massive value by giving both sides a political victory and saving the world from a nuclear war. Once again, context matters in negotiation. Here, context helps us detect the rare conditions when a lie is acceptable. And the sociopolitical context of Kennedy's lie helps us understand that this was a rare lie that created value.

Philosophical Perspectives on Ethics in Negotiation

Not all philosophical perspectives would let President Kennedy off the hook for lying about the missiles in Turkey. Deontology, a philosophical perspective associated with Immanuel Kant, argues that we are morally obligated to follow universal moral laws, such as "Don't lie." These moral laws are based on rules that are deemed to make the world better if we all follow them (what Kant called a "categorical imperative").[3] To deontologists, lying is simply out of bounds—no exceptions. That means no untrue compliments about someone's appearance. No lies to prevent a nuclear Armageddon. And when the Nazis show up at your house looking for "the Jews," no lying to hide the fact that you are protecting Jewish friends in a secret part of the house. Of course, there are advantages to never telling a lie: other people will learn to trust you, which will make your statements more credible. But not avoiding a nuclear Armageddon and not protecting your friends from evildoers would remain a problem.

In contrast to deontology, the philosophical perspective of utilitarianism judges an action based on its cumulative expected impact on creating the most pleasure and minimizing the most pain, aggregated across all.[4] According to utilitarians, the pleasure and pain of all should be considered equally. That means no extra value for your own pleasure or that of members of your in-group (including your family, coworkers, and fellow citizens). If you're a utilitarian, you place equal value on everyone's outcomes: people in your neighborhood and those across the world; those in your religion, members of other religions, and atheists; those in your organization and your competitors; and both friends and opponents on the other side of the negotiating table.

Utilitarianism is a bit demanding—too demanding, some would say—in not allowing you to give special consideration to your child, for example, over others. I personally find the idea of creating the most value for all, and not being limited by my own biases and preferences, appealing. I like the North Star of creating value over a simple rule like "never lie." Utilitarianism would be supportive of always getting to the Pareto-efficient frontier in negotiation, since that is where the most value is located. Utilitarians would be opposed to lying in the vast majority of negotiations, since it is harder to find value-creating trade-offs when one side is spreading false information to the other. Utilitarians would not want any of the pie to be squandered due to a focus on value claiming or unethical behavior. This focus on creating the most value, both in specific negotiations and in life more broadly, is my rationale for not lying in nearly all my negotiations and for encouraging others to not lie. Not only do lies make it harder to get to the Pareto-efficient frontier, but they harm relationships, reduce your credibility as someone who can create value, and weaken your working relationship between counterparts—all of which will further reduce value in the future. But utilitarians do not have a simple prohibition against lying, and many (including me) would agree that President Kennedy's lie about the missiles in Turkey was warranted.

The distinction between deontology and utilitarianism is clearest on the matter of lying. But in negotiation, deception comes in many forms, making the ethics of lying more complicated to assess. Some negotiators fake their emotional reaction to the other side's offer, misdirect the other party without making a false statement, avoid answering questions from the other side, and/or fail to correct their counterpart's false assumptions. Deontology is unclear on whether you are violating a duty when, to gain an advantage, you fail to correct your negotiation opponent's false assumption. By comparison, utilitarianism is clear: if your failure to be more transparent and honest reduces your ability to create value with the other party, then your action is unethical. The focus is not on whether you follow a rule but on the likely impact of your action on creating the most value possible.

A third perspective on ethics that's relevant to negotiation is over 2,400 years old and comes from Aristotle.[5] Rather than defining an act as moral or immoral, as utilitarianism and deontology do, Aristotle's virtue ethics focus on the moral character of the actor—in our case, the negotiator—and, specifically, the kind of person they would like to become. Aristotle saw humans as works in progress, always in the process of developing themselves on a variety of dimensions connected to morality. While he didn't include having a value-creating mindset as a core virtue, the world clearly would be better off if you sought to create value in your negotiations. Thus, internalizing the idea of creating the most value for all is a move toward the Aristotelian goal of improving oneself morally.

Without attempting to resolve core philosophical disputes about morality in this book on negotiation, I argue that negotiators are more moral when they act in ways that increase the resources available to all. In my view, the moral virtues that negotiators should want to develop are those that produce opportunities to create more value.

Psychological Perspectives on Ethics in Negotiation

While the topic of ethics has been in the hands of philosophers for generations, psychologists and organization scholars picked it up in the new millennium. Psychologists focus on the decisions that people make in contexts with ethical implications, including negotiation. When we think of someone behaving unethically in negotiations, our first image typically is of a person telling an obvious lie—making an affirmative statement that they know is not accurate, such as "This car has never been in an accident." You're already familiar with my view that you shouldn't lie in negotiation unless you are saving the world from a nuclear war or seizing some other once-in-a-lifetime opportunity to create great good. Lying harms your reputation, destroys relationships, and makes it harder to create value. The tactical advantage gained from claiming value simply isn't worth it, and from an ethical standpoint, the costs are too high. Yet many of the unethical behaviors you might engage in do not involve an explicit lie but rather would reduce value, thus making them unethical from a utilitarian perspective.

Mahzarin Banaji, Dolly Chugh, and I use the term "bounded ethicality"[6] to refer to the systematic and predictable psychological processes that prompt people (including negotiators) to engage in ethically questionable behaviors that are inconsistent with even their *own* preferred ethics. In negotiation, bounded ethicality leads us toward behaviors that destroy value overall and clash with our own conscious beliefs about right and wrong. The core argument of bounded ethicality is that many unethical behaviors that people engage in during negotiations result from ordinary, unintentional psychological processes, not from deliberate deception.

The same is true of our negotiating counterparts. When they engage in unethical behavior, we tend to assume they are deliberately trying to cheat us. The realization that we ourselves act unethically without intention suggests we need to discard the common assumption that any undesirable behavior we observe from a negotiation opponent is due to them having especially low ethical standards.

If you want to act ethically in your negotiations, you need to understand the common ways that honest people violate their own moral standards without conscious awareness.

Conflicts of interest. "It is difficult to get a man [*sic*] to understand something when his salary depends upon his not understanding it," the writer Upton Sinclair once wrote.[7] This quote turns out to be a very accurate description of human behavior generally and in negotiation specifically. Specifically, it highlights the risks of conflicts of interest. Because of their financial incentives, surgeons are more likely to view surgery as the best treatment for a patient than are physicians who do not operate. Similarly, salespeople often honestly believe that their company's product is superior even when that might not be the case.

Conflict of interest comes in two forms. The most obvious form is when a salesperson's desire to earn a commission and impress their manager conflicts with their desire to provide accurate information to a buyer. This type of conflict of interest can lead the salesperson to *intentionally* overstate the quality of their product or service. The more pernicious form of conflict of interest occurs *unintentionally*, as when a salesperson who desires to be ethical honestly believes their mediocre product is fantastic. As a result, when the salesperson deceives the buyer, they have no intention to be deceptive; they believe their inaccurate information. We have self-serving tendencies to view what we would like to be true as being truer than reality dictates. But when a salesperson says their products are the best on the market, and a potential buyer can't distinguish those products from the competition's, the buyer might not only refuse to make a purchase but also question the seller's ethics.

Asymmetric views of what's fair. Today, there is broad agreement that the climate is changing, that human behavior is a significant contributor to climate change, and that we ought to be working hard to reduce our negative impacts on the environment. Most of us also would agree that society's failure to adequately respond to the crisis is a moral one, as the costs of climate change will fall on future generations.

If we agree that those of us alive today need to change our behaviors, we are left with the task of divvying up responsibility for making these changes across nations. Which countries should commit to which changes? Emerging nations blame developed economies for our industrialization and excessive consumption. They argue it is unfair for developed economies, many of which have benefited from more than a century of economic development, to demand that emerging economies take steps toward climate change reduction. Meanwhile, developed economies blame emerging nations for burning rainforests, overpopulation, and heavily polluting forms of economic expansion. The U.S. government, in particular, justifies its failure to be more involved in developing worldwide solutions by accusing China and India of not taking enough responsibility for their current and future greenhouse gas emissions. And what about low-lying coastal countries that face catastrophic impacts from climate change—should other countries help them out?

Like many negotiators, countries tend to be biased in a self-serving manner—that is, to be egocentrically biased—when considering viable solutions to climate change. Egocentrism refers to the tendency to make judgments regarding allocations of blame and credit that are biased in favor of your group. Countries may indeed want a climate change agreement that is fair to all, but their view of what is fair is biased by self-interest. Egocentrism leads parties to believe it is honestly fair for them to bear less responsibility for reversing climate change than an independent party would judge as fair. Climate change is worsened not by our desire to be unfair but by our inability to view information objectively.

Similar patterns of self-serving interpretations of what is fair can be found in organizations. Overclaiming credit can hinder the implementation and progress of a variety of joint ventures. When each party believes they are contributing more than they really are, this can lead to conflict over credit, arguments about the allocation of future effort, and so on. So, when your colleague claims more credit for the ideas that came out of a group discussion than you believe they deserve, consider that they likely believe they deserve the credit they are claiming. This doesn't make them right, but it does make them human.

In my research with Nick Epley and Eugene Caruso, we asked MBA students to estimate the percentage of work they personally completed in their study groups.[8] On average, the credit claimed by members of a group totaled 139 percent. In separate research, Epley and his colleagues found a strategy to reduce this overclaiming of credit: "unpacking" the contributions of others. Specifically, they asked all members of the group to think not just about their own contribution but about the contribution of each group member. When they did, overclaiming dropped by about half.[9] As this research shows, explicitly thinking about the contributions of each group member reduces the magnitude of the self-serving behavior. The key is to get group members to focus not only on what they have done but also on what each individual, considered one at a time, has done.

By the way, if you think overclaiming is unique to MBA students, consider that we replicated the same effect for academic authors of published papers: they overclaimed credit for their contributions to research projects. Much of this research builds on classic work by Michael Ross and Fiore Sicoly, who in the 1970s asked both members of heterosexual married couples to estimate the percentage of the household work they each did. On average, the amounts each couple claimed to have done far exceeded 100 percent.[10]

Parties who witness contests and disputes also asymmetrically interpret credit and blame, research shows. If you've ever seen a home-team crowd in a fury over a referee's or an umpire's call, this shouldn't surprise you. We tend to view judges' marginal decisions in predictably self-interested ways. Similarly, when I teach negotiation simulations, it is common for one party in a pair to claim that their negotiation opponent in the simulation lied to them. The other party is quick to refute this accusation, arguing that they never made a false statement and therefore never lied. Notably, the results of the simulation have no actual consequences for the participants, but they become heated nonetheless. As I probe to understand their different accounts of the same episode, I often find that the accused party said something misleading, without actually making a factually incorrect statement, such as "It is possible another offer will arrive as early as 2 p.m. today" when no offer is expected—but is possible. The recipient of the misleading communication was deceived, and feels lied to. Many negotiators make it a rule to not lie but are less strict with themselves about other potentially misleading behavior. In contrast, we tend to expect more ethical behavior from our counterparts. That is, we asymmetrically hold them to higher standards than those to which we hold ourselves and members of our own team.

The omission/commission bias in negotiations. Why do so many people fail to get vaccinated against potentially deadly diseases? This failure is both a poor individual decision and an unethical act, since the failure to vaccinate against communicable diseases can harm others. Vaccines have a very successful history of providing far more benefit than the harm they create. But there are costs: people can suffer side effects from vaccines (though these are rarely serious), and some argue that vaccines could harm them in the distant future (though the evidence suggests this is not a significant medical concern). When Covid-19 vaccines became available, after over a million people had died of the disease worldwide, scientists understood that getting vaccinated was a wise choice. Yet millions of Americans, and many more people across the world, refused to get vaccinated.

Why? Because, by and large, they were more focused on the potential harms of action than on the risks of inaction. This remained true even though the benefits of Covid vaccines far exceeded the costs.[11] This illogical preference for harms of omission (risking serious illness and death from Covid) over possible harms of action (in this case, short-term side effects of the vaccine) is known as the omission bias. When following the common rule of thumb "Do no harm," we often assume that "do" requires action, which makes harms of omission easy to ignore. And when judging the ethical behavior of negotiators, we tend to hold them accountable for acts of commission, like lying, far more than acts of omission, such as not telling a potential buyer that your car has had transmission problems for the last year.

I believe a negotiator's action or inaction should be evaluated based on the net value that action or inaction creates. So, if you mislead the other side without overtly lying (e.g., by failing to correct their incorrect assumption), you are being unethical if your choice can be expected to eliminate the potential to create value. From a utilitarian perspective, the metric for judging the ethics of an action in negotiation should be how much net harm is created through our action *or* inaction.

I've covered just a few psychological aspects of the unethical choices some negotiators make. I hope they help you see how you can behave more ethically as well as how you can better understand the actions (or inactions) of your counterparts.

Cooperation between Parties

In a number of the negotiation simulations commonly taught in MBA and executive classes, participants play the role of one company in an industry that has few players (I will assume two, but the logic works with three or four). Without talking to their competitor, each student must decide whether to charge a high or low price for their product.[12] If one firm charges a high price and the other firm charges a low price, the firm that chose the low price will gain market share at the expense of the firm that chose the high price. Clearly, both companies would be financially better off if they both charged high prices than if they both charged low prices.

The parties typically play multiple rounds before getting feedback on their performance. These price-setting simulations are applied versions of the prisoner's dilemma game, in which each party in a pair would be

NEGOTIATING ETHICALLY   79

individually better off using a competitive strategy (setting a low price), but the parties are jointly better off using a cooperative strategy (setting a high price). Cooperating creates more value for the two price setters.

In the next section, we will question the ethicality of competitors coordinating to set higher prices. For now, simply notice that both parties are better off (in terms of their own value) cooperating than competing. Similarly, when nations jointly negotiate free trade agreements, they increase the opportunity for efficient trades for both sides and set themselves up to create more value. In many contexts, increased trust and cooperation between parties enables value creation. So, we should think about how different contexts provide opportunities to build trust and cooperate more—not only to increase our own profits but also to create more aggregate value.

Parasitic Value Creation

In the price-setting simulations described above, I have observed many well-known negotiation scholars praising participants who create value for themselves by setting mutually high prices. Jointly, they make more money than pairs who focus on trying to beat the other party. Personally, I question where this value creation came from. I believe in markets and incentives, and am generally open to companies charging the prices that the market will bear. But the companies in this simulation (and their negotiators) should consider, in much the same way antitrust laws ask firms to do, whether they are creating societal value or simply helping each other extract as much money as possible at the expense of the consumer. When parties are negotiating a deal that would affect people who are not seated at the table, such as consumers or future generations, it becomes their moral obligation to consider the utility of all parties, not just those at the negotiating table.

James Gillespie and I coined the term "parasitic integration" to describe negotiators creating value by taking value away from parties who are not at the bargaining table.[13] How can you judge whether the value you create is parasitic? One criterion would be to assess the net value created: overall, is society better off as a result of the parties in the deal cooperating? If so, I do not view the deal as parasitic, though some of the value created may impose costs on others. To avoid engaging in parasitic value creation, determine all the parties who would be affected by your negotiation and how each would be affected, and assess all the benefits and harms created by the deal for all these parties—not just those at the table.

Consistent with the price-setting example above, one category of parasitic integration occurs when two or more firms collude to maintain high prices rather than honestly competing in the marketplace. Another disturbing type of parasitic value creation occurs in negotiations between special-interest groups and the elected officials who can pass laws that these groups value. These interactions can include legal discussions between lobbyists and politicians, or they can involve explicit corruption of public officials. In the United States, special-interest groups contribute enormous sums of money to political campaigns.[14] Politicians clearly benefit from these donations. If you believe, like I do, that elected officials have a moral obligation to maximize the social welfare of all their constituents, then special-interest groups destroy value by gaining an outsized voice in public policy. Negotiations between special-interest groups and politicians are often unethical because they steal value from those who are not part of the discussion.

Managing the Other Party's (Un)Ethical Behavior

Very few executives have sought my advice on how they can be more ethical. Yet many executives have asked me about how to deal with the unethical behavior of other negotiators. In this section, I draw on my work with Deepak Malhotra to provide some advice on how to manage the ethical behavior of your counterparts.[15]

In general, don't lie. We have already addressed the multiple reasons you should avoid lying in negotiation (unless, of course, doing so would help you prevent a nuclear Armageddon). Here's another reason, which we covered in chapter 4: when we are honest and transparent negotiators, our counterparts are likely to be honest and transparent in return. It's the norm of reciprocity in action: when we lie to people, they tend to lie to us. Not lying reduces the likelihood that the other party will lie to you. Being open and honest doesn't guarantee the other side won't lie, but it will motivate many to follow the social norms you set.

Work to detect lies. Despite your best efforts to create a more trusting negotiation, you will find yourself in situations where you are concerned that you are being lied to. How can you tell when your counterparts are lying? If you think you have a great intuitive ability to detect lies based on cues like excessive blinking and stammering, think again. Most of us are not very good lie detectors.[16]

Fortunately, there are strategies for detecting lies that don't involve trying to read people's body language. First, we can understand that others are more likely to lie to us when they have information that we do not—that is, when information asymmetry exists. After all, they can only get away with a lie if they know something you do not. This further bolsters the importance of preparation in negotiation. When you are well prepared for a negotiation, and the other party can tell that you are, they are less likely to try to deceive you. Your signs of preparation suggest you might be able to detect their deceptive actions.

Another strategy for lie detection is triangulation, a word you might not have encountered since high school geometry class. In geometry, triangulation allows you to estimate an unknown physical quantity (distance) by using other measurements that you do know (other distances and angles). In negotiation, triangulation is the strategy of asking multiple questions to "triangulate" on the truth. A company's net income equals its revenue minus expenses. So, if you ask for all three of these quantities, and the answer they provide is inconsistent with this formula, you now have a hint about possible dishonesty. Many liars do not tell a consistent web of lies. Triangulation allows you to discover where the truth is located.

Notice when they do not answer a question. When faced with a question they don't want to answer, many negotiators answer a related question instead, as Todd Rogers and Mike Norton documented in a fascinating article titled "The Artful Dodger."[17] Lots of people dodge questions, including politicians, CEOs in press conferences, and marital partners. As I noted earlier, people don't like to lie but may be more comfortable misdirecting your attention. The implication is that you should be on the alert for when someone doesn't answer your question directly but acts as if they did. In such cases, it is typically a good time to ask your question again, saying you didn't hear the answer the first time.

Test the other party. Former business law professor and U.S. Consumer Product Safety Commissioner Robert Adler offers another strategy for testing the other side: ask them a question that you know the answer to and that you have every reason to believe they do as well.[18] If their answer doesn't line up with what you know to be true, you have a hint that they either do not know the answer or are not answering truthfully.

When using any of these strategies, you should not be focused on blaming the other party but instead on how to create a context in which the other party is less likely to lie and you are more likely to notice if they do. By reducing the odds of deception, you foster the transparency needed to create value in negotiation.

Why Not Just Create Value and Not Worry about Claiming Value?

When prospective clients call to ask about my teaching services, they often ask whether I teach win-win or win-lose negotiations. I find the question awkward and misdirected. The question tells me they are hoping I teach win-win negotiations. After all, negotiation training that was limited to strategies for clobbering the other side (win-lose) fell out of vogue forty years ago. Yet, my answer isn't win-win. Rather, as simply and clearly as possible, I try to sum up what I've covered in the past few chapters: I explain that I teach people to create the biggest pie possible while also showing them how to claim the largest portion of the pie possible, subject to concerns for fairness, the outcomes to other party, and the ongoing relationship.

What's wrong with "win-win"? To start with, win-win is too vague. Too many negotiators reach inefficient agreements, yet claim they found a win-win deal. I want negotiators to create as much value as they can.

This is effective negotiation, and since it maximizes value creation, it is consistent with my view (and utilitarian views) of ethics in negotiation.

Why not simply focus on creating the biggest pie possible? Why let concerns about value claiming get in the way of value creation? Because a salesperson who simply focused on value creation, with no concern for claiming, would not be good at their job, would eventually be fired, and, in the long term, would have fewer opportunities to create value. Thus, even the most ethical negotiator needs to think about how to get great results for themselves and their organization to thrive and create value over time.

Effective and ethical negotiators need to eliminate their own *unintended* unethical behaviors and work to create a context in which the other side is also more likely to behave ethically. The psychology of ethics can help us assess others' behavior and check our own intuition. I hope you have found some useful nuggets in this chapter that put you on the path toward more effective and ethical negotiation.

■ ■ ■

"We have been searching for a new home, and a friend of ours is our real estate agent. We have always trusted her, but have noticed that she keeps advising us to make offers that are higher than we believe are reasonable. We are concerned that this serves her interest in getting a quick sale but not our interest in getting as low a price as possible. Should we question her ability to offer us ethical advice? Should we listen to her advice? Should we even remain friends with someone whose advice would benefit her but not necessarily us?"

"Don't assume that your friend (the agent) is unethical. You need to consider her context of receiving payment only when a deal goes through, while also being your friend. As research in this chapter shows, very nice people can act in self-serving ways without being aware they are harming others. Your friend/agent, like most agents, has a conflict of interest in giving you advice, even if she claims to represent your interests. Thus, while I think you might be right that your agent is pushing you to make overly aggressive offers in the hope of closing the deal, it is also likely that your agent suffers from bounded ethicality and honestly sees the world in a way that will also maximize her returns.

Essentially, I am arguing that your agent is human, and humans tend to see the evidence in ways that match their incentives. So, there's no need to question the agent's integrity. I do recommend that you ask your agent for a market analysis that supports their recommendation and then make your own assessment. The agent's advice needs to be understood in the context of the incentives of all the parties, including the agent. Finally, I see no basis for questioning your friendship with the agent, since there's no evidence of intentionally unethical behavior."

Chapter 6

Betting on the Future

The Role of Contingent Contracts

"I like the idea of value creating and, quite honestly, hadn't really thought that much about how to create value before taking your class. But the most important challenge I will face when I get back to work concerns a supplier who has completely unrealistic views about how valuable their services are to our company. While we do value their services, their valuation of those services is out of whack with the impact we think they will have on our company. How do I create value with a supplier that does not have a realistic sense of what their services are worth to my firm?"

. . .

National Football League (NFL) players typically start their professional careers around age 22. The average age of an NFL player is between 26 and 27, and the average retirement age is 27.6. For most players, the decision to retire from football is typically not a positive one aimed at changing to a more rewarding career but rather a necessity due to concussions, other health concerns, or a decrease in skill level. So as the 2021 NFL season started, it was unusual to see Andrew Whitworth playing for the Los Angeles Rams. Whitworth was approaching his fortieth birthday and was the oldest starting offensive tackle in NFL history. For those who don't follow American football, offensive tackles are the very large guys in front of the quarterback who try to keep the similarly large guys on the other side from getting to the team's quarterback.

Before the 2020 season, Whitworth and the Rams signed a three-year agreement for about $10 million a year. The contract was not fully guaranteed, meaning the team could cancel it early and not fully pay for the second and third years. If they chose not to pay for the second year, they would have owed Whitworth $4 million to cancel the contract.

While Whitworth was valuable, $10 million for a forty-year-old was a very high annual payment and took away from other possible team expenditures. Like most professional athletes, Whitworth remained confident in his skills, but the Rams may have seen him as overconfident. That may have been why the Rams renegotiated Whitworth's contract for the second year, the 2021 season, agreeing to a guaranteed payment of $4 million (the same as the cancellation price) and up to $4.5 million in bonuses.[1] Specifically, he would receive the bonuses if he played a specified percentage of the Rams' offensive plays and if the Rams achieved a variety of team rankings.

The contract worked: Whitworth performed well and received the full bonus. The Rams won the Super Bowl, and Whitworth received the 2021 Walter Payton NFL Man of the Year Award, which honors a player's volunteer and charity work, as well as his excellence on the field. After the season, Whitworth announced his retirement, deciding not to play the final year of the original three-year contract at age forty-one. "Andrew Whitworth epitomizes the best of people," Rams owner Stan Kroenke said. "His hard work to perform at the highest levels on the field is only surpassed by his commitment to making his communities better."[2]

While Whitworth's age may have made performance bonuses particularly relevant in his case, significant bonuses have become common in sports contracts over the last couple of decades. Even top quarterbacks like Patrick Mahomes (Kansas City Chiefs) and Dak Prescott (Dallas Cowboys), who earn tens of millions of dollars in guaranteed income, can earn millions more based on their own performance and their team's.

One particularly stunning bet on performance, also known as a contingent contract, dates back to 1997, when the National Basketball

Association's (NBA) Chicago Bulls agreed to a very unusual deal with star Dennis Rodman. The Bulls had just won their fifth championship in seven years, in large part thanks to the amazing play of Michael Jordan.[3] After this fifth championship season, Bulls fans waited many weeks to learn whether Jordan would play another season. And as the Bulls waited, they held off on re-signing Rodman. While everyone agreed Rodman was a great rebounder and defender, he was also viewed as unpredictable. A showman with a disdain for professional norms, he had a propensity to miss games—sometimes suspended for his most egregious behaviors, at other times kicked out of games for fouling opponents. In fact, Rodman had missed twenty-seven of the eighty-two regular-season games in the previous season. If Jordan signed on for the next season, the Bulls wanted Rodman for his rebounds and defense, creating the potential for another championship. But they also wanted Rodman to be more reliable. If the Bulls didn't re-sign Jordan, they were unlikely to be competitive the following year, and the speculation was that they would pass on signing Rodman.

We Bulls fans were happy to learn that Jordan signed again for a record-setting salary, as discussed in chapter 2. Jordan's deal set up the fascinating negotiations with Rodman that followed.

Rumors in the media suggested the Bulls had offered Rodman $4–5 million, while he sought a salary in excess of $10 million. The result of their negotiation was the most extensive contingent contract in sports history: a guaranteed salary of $4.5 million per year, plus up to another $6 million per year in bonuses.

The bonuses included $1 million for playing in all playoff games and $500,000 for winning another rebounding title—fairly typical bonuses for an NBA player. The really interesting contingency focused on the point of contention between the Bulls and Rodman: his absences. The contract provided Rodman an additional $185,000 for each game he played above fifty-nine. The contract worked. Rodman quit fouling out of games, and he quit getting suspended. In fact, he played in eighty of the season's eighty-two games (missing two games due to injury). The Bulls won another championship, Rodman won his seventh consecutive rebounding title, and his total compensation for the year exceeded $10.1 million.

These sports stories involved performance bonuses. They also fit into a broader range of negotiated solutions called contingent contracts, which are also referred to as profit-sharing agreements, risk-sharing agreements, and bets. Chapter 4 focused on how to create value through wise trades across issues. Contingent contracts trade off what will happen if a specified event happens in the future against what will happen if it does not. It is common for negotiators to have difficulty reaching agreement because they have different expectations about a future uncertain event. A contingent contract can help them overcome such differences and reach a deal.

As I mentioned in chapter 1, I get many calls asking for advice in tough negotiation contexts, and no one calls because they want me to help make a good negotiation great. Rather, they are facing some difficulty. In over half of these negotiations, the context that makes these negotiations difficult is that the parties have a difference in stated expectations about what will happen in the future. An understanding of the specific context allows negotiators to identify how each side can reach an agreement based on their own expectations about the future. Arguing about the future rarely helps the parties resolve their differences. But bets, or contingent contracts, can provide a useful pathway to mutually beneficial resolutions.

It's not news that you can motivate employees to perform well with pay-for-performance incentives. But you might not have thought about the ways in which a broader range of disagreements about the future can be solved through the creation of novel negotiation contracts. This chapter presents the many advantages of contingent contracts, as well as their limitations. They are by definition dependent on context.

The Benefits of Contingent Contracts

There are at least four clear benefits of including contingent contracts in your agreements. These include their ability to resolve honest differences of opinion, diagnose bluffs, align incentives, and reduce risk.

Resolve honest differences of opinion. Sellers often claim their products or services are the best available and then complain when their customers expect them to compete on price. "It isn't fair," they say. "We make a better product, so we deserve to charge more." They may be right, but buyers tend to think of the same product or service as a commodity and feel indifferent between the multiple options on the market. Buyers often have less information than the seller about the seller's products and can't see the differences between the products of different sellers. As a result, they rely on price to make decisions. Wise, if counterintuitive, trades occur when parties capitalize on these different expectations rather than arguing about them.

When sellers ask me how to get buyers to stop treating them like a commodity, I advise them to stop acting like a commodity. Sellers whose products are not that different from those of the competition often still try to highlight the uniqueness of their product. Yet buyers hear from too many sellers that their product is truly superior. If you believe your product or service is better than the competition's, think about how you can put your money where your mouth is. What can you guarantee the buyer, along with a financial commitment that you will reduce or refund part of the price if you don't live up to your claims? Ideally, the claim should be measurable and something the competition cannot match, such as "no more than 20 percent of the patients who are prescribed our medication will end up in the hospital." The fact that the competition doesn't have a product that allows them to match your guarantee will provide the buyer with information about which seller truly believes in their product and which is bluffing.

As a buyer, how can you prompt a seller to offer such a guarantee? Start by asking them how you should measure the superiority of their product or service. Then ask whether the payment they are requesting can depend in part on their ability to meet that claim. Sellers who truly believe in their product will work with you to put together a deal that depends on their product's performance.

Consider the case of an online retailer that is looking to contract with a web developer to improve the retailer's online platform. With its limited technical skills, the retailer has less information than web developers do about what to expect from them, in terms of improved sales from the upgraded platform. The retailer also values follow-up support from the web developer after the new platform goes live and issues crop up. The various web developers selling their services make a variety of claims, some measurable, some not. A truly excellent web developer would be wise to consider trying to negotiate a lower up-front fee in exchange for significant profit sharing based on the retailer's growth. The lower up-front fee will be very attractive to the retailer, and the developer's willingness to delay much of their payment until after delivering performance improvements will signal they truly believe in their product. On the other side of the table, the retailer might consider asking prospective web developers to lower their up-front payment in return for sharing the profits gained from growth. Developers' responses will give the retailer information about who actually believes their services will enhance sales.

An interesting domain for thinking about contingent contracts is consulting. It is common for a consulting firm to provide a service, receive its fee, and disappear before any evidence of the project's value emerges. Many consulting firms would prefer their clients focused less on the hours they will devote to the project and their billable fee per hour and more on the value they will provide. I personally like the logic of firms receiving a higher fee based on the value that their services create for a client (e.g., increased sales). Consulting firms that believe they will provide a high level of value to the client should consider proposing a fee structure that depends on that value actually being realized. Many clients would be happy to share the upside of the value created. If you are the client, and a consulting firm wants to charge you based on hypothetical value, think about how that value could be measured and propose payment based on you realizing that value.

Contingent contracts take advantage of overconfidence, a common bias in negotiation. University of California, Berkeley professor Don Moore highlights the ubiquity and downsides of overconfidence in his book *Perfectly Confident*.[4] He argues that great decision makers, including great negotiators, intentionally try to avoid overconfidence. But sometimes it's our counterpart who we think is overconfident. Sellers often unintentionally overestimate the value of what they are selling. Rather than arguing about whether the seller is overconfident, you can propose a contingent contract that allows them to bet on their beliefs.

Diagnose bluffs. Sellers often make claims about the quality of their product or service, and buyers don't know whether to believe them. Returning to the potential web developer, let's assume she claims her ideas for a new platform will increase sales by at least 15 percent. Let's also assume that she quotes a fixed price of $10,000. Rather than accepting the $10,000 price, the retailer might consider countering with a fee of $5,000 up front, another $5,000 if sales increase by at least 12 percent within a year, and a third payment of $5,000 if sales go up by 15 percent within the first year. If the web developer believes her claim, she is likely to accept the offer. A contingent contract allows the parties to reach an agreement despite the retailer's inability to assess the quality of the web developer.

The really interesting story is what happens if the developer tells the retailer that their proposal is interesting but that she doesn't like complex agreements. This response provides a good hint that she isn't so confident of her claims. When you offer the other side a counterproposal that includes a contingent contract that should be attractive if they believe their own claims and they reject it, you have reason to suspect they might not have believed their claims in the first place. More generally, contingent contracts are a powerful tool for identifying bluffs in negotiation. When the other side makes a claim, and you ask for a guarantee on that claim, and they are bluffing, they will typically back away from the claim.

Align incentives. As we saw earlier, bonuses create incentives for athletes to perform at the highest level. More broadly, well-designed contingent contracts create incentives to perform after the contract is signed. If the web developer is paid based on sales on the retailer's site, she has more of an incentive to devote the extra effort to making the platform as successful as possible.

The most common incentives involve sales employees who are paid based on what they sell. And as I've mentioned, the idea of performance-based pay is hardly new. But I hope the organized presentation of contingent contracts will open your eyes to the possibility of applying them to a broader range of contracts. To take one fascinating application of contingent contracts, World Bank economist Shireen Mahdi describes the challenge of getting coffee pickers in Tanzania to pick the best beans.[5] If rewarded just on weight, the pickers are incentivized to pick beans early. Yet, the value of the beans won't be assessed until a couple of steps later in the distribution system. Mahdi highlights the benefits of paying the community of pickers in part based on the eventual quality rating of the beans. I observed a similar challenge in a coffee-growing region of Costa Rica, where pickers were paid based on the weight of the beans collected. Community leaders there were trying to get the workers to stop putting rocks in the coffee containers they used to collect beans. The type of contingent contract that Mahdi proposed may have helped.

Another domain where contingent contracts are useful is the construction of buildings. Whether a home, store, or factory is being built, the buyer in these construction contracts will want to know when it will be ready. For a homeowner, the completion date will determine when they should sell their existing home or end their rental lease. Construction delays could be costly, and it's not unusual for contractors to fall behind. A contingency based on completion date may aid the buyer's planning. My experience is that builders don't like the idea of being imposed "penalties," so you might think about how you can instead frame the contingency as a potential bonus, where you pay the builder an additional fee if they deliver the completed project by a specified date.

Reduce risk. Contingent contracts are bets, and most people think of bets as increasing risk. While contingent contracts can increase risk for some negotiators, for others, they can decrease financial risk and decrease the risk of impasse in the negotiation process. In the negotiation between the web developer and the retailer, the retailer's proposed contingent contract may well reduce the risk of impasse. If the retailer would not pay the $10,000, but would agree to the contingent contract, the contingent contract provides a pathway to a possible agreement. For the retailer, the contingent contract reduces their risk, as they only have $5,000 at stake if the web developer's service is not effective. And while the contingency may create some new risk for the web developer, it is potentially a good risk—a bet that she thinks is likely to net her $15,000 rather than the $5,000 minimum.

As we've seen, contingent contracts offer multiple potential benefits, though you may not know which benefits you will receive from proposing one. For example, if a seller makes an extreme claim about their services, you may not know whether your offer of a contingent contract will allow two honest people with different expectations to bridge their divide or whether you will diagnose their bluff. Fortunately, you don't need to know. You simply need to confront the different expectations with a contingent path forward.

Overcoming Barriers to Contingent Contracts

As you can tell, I am an enormous fan of using contingent contracts to confront differing expectations about the future in negotiation. And for many students, these ideas raise new possibilities for creating productive agreements in the future. But it is also true that this idea, more than most in this book, receives significant pushback from my students. Some have very negative views of contingent contracts based on a past context where a contingency turned out poorly—because they either lost the bet imbedded in a past contingent contract or ended up with a lawsuit as a result of differing interpretations of the contingency a couple of years after the contract was reached. In this section, I discuss the concerns people often raise about contingent contracts and explain how to deal with them.

They know more. One of my executive students responded to the concept of contingent contracts with annoyance, explaining that one cost him over $1 million. Basically, he lost the bet embedded within a contingent contract and concluded that he didn't like them. I asked more about the bet, and he confirmed that the other side knew far more than he did about the uncertain event in the future. His story highlighted a basic rule of gambling that applies to contingent contracts: in contexts where the other knows more than you do, don't bet against them!

That doesn't mean you shouldn't negotiate with people who know more than you do. We often negotiate contracts with service providers who know more than we do about the service they're providing. When they know more and are willing to agree to a contingent contract, this provides insight into their knowledge about the future uncertainty. The less-informed party should imagine that the other party proves to be correct. Is that good news or bad news for you? In many cases, the other side being right means a better outcome for your side.

Ambiguity. Another executive reported to a class I was teaching that she ended up in a protracted legal dispute over how to interpret a contingent contract when the supplier performed at the level required to kick in a bonus clause. As I learned more, it became clear that the parties had agreed to a poorly articulated, vague bet—that is, it was hard to interpret who the winner would be.

It would be a mistake to agree to a contingency based on "satisfactory performance." The ideal contingent contract is one that will be resolved by an objective measure, preferably from an independent source, such as the closing price of the S&P 500 at the end of a specific date, or the exchange rate posted in a specific newspaper on a particular date. When you rely on data from one of the companies in the contract, the data should be available to the other party, and you should specify in advance a method for resolving a dispute if the parties disagree about whether a contingency was met, such as arbitration. Contingent contracts require the due diligence that should go into creating any important contract, with a dose of extra attention to how you will assess the outcome at some future date.

Rewarding A while hoping for B. Another problem created by contingent contracts parallels a problem that emerges when organizations set goals for their employees. Specifically, when the organization sets one goal, the employee may underperform on some other dimension.[6] We have all heard about the educational problem of "teaching to the test," where learning is hindered when instructors focus solely on what will be on the test. The title of management scholar Steve Kerr's well-known article, "On the Folly of Rewarding A, While Hoping for B,"[7] illustrates this problem. Similarly, there have been many stories in the news of faulty incentive systems leading executives to make bad long-term decisions for their firms to achieve short-term financial results.

During the 2020 NFL season, Tampa Bay Buccaneers receiver Antonio Brown had caught thirty-four passes before the last game of the season. Brown had a contingent contract that would give him an additional $250,000 if he caught at least forty-five passes for the year. During the last game, against the Atlanta Falcons, Brown was having a great day. With just 2:14 left, he'd caught eight passes, and the Buccaneers held an insurmountable 44–27 lead. Normally, a team with this type of lead chooses safe running plays to run out the clock. But Tom Brady, the Buccaneers' star quarterback, threw three easy passes to Brown, allowing him to collect his bonus.

Brady's actions were relatively harmless but cost his team $250,000, which went to Brown. But we could easily imagine far more harmful stories where an employee engages in unethical behavior to collect on a bonus. This highlights that any negotiator should think through how a contingent contract might affect the other party's behavior before signing. You should always assess whether a proposed contingency contract is *incentive compatible*—that is, whether the incentives created are compatible with the spirit of your agreement.

Armed with an awareness of the barriers to effective contingent contracts, you should be prepared to respond to different stated expectations about future performance in your important negotiations.

■ ■ ■

"I like the idea of value creating and, quite honestly, hadn't really thought that much about how to create value before taking your class. But the most important challenge I will face when I get back to work concerns a supplier who has completely unrealistic views about how valuable their services are to our company. While we do value their services, their valuation of those services is out of whack with the impact we think they will have on our company. How do I create value with a supplier that does not have a realistic sense of what their services are worth to my firm?"

"I hope this chapter has helped you see a pathway to dealing with the challenging context of an unrealistic service provider.

I recommend not arguing with them but rather saying that you are not as confident as they are about the impact their services will have on your firm. Then suggest a much lower up-front payment than they were hoping to receive, accompanied by a large performance bonus if their services are as effective as they claim. Be careful to make the contingency clear and measurable. Also, do not treat the bet as adversarial. Rather, treat it as a mechanism that keeps you both working in the same direction on implementation. Mention that you hope they receive the contingent payment, as this would mean their services would be extremely valuable to your firm."

Chapter 7

The Context of Disputes

"Like you, I live in Cambridge, Massachusetts. I also work for the city of Cambridge. A few years ago, the City Council passed a new law that pushed the city forward by requiring it to build 22.6 miles of bike lanes through the town, including on the most significant commercial street, Massachusetts Avenue. Overall, Cambridge is proactive about improving the environment. Yet, now that we are implementing the law, pedestrians are unhappy about the risk of being hit by bicycles, and businesses have turned hostile since parking spaces in front of their stores were eliminated to create the bicycle lanes. Lawsuits are pending, and lots of resources are being wasted. Since the law was passed by the democratically elected City Council, why are so many people so angry now, and what could have been done to move more effectively toward a bicycle-friendly environment?"

• • •

For many of us, the Covid-19 pandemic disrupted our work lives. For example, I never expected to teach negotiations online, but soon I was regularly teaching on Zoom (and learned to love it!). I had conflicts with students about how they would coordinate their work with classmates, expectations for "classroom" behavior, and so on. I am sure you ran into new challenges during the pandemic as well. You may have encountered situations where you needed to negotiate with others about how to adapt to Covid, and walking away wasn't an option: if you didn't reach a deal, the conflict would get worse. In some cases, you might even have ended up in court.

Disputes stand in contrast to negotiations over purchases of new products. When negotiating a purchase, both sides typically have the option to walk away and never see the other party again. When parties are in conflict, and walking away isn't a viable option, scholars typically refer to efforts to resolve the situation as dispute resolution (or conflict resolution) rather than negotiation. These dispute-resolution contexts are qualitatively different than the negotiations we have focused on so far in this book. For one, disputes often have a different feel than negotiations. Disputants often have very different views of how the disagreement came about and how it should be resolved, yet they need to continue to interact. Not being able to walk away and work with a different buyer or supplier makes disagreements more emotional. Disputants often feel trapped, with no easy exit strategy.

Business disputes are common following a dramatic change in the political or economic environment, such as a pandemic or a recession. In such cases, parties previously negotiated an agreement that entailed an implicit or explicit understanding about the future that was upended by a crisis or other significant shift in the outside world. Simply walking away wasn't possible, and some form of renegotiation or dispute-resolution process lay ahead for the affected parties. In this chapter, I explain how the context of disputes differs from most of the other negotiations I write about in this book and outline ways of thinking about disputes that are both effective and ethical.

Project Restart

On March 13, 2020, the English Premier League (EPL) suspended its 2019–20 football season after a player and a manager tested positive for Covid. As you'll recall, uncertainty surrounded almost every facet of life at this time; for the EPL, this included when government regulators would allow a return to play. The EPL also faced internal conflict over whether and how to resume the season. Project Restart was an effort to

TABLE 7.1. English Premier League Standings as of March 13, 2020 (time of league suspension)

Position	Club	Played	Goal Difference	Points
1	Liverpool	29	+45	82
2	Man City	28	+37	57
3	Leicester	29	+30	53
4	Chelsea	29	+12	48
5	Man Utd	29	+14	45
6	Wolves	29	+7	43
7	Sheffield Utd	28	+5	43
8	Tottenham	29	+7	41
9	Arsenal	28	+4	40
10	Burnley	29	−6	39
11	Crystal Palace	29	−6	39
12	Everton	29	−9	37
13	Newcastle	29	−16	35
14	Southampton	29	−17	34
15	Brighton	29	−8	29
16	West Ham	29	−15	27
17	Watford	29	−17	27
18	Bournemouth	29	−18	27
19	Aston Villa	28	−22	25
20	Norwich	29	−27	21

Source: Nour Kteily and Deepak Malhotra, "Project Restart: Deciding the Future of English Football," HBS No. 921-050 (Boston: Harvard Business Publishing, 2021).

resolve this dispute. An excellent case written by my friends and colleagues Nour Kteily and Deepak Malhotra, which I have taught many times, tells the story.[1]

When the season was suspended, the twenty clubs in the league had played either twenty-eight or twenty-nine of their originally scheduled thirty-eight matches of the season (two matches against each of the other nineteen clubs). In the EPL, team rankings are determined by a point system: teams get three points for every win and one point for every tie. At the end of the season, if two or more teams have an equal number of points, their goal difference (the number of goals the team scored minus the number of goals scored by their opponents) across the season is the tiebreaker. Nour and Deepak's case provides the data for table 7.1 that shows the league standings as of the March 13, 2020, suspension date.

If the EPL season was not completed, all the clubs would owe an enormous sum of money to broadcasters. Broadcasting fees represented a significant chunk of the clubs' budgets. In addition, club rankings were hugely consequential from a financial perspective. At the end of the season, the top five clubs qualify for prestigious and lucrative European competitions. Of even more consequence, the three clubs at the bottom when the season ends are relegated (or demoted) to a second tier in the English Football League. There are four tiers of the English Football League, with the EPL at the top; at the end of each season, the top three clubs in the three lowest tiers move up a tier, and the bottom three clubs in the three highest tiers move down a tier. Relegation is an embarrassment to the club's fans and reduces expected revenue for the next year by tens of millions of British pounds.

In the spring of 2020, a dispute emerged among the twenty teams in the EPL about whether the season would be completed and, if not, how clubs at the top would be selected for the lucrative European competitions that would occur after the 2020 English season and how clubs at the bottom would be chosen for relegation. If the season was not completed, how would the final rankings be determined? These decisions about the future of the EPL season would need the buy-in of Greg Clarke, chairperson of the English Football Association (which oversees all four English leagues and has veto power over major decisions), and would include the owners of all twenty clubs in the EPL.

One simple option would be to take the existing rankings as final. That would relegate Aston Villa, despite the fact that if the team had played one more game and won, it would have moved from the nineteenth to the sixteenth spot. If Aston Villa was relegated based on the existing rankings, the club would likely sue and make a strong argument that it never agreed to relegation based on an incomplete season and an arbitrary rule for judging which teams are at the bottom. Making Aston Villa's case even stronger, if the rankings were instead computed by dividing the number of points earned by the number of games played and adjusting for the number of home games played (i.e., a weighted points-per-match formula), a different set of rankings would emerge. In addition, given that clubs win more often when they play in their home stadium, another possible rule would be a weighted points-per-match formula that adjusted for the number of home versus away games each club played. This latter option would move West Ham into the bottom three and save Bournemouth. As you can see, the twenty clubs and the EPL leadership could not simply walk away: they needed to resolve their dispute.

The six clubs at the bottom, each of which had some significant chance of relegation if the season was completed, coalesced around the idea that the season should be canceled and the rankings declared "null and void." But, Liverpool wanted to maintain their ability to be declared champions, and all the clubs wanted to avoid repayment of funds to the broadcasters. There were also three clubs in the second tier of the English Football League waiting for promotion. If the three spots in the EPL didn't open up, the league could face a lawsuit from the top clubs in the next tier.

Whenever a dispute arises between parties under contract, they look back at the details of their agreement, company rules, or governance provisions to figure out their rights. For many negotiators, this is the first time they read the fine print. And as it turns out, all that stuff at the back of the contract can be important. In the EPL dispute, the parties looked at the league charter and found that it specified that at least fourteen of the twenty clubs would have to vote to approve any major decisions that deviated from the existing plan. Thus, the bottom six clubs needed only one more ally to have the votes needed to block any season restart that did not meet their objectives. Notably, if there had been seven clubs in contention for the bottom three spots, the coalition of weaker clubs might have been more powerful.

Clarke had veto power on any decision reached, as would any combination of seven clubs. He preferred a return to play and keeping the promotion and relegation system in place across the English football pyramid. This could be expected to maximize the overall profit and reputation of the EPL and the broader English Football Association. But some of the clubs, as well as owners and individual players, likely had different priorities, such as ensuring they were not demoted or avoiding contracting Covid.

On May 11, 2020, an online meeting was held that included Clarke and representatives from all twenty teams to reach decisions about the rest of the EPL season. Early in the meeting, Clarke implicitly asserted his veto right but committed to let the twenty EPL clubs make their own decision, as long as relegation remained part of their plan. With "no relegation" off the table, the coalition of the bottom six teams crumbled, since the coalition had been held together by a preference for finding a solution (such as "null and void") that would save them all from the risk of relegation.

On May 28, 2020, the EPL announced it had reached agreement and would return to play. To satisfy the very enthusiastic British football audience, every match would be shown on live television (normally many matches are not televised), with several matches available to all on the British Broadcasting system for free. To try to address Covid concerns, the number of matches per week would be limited to two, with more water breaks and player substitutions allowed than in the past. The games would continue to be played in the regular team stadiums with live audiences (despite the risk of fan-to-fan Covid transmission). Most players were happy for the season to resume under these terms. Matches resumed on June 17, and the season ended on July 26. Liverpool won the championship; Bournemouth, Norwich, and Watford were relegated out of the EPL, while Aston Villa, West Ham, and Brighton (among the bottom six teams when Covid hit) were able to stay in the EPL.

The EPL story is very different from negotiation stories where one or more of the parties can simply walk away. In the next section, I explore strategies for negotiating in the context of a dispute and return to how these strategies connect to the EPL experience.

Strategies for Resolving Disputes

In their classic book on dispute resolution, *Getting Disputes Resolved: Designing Systems to Cut the Costs of Conflict*, negotiation scholars William Ury, Jeanne Brett, and Stephen Goldberg argue that disputants can choose one of three approaches to negotiating a resolution to their conflict: asserting their rights, power, or interests. According to the authors, focusing on interests generally creates the best resolutions.[2] In this section, I will overview each dispute-resolution lens and add a fourth, fairness. I will apply each to the EPL dispute context and discuss how you might consider applying these approaches to your own disputes.

Rights. When a dispute arises, those involved commonly think about their rights, particularly when their rights match their preferred outcomes. A rights lens focuses on who is right and who is wrong. The answer may come from a contract that specifies each party's legal rights. Parties also perceive their rights based on other documents, including agreed-upon governance procedures and norms that specify how opportunities are allocated in an organization. These rights might be based on seniority or performance on a test. People also have perceived rights created by government entities, such as the right to liberty, equality, and access to health care and education. Rights lead us to think about the possibility of legal action. Rights tend to sound objective but are often subject to interpretation and can conflict with other rights.

When parties focus on rights, they are trying to resolve a dispute by applying some standard of contract, law, or norm to determine who should "win." In the EPL dispute, the lower-ranked clubs likely focused on their right to not be relegated before the season was completed. These clubs might also have focused on their right to veto any agreement they did not like if they had seven votes on their side. Clarke might have thought about his right to veto any proposal that was not in the interest of the broader English Football Association, beyond the EPL. In contrast, it is easy to imagine Liverpool, the club at the top of the rankings (by far), invoking its right to be declared champion and to the post-season opportunities connected to being the best team.

Power. In 2022, Tesla CEO Elon Musk agreed to buy Twitter for the surprisingly high price of $44 billion ($54.20/share). Most analysts saw this price as being well beyond Twitter's value. After the agreement was reached, Tesla shares dropped considerably. Musk tried to withdraw from the deal by making a rather bogus excuse (that Twitter had too many bots) and hired very expensive lawyers to develop his arguments in court. Most analysts believed Musk had no legal right to withdraw from the deal, and Twitter sued to force him to buy Twitter at the agreed-upon price.

If investors believed that Twitter's rights would definitely prevail in court, it would make sense for the company's stock to trade around the amount of Musk's offer, since the stock would get redeemed at the $54.20 price at the closing of the deal. Instead, Twitter stock traded in the $32–39 range. Why didn't the market match Twitter's rights? Because investors were not confident that the acquisition would come to fruition. Yet, as Musk realized his weak position in the legal system, he changed his mind and agreed to move forward with the transaction. The stock price moved much closer to the price that Musk agreed to pay, and the deal closed at the price Musk offered.

In contrast to a rights lens, a power lens to dispute resolution focuses on how dependent each side is on the other party. When you need the other side more than they need you, they have power. In negotiation, your power comes from your BATNA—what will happen to you if you do not reach a deal. In the EPL story, the lower-ranked clubs would have had more power if there had been seven in their coalition rather than six. This would have allowed this group of lower-ranked clubs to veto any proposal they unanimously didn't like, such as one implementing relegation.

Let's revisit Clarke's statement asserting his right to veto, along with the English Football Association's relegation rules. Clarke's veto would have broken up the six-party coalition that likely preferred to have the current season be declared null and void. Once relegation was assumed to be an essential element of any agreement reached, the three clubs at the bottom would want the season to continue to try to escape from the bottom three slots in the remaining games. Essentially, Clarke's rights-based statement was a power-based move to break up the coalition of lower-ranked clubs and get what he wanted—continuation of play and relegation.

It is common for rights and power to conflict, such that parties lack the power to obtain what they believe they have the right to receive. It is also common for rights and power to overlap. For example, when one party has the ability to implement a court's decision, rights and power converge. Both rights and power focus on the claiming side of dispute resolution—who gets how much—rather than on creating value.

Interests. In their book, Ury and his colleagues describe disputants' focus on interests as their attempt to understand the needs, desires, preferences, and concerns of all parties and to find a resolution that is viable for all. In some cases, the interests of the parties overlap. In other cases, a focus on interests allows the parties to understand the competing interests of the disputants more clearly. Essentially, a focus on interests is compatible with enlarging the pie by reducing the harm of any resolution. In most negotiations, we think in terms of the gains created to the parties through agreement. In contrast, disputes often have the parties framing possible outcomes in terms of what they have to lose.

Most of the ideas I presented on creating value in chapter 4 map onto the behaviors that disputants engage in when they follow Ury, Brett, and Goldberg's approach to interest-based dispute resolution. When the EPL disputants focused on how to limit the clubs' and league's overall financial losses from the pandemic, how to maintain fans' interest in the game, and how to make it safe for players to play, they were focusing on interests.

Ury and his colleagues strongly advocate for focusing on interests over rights and power. In the aggregate, they argue, an interest-based approach to dispute resolution reduces the costs of conflict, increases parties' satisfaction with their outcomes, maintains stronger relationships, and reduces the recurrence of disputes. An interest-based perspective is most likely to succeed because it incorporates the concerns of all the parties, they write.

By contrast, I argue that disputants should think about the interests, rights, and power of all of the parties rather than focusing just on interests. In chapter 4, I highlighted the need for negotiators to both create and claim value. Similarly, disputants need to consider the rights and power of the various parties as they seek creative, interest-based solutions. While I encourage disputants to make sure they do a great job of thinking through the interests of all parties, I think it makes sense to do so in the context of parties' rights and power.

Fairness. Ury and colleagues view fairness as a right. In contrast, I view fairness as a fourth lens that disputants can use to develop resolutions to their conflict. There are often many possible resolutions that consider parties' interests, in the context of their power and rights, but which is the most appropriate one? In moving toward an agreement on a possible resolution, most parties want to reach a fair agreement. The fairness of a possible resolution affects the degree to which a party can convince others that it is the most appropriate choice and that they should move forward with it. This will be particularly true in multiparty contexts, where the parties are discussing multiple approaches to resolving their conflict.

The problem with using fairness as a lens for identifying the best resolution is that parties often have different and self-serving views of what constitutes the fairest choice. Liverpool, in the first-place spot when Covid hit, is likely to have thought it would be fair for the season to end early and for it to be named the EPL champion. Last-place Norwich, meanwhile, probably thought it would be unfair for it to be relegated based on the rankings of a partial season.

How can we resolve different fairness claims in dispute resolution? For utilitarians, the most ethical (fairest) outcome would be the one that maximizes the total value received by all affected parties, not just the twenty clubs involved. This would include a consideration of the enjoyment of fans and the health risks to players imposed by any strategy. It would also ignore the rights and power of the parties, which would make utilitarianism less viable as a singular perspective for resolving a dispute. Yet, I like the utilitarian goal of striving to create as much value as possible—or, if the dispute is concerned with losses, reducing aggregate losses as much as possible. And, by focusing on minimizing aggregate losses, you will develop your reputation as a respected and effective dispute resolver.

One fascinating conceptualization of fairness comes from John Rawls, a philosopher who viewed himself as being in strong disagreement with utilitarians.[3] Rawls asks people to think about how society should be arranged by assuming a *veil of ignorance*—that is, without knowing who in that society they would be. A just society, in Rawls's view, would be one in which we make decisions without the bias of any particular role or other trait, such as how much money we have, where we live, and so on. In Rawls's words: "Among the essential features of this situation is that no one knows his place in society, his class position or social status, nor does anyone know his fortune in the distribution of natural assets and abilities, his intelligence, strength and the like."[4]

Rawls applied this idea to philosophical questions about different forms of government. In our work, Joshua Greene, Karen Huang, and I applied Rawls's veil of ignorance to more micro decisions, such as the programming of driverless cars or the allocation of scarce ventilators during the Covid-19 pandemic, theorizing that we could make fairer decisions if we could put a veil on our own identity.[5] People would make fairer decisions, we argued, if they didn't think about who they are in society, knowledge that can be predicted to bias their decisions. This biasing information would include knowledge of one's gender, race, religion, and nationality.

In the case of EPL, the key factor likely to bias clubs' perceptions of what would be a fair decision is their rankings at the time of the season interruption. As previously noted, Liverpool, in the first position, is likely to have a very different view than Norwich, in the last position, of what is fair. These differences can be predicted to be self-serving. If you were in Clarke's position and wanted to reach a resolution that created the most value and also wanted to avoid future litigation, it would be very helpful to put fairness concerns at the center of the discussion. Ample evidence shows it is impossible for people with a strong vested interest in an outcome to be objective.[6] Clarke might want to encourage all the clubs' representatives to think about what they would see as fair if they didn't consider how their own club would be affected.

If getting people to "put on a veil" when they have so much at stake seems difficult, it might also be useful to think about the typical nature of group discussions. Who tends to talk the most? In the majority of the groups I have been involved with, the people with the strongest opinions do the most talking. As people offer their biased opinions, this tendency works against an objective discussion of what is fair. In such cases, your aim could be to get the group members who are least likely to be biased to play a more central role in the discussion. Greg Clarke, for example, could encourage the representatives of Arsenal, Burnley, and Crystal Palace (clubs in the middle of the ranking) to play a central role in the discussion, as they are the parties who are least likely to qualify for the lucrative opportunities that come from finishing at the top and also do not need to worry about being relegated.

A wise disputant will consider how all parties to the dispute are likely to think about their rights, power, and interests, and what is fair. You should also be aware that parties will tend to select the lens that best serves their side's interests and are likely to believe they are simply seeking a just outcome. Anticipating the views of the other parties will allow you, as a disputant, to reason through a wise path to resolution.

While power and rights are the lenses through which disputants most commonly assess what they view to be a just outcome, interests and fairness are the lenses that are most likely to be associated with ethical outcomes. An interest lens is needed to find the trade-offs and creative solutions required to maximize the value created (or to minimize harm). And a fairness lens is helpful for sorting through the most ethical of the possible outcomes that efficiently create the most value.

Bringing Reason to Disputes

Why are disputes so often difficult, lengthy, and contentious? Why do so many people and organizations spend so much money on legal advice, only to eventually obtain a resolution that they could have reached without paying lawyers? Why do parties in conflict often focus more on berating or trying to punish the other party than on trying to reach a resolution? Part of the answer is that disputants often are trapped in a difficult relationship and can't simply walk away. When two parties are negotiating a new deal, they typically both expect to create new value from the agreement. In contrast, disputants typically are trying to decide who will suffer losses. Negotiating over losses is less fun and more emotional than negotiating over gains. And as research by Mary Kern and Dolly Chugh shows, people are more likely to cheat to avoid losses than they are to obtain gains.[7]

The emotionality associated with negotiating losses was present in the early months of the Covid-19 pandemic when some health-care professionals were forced to make difficult decisions over which patients to save. A PBS documentary captured the torturous choices that Italian physicians were compelled to make in 2020 when they didn't have enough ventilators for the patients who needed them.[8] Who should get scarce, lifesaving resources? Many physicians will advocate for the particular patient they are treating—the ventilator candidate with whom they have an emotional connection. Physicians are also likely to feel an emotional need to protect the most vulnerable in society, such as the elderly. In contrast, utilitarians favor allocating scarce resources where they will create the most good, for example, by saving as many life years as possible—which tilts the ventilator decision toward younger patients in need.

Karen Huang, Regan Bernhard, Netta Barak-Corren, Josh Greene, and I used Rawlsian logic to develop an intervention for hospital physicians and other medical decision makers on how to identify the fairest way to allocate limited medical supplies during crises like the Covid-19 pandemic.[9] One group of our study participants was asked to imagine a physician deciding whether to give the last available ventilator in a hospital to the sixty-five-year-old patient who arrived first or to the twenty-five-year-old patient who arrived moments later. Participants were told to assume that whichever patient is saved would live to age eighty, that the ventilator was equally capable of saving either patient, and that the patient without the ventilator would quickly die. We asked participants to respond to the following question: "To what extent is it morally acceptable for the doctor to give the last ventilator to the younger patient?" About half the participants viewed it as more moral to give the ventilator to the younger person, with participants showing bias toward the person closer to their own age.

Another group of participants was asked the same question, but only after first being asked to put themselves into the equation by adopting a veil of ignorance. We asked this second group to imagine they had a 50 percent chance of being the older patient, with fifteen years left to live if they are saved, and a 50 percent chance of being the younger patient, with fifty-five years to live if saved. They were asked to assess their preferred decision rule under this veil of ignorance. A significant majority said they would want the younger person to be saved. They were then asked whether they thought it would be moral to give the ventilator to the younger person. A much higher percentage (62 percent) of this group found the utilitarian course of action to be more ethical—that is, giving the ventilator to the younger person. Interestingly, older participants changed their views the most. The veil of ignorance induced people to see the most moral decision to be the one that would create the most aggregate good from the allocation of scarce resources.

The PBS documentary on the Italian ventilator crisis also highlighted how unethical it was for physicians to be put in the terrible position of making these choices. While working around the clock under frightening conditions, they were expected to make emotional decisions about who should be given a chance to live and who should not. Before crises erupt, hospitals should consider the context of life-and-death dispute resolution and establish principles for the allocation of scarce medical supplies. Such advance planning would create a better work environment for physicians and promote decisions that create more aggregate good.

. . .

"Like you, I live in Cambridge, Massachusetts. I also work for the city of Cambridge. A few years ago, the City Council passed a new law that pushed the city forward by requiring it to build 22.6 miles of bike lanes through the town, including on the most significant commercial street, Massachusetts Avenue. Overall, Cambridge is proactive about improving the environment. Yet, now that we are implementing the law, pedestrians are unhappy about the risk of being hit by bicycles, and businesses have turned hostile since parking spaces in front of their stores were eliminated to create the bicycle lanes. Lawsuits are pending, and lots of resources are being wasted. Since the law was passed by the democratically elected

City Council, why are so many people so angry now, and what could have been done to move more effectively toward a bicycle-friendly environment?"

"I have followed the bike-lane dispute in Cambridge from a distance, and your question led me to catch up on what has turned into a pretty hostile dispute in a generally cooperative city. I should also mention that I rarely ride a bike and frequently walk many miles per day in Cambridge. At least part of the conflict stems from different views about how the dispute between the bicycle constituency and other interests should play out. The bicycle constituency had the power to push for passage of the law you mentioned in 2020. The law now provides a basis for bicyclists to claim a right to the new bike lanes. It is also true that pedestrians and business owners were too silent in 2020 when the City Council was discussing this initiative. I believe the City Council also failed the community by only thinking about the arguments of the bicycle lobby and the rights that would be created for bicyclists in the future. I fully expect the Council believed it was creating benefits for the whole city. But Council members likely failed to consider the interests of all the parties, including the danger to pedestrians and the negative impact on businesses of eliminating car lanes and parking. The city would have been wise to get all the parties to the table in the beginning to negotiate a plan that considered all interests and was fair to all. There were likely bicycle-friendly strategies available that could have avoided the hostility and legal expenses that Cambridge now confronts."

Chapter 8

Transacting Online

"I have a house that I hope to rent out for the next year while I'm working on the other side of the country. I am very nervous about renting my house to strangers who might cause damage. These days, tenants are commonly found on online platforms, which might keep me from being able to meet prospective tenants in person. I have also heard that a series of short-term rentals on Airbnb would result in more revenue than one long-term rental. I only rented out the house once before, to a colleague for a month. What advice do you have for negotiating an agreement(s) with one or more parties to live in my home?"

. . .

In 1990, if you wanted to reserve a hotel room, there were two main ways to do so. You could call the hotel or the hotel chain from your landline (you didn't have a cell phone back then) and book the reservation directly over the phone. Or you could visit or call your travel agent and ask them to make the arrangements for you. By the early 1990s, techies started to use the internet, but most people continued to make room reservations by phone. In 1991, Bob Diener and Dave Litman founded the phone-based Hotel Reservations Network (HRN), which later became the online company Hotels.com.[1]

Diener and Litman built HRN after observing that hotel occupancy at the time averaged about 60 percent. They saw an opportunity to fill more rooms with customers who would pay a lower price through the aggregation of hotel rentals. They reasoned that hotels would value another distribution channel for their assets, which depreciated to zero every night the room was empty. The hotel would take a lower price for the incremental sale, the consumer would pay a lower price, and HRN would still get a significant commission.

In the 1990s, if you wanted to stay overnight in someone's home, the homeowner would typically be a relative or friend. No widespread mechanism existed for you to find a stranger's home at which to stay. Today, we can quickly find homes to rent across the globe on Airbnb, HomeAway, Vrbo, and other popular platforms.

Online platforms such as Airbnb, Uber, eBay, and Tinder have changed how parties match up and interact. These platforms have created enormous opportunities while also changing what you need to know to transact effectively.

You might wonder whether transactions on Airbnb, Uber, eBay, and Tinder are negotiations. My answer is that they are. I define negotiations as decisions made between two or more parties who do not have the same preferences. So bidding in auctions is a form of negotiation. Scanning internet sites for the best price on a new coffee maker is also a form of negotiation. And talking to people on Zoom about a multi-issue agreement is also negotiation.

In the previous chapter, I mentioned that the Covid-19 pandemic accelerated an existing trend: negotiations that take place when we are not physically present with the other party. Of course, many of us had negotiated via telephone and email in the past, and occasionally through online platforms such as Skype and FaceTime. But in 2020, many people who negotiated regularly and believed in doing so in person found themselves in front of a computer screen for most of their negotiations. And there is every reason to believe that this move toward online negotiating will last well beyond the peaks of Covid.

In this chapter, I discuss online negotiation, a communication channel that only became available in the last three decades. I will also explore the challenges and opportunities associated with transacting directly online and through platforms like Airbnb and eBay. Core negotiation concepts remain relevant online, but what we need to think about and how we need to prepare are strongly affected by the online context.

Negotiating on Zoom

When the pandemic began in March 2020, we all had new experiences as a result of interacting with others on Zoom and other videoconferencing platforms.[2] Some of us are now happy to meet with others online, while others really want to return to life before Covid. We complain about life on Zoom, yet like it well enough to question why we would need to work at the office. People who used to travel many hours to negotiate face-to-face often can't quite figure out why they spent so much time on airplanes when video works pretty well. What's clear is that many of our future transactions will be on Zoom-like platforms. How are they different from transactions conducted in person? How do you optimally negotiate via video?

In this half of the chapter, we will consider the social science relevant to negotiations among parties who are physically distant from each other. I will then discuss what to do before an online negotiation starts and then during the negotiation. Finally, we will cover additional issues to consider when your video negotiation includes teams on each side, or at least your side.

Since negotiating on Zoom is a relatively new phenomenon, there is limited peer review research available to draw on to understand exactly how video negotiations differ from face-to-face ones. But we all have fascinating anecdotes to share, and researchers have shown that having less of a social connection in your communication structure affects negotiation.

In studies of the differences among traditional modes of communication, social scientists have found that "channel richness" is enhanced as we move from email to telephone to face-to-face communication. Channel richness refers to the amount of verbal and nonverbal information that can be transmitted from one person to another during any given communication. Zoom is a richer communication form than a telephone conversation, as it includes visuals, but it is not as rich as meeting face-to-face. While we could consider many other mechanisms, we will focus on negotiations over platforms like Zoom because they have become so commonplace.

The impact of communication richness on negotiation outcomes can be seen in research I conducted pre-Covid (and pre-Zoom) with Kathleen Valley (now Kathleen McGinn) and Joe Moag.[3] We studied the impact of the richness of social exchanges in a problem where vital information is known only to one party in a two-party negotiation. Specifically, we studied a version of a negotiation simulation called "Acquiring a Company" that I wrote with Bill Samuelson. In the simulation, one party, the acquirer, is thinking about acquiring a target company.[4] The target's value to itself comes from a uniform distribution (that is, all values are equally likely) between $0 and $100/share (depending on the results of an oil exploration project). But the acquirer can better use the assets of the target; as a result, the acquirer would value the company at 1.5 times its value under the target. The quirk is that while the acquirer only knows the range of possible values ($0–$100), the target will know its exact value before accepting or rejecting the acquirer's offer.

In the original version of the "Acquiring a Company" problem, simulation participants played the role of the acquirer and decided whether to make a one-shot offer, which the target would accept or reject based simply on whether the acquirer offered them more than the firm was worth to them; the game was then over. Game theory, or the mathematical analysis of rational actors in a game, concludes that despite the acquirer valuing the company at a price higher than the target values itself, the information structure would lead to all offers having negative expected value to the acquirer; thus, game theory concludes that a rational acquirer would make no offer. This can be shown mathematically but is easiest to see in the following hypothetical thinking that Kathleen, Joe, and I provided:

Assume I offer $50 per share for the target company. The only way to gather information about the actual value of the target is to see whether my offer is accepted or not. My offer will be accepted only if the target is worth less than $50. Thus, the expected value of the company, if I can acquire it for $50 per share, is $(.5)(50)$, or $25 per share, and my expected value is $(1.5)($25)$, or $37.50 per share. Since I bid $50, my expected net return will be ($37.50 – $50.00), or a loss of $12.50 per share. In fact, since no matter what I bid, the seller will only accept those bids that equal or exceed the actual value of the target, my expected net return on an accepted bid will always be negative. This is the "winner's curse": If I win the prize, I've probably paid too much.[5]

More abstractly, if the target accepts any offer from the acquirer, this means the company is worth between $0 and the amount offered (P), creating an expected value to the acquirer of P/2. Even with the 50 percent premium, on average, the acquirer will only be worth three-quarters of what they paid (and thus, on average, would lose 25 percent of what they offer). Thus, game theory concludes that the acquirer should make no offer.

But my earlier research with Bill Samuelson shows that most people, including very smart and well-educated people, and those with positions relevant to understanding the "Acquiring a Company" task (e.g., financial professionals, business development experts, CEOs), fail to analyze the problem as game theory would suggest. Instead, acquirers tend to ignore their information disadvantage; think about the fact that the firm is worth $50 to the target and $75 to the acquirer, on average; and make offers of $50–75. These acquirers suffer the so-called winner's curse by making offers that are most likely to be accepted when the acquirers least want to make the acquisition, and they lose money on average.

If the parties in this scenario are allowed to talk to one another in person before the acquirer decides whether to make an offer, rather than the acquirer simply making a take-it-or-leave-it offer, game theory still concludes that the acquirer should never make an offer.[6] Yet, if honest information is exchanged, which the game-theoretic account does not assume will happen, there is the potential for both sides to profit through a transaction at some price between the value to the seller and the value to the buyer (which is 50 percent higher than the seller's value). Kathleen, Joe, and I found that when negotiating pairs have the chance to talk face-to-face, most of them "solve" the "Acquiring a Company" problem and reach an agreement that is mutually profitable for both sides. Face-to-face communication allows actual people, rather than game-theoretic actors, to incorporate elements of honest information exchange, cooperation, and trust into their negotiation strategies. By contrast, when the negotiators in our study used email, impasse was much more likely, consistent with game theory's predictions. And when they used the telephone to negotiate, buyers often lost money and suffered the winner's curse. Only the richest form of communication allowed for enough information sharing to create a mutually beneficial agreement.

When it comes to communication richness, Zoom lies between telephone calls and face-to-face meetings. Thus, in Zoom negotiations, people are likely to gain some of the benefit of face-to-face communication. However, parties who lack information need to think carefully about how to develop the information exchange needed to reduce their information disadvantage. Whether Zoom negotiations closely resemble an in-person negotiation or are more like a telephone negotiation may lie in how the platform is used. Are the negotiators looking at each other, or are they multitasking and looking at a second screen? Are they negotiating on their smartphone's tiny screen or on a 32-inch monitor? The better negotiators can see each other, the more likely they are to capture some of the benefits of face-to-face communication.[7]

The relationship development and trust building that are often achieved in face-to-face communication are things for negotiators to strive for when they are not negotiating in person. Don Moore and his colleagues[8] explore the context of email negotiations in a simulation titled "El-Tek."[9] In "El-Tek," the parties represent two divisions of a company that are negotiating an internal technology transfer. In the simulation, the parties can create more value by making trade-offs across issues. But virtually any agreement that students could reach would be far better than an impasse. When we teach this simulation in person, about 95–98 percent of pairs reach an agreement. But Moore and his colleagues found that when business-school students negotiated with a student from a different business school via email, more than 30 percent reached an impasse. In contrast, when the students are from the same university or are given some time to socialize in their emails before negotiating (again, exclusively via email), the impasse rate falls to well under 10 percent. The results highlight the importance of developing a relationship with your counterpart when negotiating via email, particularly when you lack a prior social connection. While this research centered on email negotiations, there is wisdom in adding extra focus on relationships and trust building when negotiating over Zoom as well.

A different challenge in online negotiation is suggested by Boaz Keysar's research showing we tend to overestimate the degree to which others understand our intended message.[10] Keysar uses the (pre-GPS) example of giving people directions to your house: you would provide directions that you thought were perfectly clear, yet they would often get lost. As Keysar's research shows, we tend to believe the information we provide is clearer than it is. Compounding this problem, many of us are not very good at telling others when we didn't understand something they said—including in our negotiations. As the negotiation context moves to lower levels of communication richness, our intended communication is less clearly transmitted, and our tendency to overestimate what others understand from us rises. When we lack the social richness of face-to-face communication, our likelihood of communicating effectively through nonverbal cues also goes down, Justin Kruger and his colleagues argue.[11] The overall message is that when we negotiate without the benefit of being in front of the other party, we should pay more attention to the clarity of our communication and consider confirming that they understood our intent.

Terri Kurtzberg and her colleagues have conducted a variety of important studies whose results highlight the uniqueness of the video context in negotiation. First, they find that video communications lead to more value creation than text communication. They also find that larger screens are associated with greater trust and richer communication—that is, laptops are better than smartphones when it comes to video negotiations.[12] In turn, the greater communication richness enabled by larger screens translates to more joint value creation than is achieved on smaller screens. And when the size of the screens of two negotiating counterparts differs, the advantage on the value-claiming side tends to go to the negotiator with the larger screen. Finally, an overlapping team of researchers has shown that when one negotiator is multitasking (specifically, checking their smartphone during an in-person negotiation), the other side trusts them less, and the multitasker performs worse than their counterpart.[13] Being distracted by other tasks is a particular problem on Zoom for all parties, given how easy it is to hide our multitasking during video negotiations.

As noted earlier, all the information I've shared on how to prepare for negotiations also applies to video negotiations. But video negotiations require some additional advance considerations. First, consider that research suggests people are more cognitively overloaded on Zoom than in face-to-face communication.[14] They might be cognitively overloaded by thinking about what they plan to tell you next, or they might be simultaneously attending to a critical email or dealing with a personal issue in their household. For this reason, your online negotiations might benefit from you taking time to think about what information you want the other side to know, and you might consider sending them an email attachment before the Zoom session to share helpful information.

Next, think about how you will start the meeting. You will want to manage time carefully, given that you (or your counterpart) may have another Zoom meeting or other obligation scheduled an hour later. Be clear about the start and end time of the meeting: does one (or both) of you have a hard stop? In addition, while you don't want to waste time, if you have little or no prior relationship with the other party, you might want to think about how you can pleasantly, yet efficiently, connect and build some trust.

If you are not the only person on your side of the negotiation, discuss with your team members who will do and say what during the negotiation. Think ahead about how you will communicate with your team while negotiating. Will you use the chat function in Zoom or another form of online communication to send messages to each other? As in face-to-face negotiations, it is generally a bad idea to surprise other members of your team. But when we are meeting in person, we generally can read each other's nonverbal cues to figure out when our side needs to caucus. Zoom negotiations require us to plan for such pauses in advance.

Negotiating without Talking

When you send a host of an Airbnb home the following message, you are negotiating: "Your listing says that you do not accept pets, but my dog is very well-behaved, and I would be happy to add a security deposit." When you contact someone about moving some items from your storage unit to your condo on Taskrabbit.com, you are negotiating. When you find someone on Upwork.com to edit your book and haggle with them over the price, you are negotiating.[15] We reach agreements to buy and sell, provide services, and make travel plans online on a regular basis. Conducting these transactions in the manner we did twenty years ago seems inconceivable.

We also find our transaction partners online. I am fascinated by how quickly my unpartnered friends swipe left and right on dating sites like Tinder. Redfin.com allows us to sort through which houses we want to look at and potentially bid on. On Booking.com, we can sort through opening (and typically, but not always, final) price offers from dozens of airlines and hundreds of hotels. Amazon and Google allow us to compare prices for hundreds of options for the same product within minutes. Being able to search more options in a shorter amount of time allows us to save time, gain more options, and often save money. Online transactions also allow us to search independent platforms (eBay, Amazon, etc.) for information about products we're considering. During the pandemic, online transactions reduced the incidence of disease by eliminating the need to be in congested locations.

Selling can also be easier online. A number of years ago, I was gifted a new high-end cell phone. Two aspects of the gift limited its value to me. First, I already had a cell phone that worked fine. Second, the new phone was more technologically sophisticated than I could appreciate. So, what should I do with the gift? One of my more tech-savvy colleagues pointed out how easy it would be to sell it online. Within the week, my phone was on its way to the winner of an eBay auction.

Yet people have concerns about online transactions, and rightly so. When we negotiate online, we are more anonymous, which will lead some negotiators to feel licensed to behave less ethically because they don't expect their reputation to suffer. I also understand from my unpartnered friends that honesty is limited on dating sites, for example.

Turning to the realm of insurance, as transactions are increasingly conducted online, insurance companies fear that customers will submit more fraudulent claims. The insurtech (online insurance) company Slice Insurance creates value by simplifying transactions for policyholders, including the claims process.[16] Among Slice's products are short-term insurance policies for people who rent homes on Airbnb. The key question facing Slice, similar to someone searching for a match on Tinder, is how to obtain truthful information from claimants. Slice concluded that claimants would be less likely to lie on video than in writing. Thus, it asks claimants to create a short video on their phone describing their claim. In addition, because ambiguous questions such as "What was the lost item worth?" encourage deception, Slice instead asks specific questions, such as "How much did you pay for the lost object?" and/or "What does it cost to replace the item on Amazon.com?" Claimants are also asked to state who else knows about the loss, since accountability to others has been found to decrease deception. Slice reciprocates the trustworthiness it hopes to inspire in its customers by electronically paying most claims as soon as they are submitted rather than delaying payment, as other insurers do. Slice is trying to turn what feels like a problem—getting honest information online—into a comparative advantage. The company believes its digital claims process reduces fraud and builds trust with customers.[17]

Fairness and equity are other important concerns that arise when we transact online. Early in the history of online transactions, many believed the internet reduced discrimination due to the anonymity it provides. Early research by economists Fiona Scott Morton, Florian Zettelmeyer, and Jorge Silva-Risso showed that the prices paid in car sales initiated online were less biased by race and gender compared to transactions conducted entirely offline.[18] It seemed that online transactions were a solution to fairness and equity. But, over time, online platforms evolved, and anonymity became a design choice made by their creators.

When Brian Chesky and Joe Gebbia were creating Airbnb in 2007–8, they started with the idea that hosts would provide lodging and a local experience for guests. Chesky and Gebbia were the service's first hosts. One of their early design decisions was to create a community feel for guests and hosts, which they tried to do in part by asking them to upload photographs of themselves to their Airbnb profiles. The thinking was that people would feel more comfortable staying in someone's home, or inviting someone into their home, if a trustworthy photo was visible to them.

A decade later, Ben Edelman, Mike Luca, and Dan Svirsky (my Harvard colleagues at the time) conducted an experiment in which, posing as Airbnb guests, they sent rental inquiries to 6,400 Airbnb hosts in the United States. They used fictitious names, half of which are statistically more common among white people (such as Brett and Todd) and half of which are statistically more common among Black people (such as Darnell and Jamal). They found that guests with Black-sounding names were approved by Airbnb 8 percent less than guests with white-sounding names.[19] Edelman and his colleagues showed that discriminatory decisions were made primarily by hosts who had never had a Black guest. The article, published in 2017, received massive media coverage and caught the attention of the U.S. Department of Housing and Urban Development, attorneys general in many states, the Congressional Black Caucus, and private attorneys who filed lawsuits against Airbnb. The uproar led Airbnb to begin making changes to the platform to reduce discrimination by hosts, while trying not to lose too many hosts and guests in the process.

Chesky admitted that he and Gebbia had not thought about how their initial platform design for Airbnb might facilitate discrimination.

As is the case with many tech start-ups, there were myriad small decisions to be made, and the potential bias of hosts wasn't on their radar. Airbnb's failure to think about this issue meant that Edelman and his colleagues drove the story, which made solving the problem more of a reactive than a proactive process. As new platforms are created, executives should be aware that online negotiations are inevitably shaped by the platform's design.

The people who create online platforms might question whether they are responsible for the actions of their users. In my view, they are at least partially responsible. Creators should think through the likely experience and behavior of users on their platform. When you choose not to regulate miscommunication on your platform, you are participating in creating misinformation. And when you allow people to discriminate on your platform, you have played a role in the resulting discrimination.

Platform creators make lots of other decisions that affect the negotiations that occur on their sites. Will you simply connect people and allow them to negotiate prices, or will prices instead be fixed? Will you create an auction format or have a dynamic supply and demand, like Uber? Will you require workers on the platform to earn a wage at or above some minimum that you could specify? What will you enable users to learn about the people on the other side of their negotiations? Will reviews of buyers, sellers, and/or products be available on your site? As these questions make clear, companies that create platforms are making dozens of decisions that will affect the structure of negotiations among their users.

Online Has Changed the Game

Most of us were gradually shifting from face-to-face transactions to online transactions in the past decade or two, only to take a big leap in this direction during the pandemic. Our core negotiation goals are often the same online, but how we best implement transactions has significantly altered. The online context may represent the biggest contextual change in how many of us negotiate. If we are negotiating on Zoom, the core tasks of preparing for negotiation remain. But important Zoom negotiations require an extra layer of preparation. In particular, we need to think through what information we want the other party to have access to and how our team will communicate.

When preparing for important transactions on online platforms, recognize that not all platforms are the same and that key design features can work for or against you. Also think about the platform itself as an intermediary with a set of goals of the platform creators, separate from the buyer and seller. In traditional negotiations, agents often don't share the goals of their principals. Now we need to think about the organization creating the platform as a party to the negotiation as well.

• • •

"I have a house that I hope to rent out for the next year while I'm working on the other side of the country. I am very nervous about renting my house to strangers who might cause damage. These days, tenants are commonly found on online platforms, which might keep me from being able to meet prospective tenants in person. I have also heard that a series of short-term rentals on Airbnb would result in more revenue than one long-term rental. I only rented out the house once before, to a colleague for a month. What advice do you have for negotiating an agreement(s) with one or more parties to live in my home?"

"Keep in mind that many people rent out their homes online, and most of the time, it works out just fine. But if you remain concerned, one option would be to list your home with a traditional real estate agent in your town, which should allow you to meet the prospective tenants and could provide some reassurance. That said, it is certainly true that much of the rental market is most easily accessed online through platforms like Airbnb.com, HomeAway.com, and SabbaticalHomes.com. These platforms structure transactions in slightly different ways, and you might want to invest a bit of time in checking out the differences. Some, especially those specializing in short-term rentals, will allow you to see reviews of potential tenants. It is also true that lining up many shorter stays is likely to generate more revenue than one long-term visitor (the nightly price for shorter stays tends to be higher), but this also requires more management and greater tolerance for more people coming through your home. My main recommendation is to identify multiple strategies for the use of your home while you are traveling. Then, think through what you really care about and decide the best third-party mechanism—such as a realtor, perhaps a university housing office, or one or more of the many online platforms—to help you achieve your objectives. Most likely, this will work out great, perhaps with a small bump or two. So, concentrate on having a great year away."

Chapter 9

Beyond Two Negotiators

"Last week, we were skiing at Sugarbush Mountain in Warren, Vermont. The weather wasn't good for skiing one day, so we visited the next town over, Waitsfield. As we passed a real estate office, we saw a charming farmhouse advertised in the window. With time to kill, we walked in, chatted with a real estate agent, and at the end of the day, met with them again and saw the house. We loved it! It needs a fair amount of work, but my partner and I enjoy doing many of the tasks that are needed. The agent followed up by sending us information on comparable sales in the area and informed us that the house was being sold by three adult children who grew up in the house, which they inherited from their recently deceased parent. The house was listed for \$499,000, and the comps that the realtor sent suggest that \$470,000 would be a good estimate of the market value of the house. How do you recommend we proceed?"

▪ ▪ ▪

In chapter 5, we considered the role that a lie played in a pivotal moment during the Cuban Missile Crisis. Another fascinating story from the same crisis involved a group negotiation that occurred on a Soviet submarine—a negotiation in which Vasili Arkhipov may well have saved the world. Amid the crisis, on October 26, 1962, a U.S. ship, the USS *Beale*, identified a Soviet submarine, *B-59*, and dropped depth charges (explosions) to try to force the sub to surface. Unbeknownst to the U.S. government, the submarine was armed with atomic warheads. The Soviet ship's captain, Valentin Savitsky, did not understand that the depth charges were meant as a signal to surface. There was also a communication failure between the Soviet submarine and its command structure.

Savitsky falsely concluded that a war had started. Rather than surface in response to the threat from the USS *Beale*, he favored launching the sub's nuclear warhead at a U.S. target: the USS *Randolf*, a giant aircraft carrier leading the eleven ships in the U.S. blockade of Cuba. Exhausted and panicked, and assuming his submarine was doomed, Savitsky ordered the nuclear weapon—as strong as the one dropped on Hiroshima—to be made combat ready. "We're gonna blast them now!" he reportedly said. "We will die, but we will sink them all—we will not become the shame of the fleet."[1]

Fortunately, Savitsky did not have the authority to order the launch of the warhead on his own. He needed the approval of two other captains on the submarine. Ivan Maslennikov, another captain, approved the strike. But lower-ranked deputy captain Vasili Arkhipov, the third vote needed, said no. Foreseeing that launching the missile could trigger a nuclear war, Arkhipov put his life and career on the line, and refused to go along with Savitsky's decision.

Many historians believe that if Arkhipov had not been there to prevent the nuclear torpedo launch, nuclear war would have broken out between the United States and the USSR. "The fate of the world would have been very different: the attack would probably have started a nuclear war which would have caused global devastation, with unimaginable numbers of civilian deaths," Edward Wilson wrote in *The Guardian*.[2] As someone who was within striking distance of the missiles that were ready to launch, I, like millions of others, may well owe my life to Arkhipov. But we also owe a debt of gratitude to the Soviet military officials who created the rules of engagement that required unanimous agreement for the submarine to launch its nuclear warhead. If the commander of the ship, Savitsky, had had the authority to launch, the world could have been destroyed. If the rules of engagement had been that two of the three captains had to agree, the world could have been destroyed.

The requirement of unanimity to launch a nuclear warhead, coupled with Arkhipov's bravery, saved us.

The discussion aboard the Soviet submarine consisted of a negotiation between three parties under defined rules. In this chapter, we will look at negotiations involving three or more individuals who have different preferences. Many aspects of negotiation become more complicated as the number of parties increases beyond two people. It becomes more complicated to develop trust. Coalition formation becomes core to the results of the negotiation. And the rules that govern decision making become very important. This chapter explores a variety of contexts that grow more complex as the number of negotiating parties rises beyond two.

Negotiating with Agents

Imagine you have accepted a new job in a new city. Time is limited, but you would like to buy a condo. Where should you look for guidance on one of the few weekends you have available to house hunt in your future city? Many people in this situation search for a real estate agent, often by asking a friend or colleague for a recommendation. Agents are needed in many contexts, and it is important to understand that they are another party to the negotiation. Real estate agents earn their living from our housing purchases—through 2023, 5–6 percent of the closing price (this is in flux, based on recent changes in the industry).[3] Similarly, investment bankers act as agents in the sale of companies and are paid when a transaction occurs. Literary agents earn their living by closing deals between the authors they represent and publishers, typically earning 15 percent of the amount due to the author.

In many negotiation contexts, agents (realtors, literary agents, investment bankers) have created norms about how transactions will occur, such that many parties use their services without considering other options. Would buyers and sellers be better served by a well-designed website listing houses for sale, where sellers pay far less than the amount commonly paid to a real estate agent? While this idea is appealing to many, websites like Redfin.com have had limited success in taking over the market for combining buyers and sellers from traditional real estate agents.

So, why do buyers and sellers use agents? One reason is that agents often have more expertise than we do. Attorneys act as our agents in legal matters because they know relevant case law, and the cost of gaining the legal knowledge needed to defend oneself or to prosecute another party would be huge. And, while we can easily browse all the houses on the market in our area through online sites like Redfin, Trulia, and Zillow, the best-connected agents may also know about new properties that can't yet be found online, or they may know something about a property that hasn't been disclosed in the online listing. In a seller's market, that market knowledge can be critical. In the publishing business, some publishers give preference to work submitted by literary agents, reasoning that if an author has convinced a well-respected agent to represent them, the book is of higher quality. As a result, many authors view getting an agent to be an important first step in the publication process. Finally, thanks to their emotional distance from your negotiations, agents across contexts can protect you from making irrational decisions and escalating conflict by nudging you toward more deliberative thinking. And, in the case of attorneys, an intermediary can protect you from people you are better off not dealing with directly—an especially critical role for divorce attorneys.

While agents can play an important role in negotiation, they come at some cost. An agent's commission or fee shrinks the amount of the pie that goes to the principal, unless they create value that the negotiators couldn't create on their own. Shrinking the pie going to the principals can make it more difficult for the parties to reach an agreement and increases the likelihood of an impasse.[4] Thus, when deciding whether to work with an agent, buyers and sellers should assess the value that an agent is expected to create versus their cost.

An agent is essentially another party in the negotiation. It is typically impossible to perfectly align your agent's incentives with your own. Imagine you are thinking about buying a house. You are not in a hurry to buy and care a great deal about not overpaying. What about your agent? As we saw in chapter 5, real estate agents can have incentives to close deals as quickly as possible, and they receive slightly more money from higher prices.[5] These conflicts of interest could tilt the agent toward advising you to move faster and pay a higher price.

Most people recognize the conflicts of interest faced by other people's agents but tend to think their own agent is not conflicted. We personalize our agent and, with a dash of overconfidence, reach the false conclusion that our agent's conflicts of interest are a minor problem for us. This may sound cynical, and you might be wondering if I dislike all agents. No! I have friends who earn their living as agents. I have happily and successfully used agents to buy and sell houses, and to help me find a publisher on multiple books. The issues in this section should not be seen as a criticism of the ethics of agents. Rather, I encourage you to understand the strategic position of agents in the negotiation process. Any advice you receive from an agent that nudges you away from your best interests is probably occurring without the agent's awareness that they are violating their fiduciary interest to you. Rather, agents generally believe that their biased advice is unbiased. So, when your real estate agent advises you to raise your offer beyond what you think is optimal, the point is not that they are corrupt but that they are human, and therefore implicitly biased in a self-serving direction. When we are motivated to see data in a direction that will benefit us, we are incapable of providing others with unbiased advice.[6]

In some domains, intermediaries, such as financial advisors, are required by law to disclose their conflicts of interest. Consumers tend to erroneously assume that such disclosures mean their intermediaries will rise above their conflict of interest. In fact, ample research shows that disclosure may actually *increase* the problems that arise from conflicts of interest.[7] In a study by Daylian Cain and colleagues, participants simulating the role of advisor were required to tell those playing the role of client that they, the advisors, had different financial incentives than the client. Unfortunately, the disclosure led the advisors to be *more* self-serving, since the people they were advising had been warned about the conflict of interest. Yet, the simulated clients believed that disclosure made their advisor more ethical—which was not the case.[8]

So, what's my advice to a home buyer on using agents? You may well want to use an agent, especially if you are searching for a new home in a seller's market, to have access to a greater range of options. While your agent may know things that you do not, verify the agent's advice from unbiased sources. If they make a statement about the market, ask them to back up their claims with objective data. If you get to the point of making an offer, and will not personally be present for the negotiation, ask your agent for regular updates and factual information about what transpired. You might also consider asking your agent for direct access to the parties on the other side, even if your agent advises against doing so. Finally, avoid the common tendency to view your agent as a trusted advisor who should be privy to your reservation price. This might sound cynical, but a study led by Harvard Business School professor Kathleen McGinn showed that selling prices were lowest when an agent only knew the seller's reservation price and were highest when the agent only knew the buyer's reservation price. Agents benefit from confidential information at their clients' expense.[9] Generally, share no more information with your agent than you would with the party across the table. Though it may be difficult, particularly if you like your agent, consider your agent first and foremost a party to the negotiation, not your partner in the negotiation.

Cooperating beyond Two

If we scan for the world's biggest negotiation failures, we can easily identify ongoing conflicts in places like the Middle East and Kashmir, where decades pass with little movement toward lasting peace. An even more significant negotiation failure may be the international community's inability to reach a binding and effective accord on reducing climate change. Across multiple international summits, global negotiations have failed to achieve meaningful results for decades. When the international community has reached agreement, as in the 2015 Paris Climate Accords, implementation has been a problem; the representatives at the international negotiations often have not had the power to force their countries to implement the agreement. Most people who believe in science understand that climate change is occurring, that humans are causing it, and that we have a moral obligation to future generations to act now to stop it. Yet, nations continue to fail to reach a binding resolution on how to reduce our impact on climate change. If so many people around the world agree that change is warranted, why can't we reach a more sensible agreement?

One key challenge is identifying which nations must make the necessary changes. Who is most responsible for the climate change that has occurred already? Nations differ in their assessments of how to dole out the blame. According to emerging nations, developed economies' industrialization and excessive consumption created the problem. Meanwhile, many in the United States and other Western nations blame the global failure on China and India accepting too little responsibility for their current contributions to climate change. Developed economies also blame emerging nations for burning rainforests, overpopulation, and unchecked economic expansion.

Our failure to act can be explained in part by most of us not valuing future generations as much as we claim we do. Another significant part of the challenge is that even if we can all agree that the world needs to address the problem, we may disagree about who is most responsible and what actions different parties need to take. In chapter 5, I discussed a prisoner's dilemma problem involving two parties who are individually better off competing but collectively better off cooperating. As the number of parties increases in negotiation, cooperating becomes more difficult. Psychologist Robyn M. Dawes defined social dilemmas as multiparty contexts in which "(a) each individual receives a higher payoff for a socially defecting choice . . . than for a socially cooperative choice, no matter what the other individuals in society do, but (b) all individuals are better off if all cooperate than if all defect."[10] Just as in the prisoner's dilemma problem, the three or more parties are individually rational by defecting on group cooperation while collectively better off cooperating with the group.

Over a half century ago, ecologist Garrett Hardin introduced the phrase "the tragedy of the commons" when describing a situation in which a group of herdsmen grazed their animals in a common pasture.[11] Each herdsman is better off increasing the size of his herd because each additional animal represents personal profit to him. But if too many animals graze, the pasture is damaged, and all the herdsmen are harmed. The herdsmen have a collective interest in setting individual limits on the total number of animals grazing in the pasture that match the rate of pasture replenishment, while each herdsman's interest is to marginally increase the number of animals that graze. As each herdsman responds to the short-term incentive to increase the size of their herds, the commons is destroyed. Similarly, as each country pollutes to grow its economy, the long-term future of the world is degraded.

In Hardin's story of the commons, the herdsmen have similar interests and have herds of similar size. In such so-called symmetric dilemmas, it is easier for parties to use a fairness norm of equality—that is, to agree to divide the resource equally. In contrast, when asymmetry in interests and outcomes exists, as in global climate negotiations, ambiguity arises concerning what a "fair" solution would be. When we are faced with ambiguity, our judgments are biased in a self-serving manner. Each party honestly believes it would be fair for others to sacrifice more and for their own side to sacrifice less than an independent analysis would suggest.[12] The net result is that most parties will fail to fairly contribute to solving the problem, given their perceptions of insufficient action by others.

It will be very difficult to get the most important actors to implement a fair resolution on climate change without an international body (such as the United Nations) gaining more authority and without weighting the voices of less-biased nations more heavily. As long as the United States and China draw their own conclusions about what would constitute a fair solution, self-serving biases are likely to be a barrier to implementation of a fair resolution. Countries need to apply Rawls's veil of ignorance and be willing to make the sacrifices necessary to put in place what an unbiased assessment would suggest—a significant contribution to solving this existential risk.

Negotiations within Organizations

Organizations exist to create synergies beyond what their members could create on their own. Many decisions within organizations are made by multiple employees who do not have identical preferences and views. Given my definition of negotiation as a decision involving two or more people who do not have identical preferences, these organizational decisions are negotiations. The best decisions in these contexts, I argue, are those that create the most aggregate good for the organization. This probably doesn't sound controversial. Yet when most of us join a group meeting where an important decision must be made, we focus more on building a winning coalition for our preferred outcome than on using the different areas of expertise found in the group to search for the best aggregate decision. In this section, we examine how people who may not agree can reach great decisions.

In my most recent book with Don Moore, *Decision Leadership*, we argue that a critical challenge for leaders is to nudge members of their organization to focus on making the best decisions possible.[13] How can you do this when different members of the organization have access to different information? As you think about this question, consider that Daniel Kahneman and his colleagues highlight in their book *Noise* that executives are very "noisy" when making a wide variety of assessments. They describe noise as unwanted variation across individuals. Not only is there a great deal of noise in executives' estimates, but the noise is far larger than executives expect. For example, Kahneman and his colleagues document that insurance executives who estimate the appropriate premium to charge or the value of a claim typically expect they will, on average, differ from their colleagues by no more than 10 percent. In fact, the actual average variation between executives is closer to 50 percent.[14]

How can you best aggregate assessments from people who have very different, noisy views? To answer this question, think about what typically happens in your organization. For many of us, the leader maintains decision-making authority and underweights input from others. Notice that in the Cuban Missile Crisis, this would have led to Savitsky firing the nuclear warhead. Another common scenario in organizations is following the will of the majority. Here again, this would have led to the nuclear weapon being fired. Alternatively, decision makers could sit around talking until they reach a unanimous decision, but requiring unanimity could prevent them from ever making many necessary decisions.

How else might numerous people in an organization reach agreement? You may have heard of "the wisdom of crowds," an idea popularized by journalist James Surowiecki in his 2004 book of the same name.[15] Based on research, case studies, and anecdotes, Surowiecki concludes that groups typically reach better decisions than individuals because they are able to aggregate information from all members, and the errors on the high side and low side cancel each other out. More recently, Rick Larrick and his colleagues concluded from their review of a great deal of research evidence that very simple rules for aggregating group judgment, such as using the mean or median decision, generally outperform having the leader make the decision or having the leader select the individual whom they think will make the best decision. They give the example of the *Wall Street Journal's* annual forecasting competition. In these competitions, the *WSJ* asks approximately fifty economists to predict key economic outcomes for the upcoming year. As Kahneman and colleagues would predict, there is lots of noise in their answers.[16] So if you wanted to obtain a best estimate of one of these economic quantities, based on the economists' many predictions, what would you do?

One of the greatest advisors in history was Socrates. He advised Plato, who went on to advise Aristotle—pretty good credentials for an advisor. With regard to finding good advice for making a decision, Socrates offered: "First of all ask, whether there is any one of us who has knowledge of that about which we are deliberating? If there is, let us take his advice, though he be one only, and not mind the rest; if there is not, let us seek further counsel."[17] So, if you were to follow Socrates's advice, you might choose the estimate from the economist who was the most accurate the previous year, the most accurate economist averaged across the last three years, or the most well-cited or well-recognized economist.

By contrast, the wisdom-of-crowds argument would advise averaging all the economists' predictions. Many people react negatively to this simple advice, as the average would include some very ill-informed opinions. Giving the predictions of ill-informed people equal weight as the predictions of really smart, informed people sounds off to many. Yet, data suggest that the wisdom of crowds outperforms most methods for identifying the best prediction.

Rick Larrick's research team argues that you can reap the benefits of selecting experts and the statistical benefits of averaging through their select-crowd strategy, which involves averaging the opinions of a small number of experts.[18] Larrick's research shows that choosing the best person in advance (based on prior accuracy) works in some contexts, and averaging a large crowd works well in others, but their so-called select-crowd strategy has robust results across many contexts. Another advantage of the strategy is that people tend to be much more receptive to the idea of averaging experts' opinions than to the idea of averaging many opinions, including some that are ill-informed. In the *WSJ* context, averaging the predictions of all the economists is better than selecting the prediction of a random economist or choosing the best predictor from the previous year. And averaging the top five predictors from the previous year provides even better estimates than averaging the predictions of all the economists.[19]

I am quite convinced by Larrick's analysis of the benefits of averaging opinions. But my own experience in many group meetings suggests that we can also improve our decisions and estimates by dramatically improving group processes. Consider that many groups start with the person most central to a project (or a leader) offering their views and then asking for reactions. The initially stated opinion or conclusion becomes an anchor that keeps the rest of the group from offering independent assessments and undermines the crowd's wisdom. The strength of the wisdom-of-crowds and the select-crowds strategies comes from individuals making independent assessments not influenced by a common source (the leader's or speaker's assessment). If one person's initial opinion affects others' subsequent opinions, independence and the wisdom of the crowd are destroyed. This suggests that groups need to be structured to give all decision makers the facts they need and to get their opinions before they hear a presenter's or leader's opinion.

Finally, a few words on who should belong to the crowd. People with more expertise are preferred. Diversity should also be prioritized—not just for the sake of inclusion but to reach better predictions. That's because similar experts have similar biases. I am often struck by the inability of people in my liberal city of Cambridge, Massachusetts, for example, to understand the views of more conservative Americans on political issues. So, averaging the opinions of a group of Cantabrigians (yes, that is what we are called) wouldn't solve the problem of better understanding the American populace. When you have diverse experts, their different biases cancel each other out, creating the power of the crowd. If a small group is well managed, the use of selected experts provides a great strategy for making good decisions.

Coalitions in Negotiation

We've just seen the value of getting key organizational decision makers to focus on what is best for the organization as a whole rather than on building a coalition that allows one side to dominate the decision-making process. Journalist Ken Auletta's bestseller *Greed and Glory on Wall Street* documents the disintegration of Lehman Brothers, a major Wall Street investment firm, due to a power struggle between two coalitions, the "traders" and the "bankers."[20] The traders, focused narrowly on increasing their own short-term wealth, were eager for firm profits to be distributed. To get their way, they built a "winning" coalition, only to deplete the firm's resources and destroy its long-term viability, leading to bankruptcy. Cornell professor Elizabeth Mannix views coalitional behavior within organizations as a form of defection from the interests of the broader organization by members who push only for the coalition's interests.[21] In a well-functioning organization, all key decision makers would be focused on what is best for the organization. But leaders often focus instead on their smaller coalition's interests.

Consider the role of coalition dynamics in different forms of democracy. The United Kingdom (UK), a parliamentary democracy, is divided into a number of districts, each of which elects one Member of Parliament (MP) to represent it in the House of Commons. If one political party wins more than half the seats in the House of Commons, that party's leader forms the government and becomes prime minister. When none of the parties win at least half of the seats in the House of

Commons, two or more parties can coalesce to create a majority that governs the country. If one or more parties in the coalitional majority later withdraw their support so that a ruling majority no longer exists, the government falls, and new elections are called. No political system is perfect, but one limitation of a parliamentary democracy is that political parties tend to focus on getting into power rather than on developing policies that are best for the country. A common complaint from sectarians in Israel, which has a parliamentary democracy, for example, is that the governance processes give too much weight to the preferences of the extremely religious (for example, requiring businesses to close on the Sabbath). This results from the fairly equal balance between the major parties. The religious parties have the power to create a multiparty majority by combining with the party that will make the greatest concessions to the preferences of the extremely religious.

Even within a two-party system like the United States, we can see the role of coalitional dynamics. On August 16, 2022, President Joe Biden signed the Inflation Reduction Act (IRA). The U.S. Senate had approved the package on August 7 by a narrow 51–50 vote (with Vice President Kamala Harris serving as the tiebreaker), and the House of Representatives easily approved the legislation on August 12. The IRA included $437 billion of new investments in climate change mitigation, clean energy, health care, and prescription drug reform, as well as $300 billion for projected reductions in the national deficit. To pay for these costs, the act also included a 15 percent corporate minimum tax, a 1 percent fee on stock buybacks by corporations, savings from allowing the government to negotiate drug prices (which, bizarrely, it had been prevented from doing for many years), and anticipated improved tax collections by hiring 86,000 additional Internal Revenue Service employees.

While the IRA was the most significant climate investment in U.S. history, the bill was a slimmed-down version of Biden's earlier proposed bill, Build Back Better (BBB). BBB never came close to gaining the support needed for passage in the Senate. (For non-U.S. readers: for a bill to become law in the United States, it must receive majority support in the House and Senate—with the vice president casting the deciding vote if there is a 50-50 tie in the Senate—and be signed into law by the president.) As of 2022, the Democrats had the majority in the House, and all Democratic House members and the president supported both the BBB and IRA, as well as every iteration between the two bills. All fifty Republican senators, meanwhile, were opposed to the BBB and IRA bills. Two of the Democrats' fifty senators, Kyrsten Sinema of Arizona and Joe Manchin of West Virginia, were noncommittal about whether they would support either bill, which was critical to the Biden administration's political success.

Just a month before the IRA became law, both Sinema and Manchin indicated they would vote against it, putting the bill in jeopardy. With the Democrats in control of the White House, Senate, and House, this likely failure was an embarrassment to Biden and the Democratic Party, and it suggested the Democrats were incapable of passing important legislation. The problem was a coalitional one: the Senate Democrats were not a monolithic actor. Sinema and Manchin repeatedly withheld their commitment for the Democrats' proposals, likely fearful their support would alienate voters in their historically conservative states and lead them to lose their next elections.

Ultimately, in exchange for his vote on the IRA, Manchin demanded legislation that would pave the way for massive expansion of oil and gas drilling on federal lands and in federal waters, and for federal support of a pipeline project of value to West Virginia. Once the Democrats agreed to a deal with Manchin, they needed Sinema's vote. She demanded a concession that her largest supporters (venture capital and private equity) lobbied for: to kill the elimination of a tax break called the "carried interest loophole," which benefits only the ultra-wealthy by taxing private equity and venture capital income at an inequitably low level.

The changes Manchin and Sinema demanded provided some benefit to the citizens of West Virginia and the financial lobbyists who bought Sinema's support at a far greater cost to the country as a whole. But, that is the nature of decision making in groups governed by coalitional behavior. Manchin and Sinema defected on what was best for the United States for their own political benefit. The Democrats could have done a better job of anticipating Manchin's and Sinema's objections. Rather than negotiating with them at the end of the process, the Democrats could have offered concessions on the front end when Manchin and Sinema would have felt less powerful. More broadly, thinking about the coalitional behavior of all of the parties is critical in complex, multiparty negotiations.

Negotiating as a Team

In this chapter, we've explored a variety of complex negotiation contexts where the complexity comes in part from the presence of more than two parties. In this final section, we focus on the common context of negotiations between two parties, where one or both parties bring a team to the negotiation table rather than just an individual. When my colleagues and I teach our one-week "Changing the Game" executive program at Harvard, we run two of the simulations as team negotiations, one early in the program and one to end it. Early in the program, when the executives first try negotiating as a team, I observe two interesting aspects of how they respond to negotiating in a group. First, many executives prefer negotiating alone rather than as a team. Second, the time they spend preparing as a team is not as useful as it could be. When we close the program with the second team negotiation, the executives have learned more about how to prepare and about the benefit of team negotiations. As a result, their preparation process is much more impressive, and they value their team members far more than they did at the beginning of the week. They also access the strengths of their negotiation partners to negotiate better agreements. This section focuses on what the executives learn about the benefits and limitations of negotiating as a team, as well as how to manage the limitations.

Negotiating as a team offers a number of benefits over going it alone. A team provides more collective knowledge and skills than any one individual has alone. Diversity on a team helps, as it embodies the team with unique skills and knowledge rather than redundant ones. Many of us are drawn toward adding team members who are like us when we would benefit more from including people who can complement our skills. So, when creating a negotiating team, think about who possesses information you might want to have available and who has cognitive skills that would be beneficial to draw from on your side of the negotiation. Look beyond friendship and recruit individuals who have the experiences, negotiating skills, technical expertise, and interpersonal skills you need.

In chapter 13, we will discuss negotiation preparation in detail. Here, I simply highlight some aspects unique to team negotiations. In the first team negotiation in "Changing the Game," my experience is that these sophisticated executives offer many interesting insights about negotiation and how their past experiences inform their ideas. However, they often fail to conduct a clear analysis of their BATNA, reservation price, and, more importantly, the BATNA and reservation price of the other party. A positive feature of team negotiations is that it provides thought partners to help you work through and articulate your ideas about these key parameters of any important negotiation. Being explicit in your analysis will lead you and the other members of your team to use your deliberative thought processes rather than relying on your less effective negotiation intuition. In addition, team members often have different information that allows you to better understand these key elements of your negotiation analysis.

Being on a team also creates potential problems. Many negotiators have been frustrated to hear their teammates say things during a negotiation that they view as a mistake, such as accidentally giving away the team's reservation price. To lessen this possibility, you and your team should aim for consensus on critical issues you might face in the negotiation during the preparation stage. During your preparatory meetings, decide which information you are willing to share with the other side; otherwise, your counterparts across the table might take advantage of any cracks that emerge in your team. It is also important to think through who will do what during the negotiation. Are you going to have one primary spokesperson, or will different team members handle different parts of the negotiation exchange? The answer likely will depend on the various types of expertise found on your team. It's critical to talk through these issues in advance so that there are few unpleasant surprises at the negotiating table.

You should also think through who will provide technical knowledge, who will crunch the numbers to determine the overall value of the other side's offers, and—perhaps most overlooked—who will be actively listening to and observing the other side. Negotiation is a cognitively tough task: it requires us to listen and get ready to speak at the same time. Negotiators often are too busy thinking about what they will say next to fully listen to the other side. Negotiating on a team allows you to allocate the role of active listening to a specific team member. When debriefing negotiation simulations, I commonly hear one negotiator complain about the information the other side didn't provide, only for the other side to clarify that they did indeed provide that information. Listening is underrated in negotiation (and in other aspects of life). Being on a team allows you to plan how to best hear your counterparts.

Your team should also think through the negotiation process. Do you have the information needed to be able to put the first proposal on the table (as discussed in chapter 2), or do you need to learn more? If you are going to make an opening offer, what will it be? What will you do if you learn new, key information from the other side? Will one team member have the authority to respond, or will you need to caucus to discuss what's happened so far, handle any internal disputes that arise, and plan your next moves?

Overall, in team negotiation, it's important to think through the many benefits available to the team but also to make sure you are ready to gain the benefits of the extra minds available to you.

In this chapter, many of the ideas we have discussed about two-party negotiation have reappeared but in more complicated form. Contexts that involve more than two individuals typically create the need for added preparation to understand the interests of all the people and parties at the table. Many of our most important negotiation contexts will involve more than two parties. Thinking about the processes involved, as well as the extra interests to consider, creates more challenges but also more opportunities.

■ ■ ■

"Last week, we were skiing at Sugarbush Mountain in Warren, Vermont. The weather wasn't good for skiing one day, so we visited the next town over, Waitsfield. As we passed a real estate office, we saw a charming farmhouse advertised in the window. With time to kill, we walked in, chatted with a real estate agent, and at the end of the day, met with them again and saw the house. We loved it! It needs a fair amount of work, but my partner and I enjoy doing many of the tasks that are needed. The agent followed up by sending us information on comparable sales in the area and informed us that the house was being sold by three adult children who grew up in the house, which they inherited from their recently deceased parent. The house was listed for $499,000, and the comps that the realtor sent suggest that $470,000 would be a good estimate of the market value of the house. How do you recommend we proceed?"

"First, Waitsfield is a beautiful town, and the Mad Taco makes great enchiladas. On to your question. There are various people involved in your negotiation context, and you need to deal with them in different ways. First, you are negotiating with your partner. I recommend that you and your partner coordinate on what you want in a new home and your negotiation strategy before meeting with the realtor. Then, I wouldn't move forward on the specific home that you stumbled upon due to the canceled skiing without doing a more thorough search of similar houses in the many ski towns in the area. You might find other options that meet your needs. Even finding a second choice that you love almost as much as the Waitsfield farmhouse will help you develop a strong BATNA. I also recommend not limiting yourself to the realtor's selected comps but instead asking for a list of all homes that have sold in the area between $400,000 and $600,000 over the last two years (you can also find this information online on sites like Redfin). Do your own analysis rather than relying on the potentially biased data the realtor selected. Finally, you might want to meet the siblings selling the house. Do they still love it? If so, would they sell it for a lower price if you allowed them to use the house a few weeks a year while you are traveling? Direct discussion between principals often allows you to discover value-creating options that are hard to find with an intermediary in the middle. I hope you find a great home, whether the one you fell for or another option."

Chapter 10

Changing the Game

"We are about to put our house on the market. Our agent recommends that we list it on a Thursday, hold an open house on Sunday, and then not consider offers for three days, until Wednesday at noon. She argues this will increase the likelihood of having multiple offers to consider at the same time. She even recommends that we leave town so she can claim we aren't available to consider offers that might come in earlier. My spouse doesn't like the idea of waiting until Wednesday to consider offers, for fear we will lose a buyer who is unwilling to wait to get involved in what feels like an auction. Who is right, my spouse or our agent?"

. . .

One Friday night a few years ago, a friend of mine sent me an email, asking for negotiation advice. The day before, she and her partner had put their condo in Cambridge, Massachusetts, up for sale in a hot market with a list price of $989,000. An open house was scheduled for Sunday, and buyers were told that no offers would be considered before Tuesday at noon. The hope was to generate multiple offers and trigger a bidding war, though my friend said they were open to having their "socks knocked off" before then with a great offer. She was anxious for the condo to sell quickly. The condo had "tons of showings" so far, she told me in her email, and they had just gotten a great offer: $1,125,000 with an expiration of Sunday evening. The offer waived the right to an inspection of the condo and highlighted why financing was unlikely to be a barrier for the buyer. My friend and her partner were happy to receive what seemed like a very high offer, but they were concerned: Did this suggest their agent had seriously undervalued the condo?

The agent provided his opinion of the offer in this email to my friend:

> WOW! I think these are your buyers! You should seriously consider this offer or counter at $1,150,000 to see if they bite! Nice personal letter/photo etc. 10K for initial deposit, usually $1,000. Wow, $102,500 dollars "non-refundable" at the Purchase & Sale Agreement. Usually only 5% down payment for P&S etc. If they default can we split it . . . lol No, seriously you may think someone would, could pay more etc. But we don't have a crystal ball. So don't lose them.

Not surprisingly, the agent was eager to close the deal. To try to induce my friend to do so, he was warning her about the uncertainty of the situation and offering advice that was not very creative.

"Would love your input on how to proceed," my friend wrote. Specifically, she wanted to know if she should take the offer, counteroffer, or reject it and wait for the open house.

I regularly receive emails and calls from friends asking for advice on their real estate negotiations, but this one was particularly intriguing. My intuition was that the agent had listed the condo for at least $100,000 too little and was still undervaluing the condo as they weighed the early offer. Like many agents, he appeared to be eager to close the deal quickly and earn his commission. Yet, I knew my friend would be upset and anxious if my advice led her condo to remain on the market for a significant amount of time.

Borrowing from a strategy I learned from my Harvard Business School colleague Guhan Subramanian, I proposed that she and her partner counter with:

1) A request for the prospective buyer to make their offer legally binding through the following Wednesday.
2) In return, offering the prospective buyer a chance to beat the best offer the sellers receive by $25,000, if they receive a higher offer by Wednesday.
3) The sellers would commit to accepting the current offer if no higher offer arrives.

This strategy is rooted in common practices in mergers and acquisitions negotiations. Typically, a company that is ready to be sold seeks an array of possible acquirers to create competition and a favorable price. But, sometimes, one potential acquirer makes an early offer and also provides the seller with a "go-shop provision." This provision binds the potential acquirer to their offer but allows the seller to seek other offers during a specified time period. In return for the buyer's openness to the seller's search for a higher offer, the buyer has the right to match or beat the highest offer the seller obtains and to close the acquisition.[1]

Applied to my friend's problem, this go-shop provision would give the buyer a guarantee that they would have the option to buy the condo, and it would give my friend an opportunity to find out what the broader market would provide. My friend adjusted my suggested final premium down from $25,000 to $10,000 and sent the following counterproposal to the buyer:

> You officially extend your offer, as is, to Tuesday, August 16 at 9 p.m. In exchange, we will give you right of first refusal: if we obtain an offer that beats yours, before accepting it, we will give you the opportunity to beat it by $10K, in which case the condo is yours. If no better offer comes in, then we simply execute your current offer. This arrangement gives you the certainty of knowing that if you want the condo, you will have the final opportunity to get it. It also means you only pay more if there is a competing offer.

The buyers accepted the proposal. My colleague and her partner received multiple higher offers, created an auction, and took the highest price offer, $1,200,000, to the original bidder, who used their option and beat the best offer by $10,000. My friend and her partner were delighted, as they received $60,000–85,000 (minus the agent's 6 percent commission) more than if they had followed their agent's advice. The key to reaching this outcome was to think systematically about the process that would guide the transaction. Finally, it is interesting to note that I have never heard of this process being proposed by a real estate agent.

While this story occurred recently, it highlights a theme that has been core to the teaching of the Negotiation, Organizations & Markets unit at the Harvard Business School for at least a couple of decades. I formally joined HBS in 2000 and soon created and led a new executive program on decision making and negotiation, starting in the spring of 2001. My colleague Adam Brandenburger was part of the teaching team I recruited for this new program. Adam argued that we should be teaching people not just to make good decisions and to negotiate effectively but also to change the game they are playing for the better, when needed. Adam convinced me, and we called the program "Changing the Game." For more than two decades, it has been one of the most popular focused programs that HBS has offered. I believe the theme of changing the game has been core to the program's success.

Participants are surprised by the opportunities the program presents to change the game, rather than simply to play a well-specified game. Most people think of negotiation as a process in which two parties exchange offers on a predefined issue (such as price) or issues (such as salary, starting date, and initial job assignment). Changing the game creates a different context for offers to be made by changing elements such as the parties at the table, the issues to be negotiated, and the negotiation process. So far, this book has highlighted how the game—that is, the world—has changed around us. In this chapter, we look at opportunities you may have to shape the game you play.

Does an Auction Make Sense?

We often accept the norms provided to us about how a transaction should transpire. At the grocery story, we either accept or reject the store's final offer on a jar of peanut butter—or what is called a fixed price. Few people consider offering the checkout clerk a lower price. In contrast, when we enter a car dealership, we fully expect to negotiate the price of our chosen car. And when a literary agent is selling their client's manuscript to a publisher, they typically do their best to drum up an auction. The agent specifies features of the desired agreement, typically with standard industry terms, except for the author's advance. Then, using an auction process, the agent tries to attract multiple bids and sell to the publisher that offers the most money.

The process of a negotiation is created by a set of choices that we and our counterpart make. Too often, we accept this process without considering whether a different process would lead to better results for us and possibly also the other side. Great negotiators not only implement the negotiation game well but change it to maximize their outcomes.

Most readers have experience buying fixed-priced goods and negotiating, and less experience running or participating in auctions. But if you purchased products online at the turn of the millennium, it is quite possible you participated in auctions on eBay. Back in 1995, the early days of the World Wide Web, Pierre Omidyar created a website called Auction Web where people could sell collectibles to one another. He put the first items up for auction and was surprised when his broken laser pointer sold for $14.83. Omidyar contacted the winning bidder to ensure he understood that the laser pointer was broken; the buyer explained that he was trying to make his own pointer with used parts.[2]

Soon, eBay was born. Early on and until today, the site has offered sellers the choice to sell items at a fixed price of their choosing or through an auction process. But eBay became famous as the first online auction site, and its popularity boomed: by 2000, it had 12 million registered users and was hosting more than 4.5 million auctions on a typical day.[3] This was before Facebook, YouTube, Twitter, and Instagram were available to entertain us online, so bidding in online auctions was a popular form of entertainment. I purchased a bunch of rugs in eBay auctions—it was fun. But with the rise of social media and other internet time wasters, auctions slipped as a form of online entertainment; by 2022, fewer than 15 percent of eBay listings were auctions. Consumers now look for convenience in online shopping, not games.

The internet also moved corporations toward procuring the materials they need for production in online auctions. With the development of online technology, large corporations discovered the power of online auctions to obtain better prices in a shorter amount of time than before. In these "reverse auctions," the winning bidder was typically the supplier with the lowest price (rather than the buyer with the highest price). Companies would either create their own technical capabilities for holding auctions or hire an online intermediary to manage their auctions. Those holding an auction would issue a request for proposals, allow potential suppliers to visit a website to learn more about the products or services being sought, provide a deadline for bids, and specify the process that would be used to move from bids to contracting with a chosen supplier. This latter process could involve simply selecting the best bid, negotiating with the lowest bidders, or moving on to a second round of the auction (perhaps telling all remaining bidders the price they need to beat to stay in the process).

Many organizations found they could obtain much lower prices through an auction process than by negotiating with suppliers one by one—the same reason my friend wanted an auction to develop for her condo. Some buyers valued auctions not just for driving competition but for creating opportunities for those who had been excluded from the supply chain in the past based on their gender, race, or ethnicity. Buyers also saw auctions as helpful in reducing corruption in the supply chain, which could take the form of a procurement officer getting an illegal kickback from a supplier. For these reasons and others, many federal and state regulations that required auctions for specified procurement activities were put in place.

At the same time, many organizations found that while auctions generated good procurement prices, the quality of the goods and services offered by the company that submitted the low bid could be unsatisfactory. And in some organizations, internal conflicts arose around auctions. Specifically, the division seeking to acquire specific goods or services might prefer a certain provider, while the procurement group had incentives to go with another provider to lower costs. In addition, some high-quality suppliers made it a policy to not participate in auctions because they didn't want to be commodified.

Procurement professionals tend to be divided between those who love versus hate e-auctions, I've found. As with so many other negotiation issues, whether e-auctions are helpful or harmful depends on context. A number of scholars, including Patrick Bajari and his colleagues, and Guhan Subramanian and Richard Zeckhauser, have outlined factors that define this contextual insight.[4] Here are some of the contextual features that a mechanism setter, such as a procurement officer, might consider:

1) How many serious bidders do you expect if you conduct an auction? The more bidders, the better the price you are likely to get from an auction.

2) Do you have a strong preference for a particular supplier? Obviously, a negotiation format will be more effective if you would prefer to hire a specific supplier.

3) Do you care about factors beyond price? Auctions are easiest to implement when all you care about is getting the best price. But if you also value product quality, delivery timing, establishing a long-term relationship with the supplier, or other issues, then auctions become more difficult (but not impossible) to implement. In addition, auctions are not the best mechanism for value creation.

4) What is your tolerance for risk? Once you set up an auction, the transaction becomes more difficult to control. Can you accept uncertainty about who will submit a bid and the competitiveness of these bids?

Above all, keep in mind that auctions are a choice rather than a foregone conclusion and that they are not uniformly good or bad. Rather, the effectiveness of auctions is determined by the predictable contextual factors discussed above. Subramanian also highlights that whether to negotiate or hold an auction is not a dichotomous choice. He coined the term "negotiauction" to describe a process that brings multiple bidders into the process yet maintains much of the control and advantages of a negotiation.[5] A negotiauction, from a seller's perspective, would typically include identifying multiple bidders; having one-on-one meetings with each bidder (which would include letting them know about their competition); and running multiple rounds of bidding using an auction format. Or the process could begin with an auction and continue with one-on-one negotiations with the top few bidders. As Subramanian notes, negotiauctions allow the mechanism setter to create the competition found in auctions while allowing opportunities for value creation in one-on-one discussions and prioritization of bidders. Notice that the story of my friend's condo sale was a negotiauction— she negotiated with one bidder and then opened up an auction with more. Negotiauctions can take a wide variety of forms, but they all strive to combine the competitive benefits of auctions with the ability to negotiate directly with one or more potential buyers.

Bidding in Auctions

So far, our discussion of auctions has largely taken the perspective of the party that is thinking about hosting an auction. Bidding in auctions also requires some unique insights. One of the most significant outcomes for a bidder in an auction is the *winner's curse*. In chapter 8, in the "Acquiring a Company" problem, I discussed the winner's curse in terms of what happens when a negotiator fails to think through the implications of the other side accepting their offer. Here, I discuss the winner's curse in the context of not thinking about what you can infer from being the most competitive bidder in an auction.

Imagine that your company aggressively outcompetes many other organizations in an auction and successfully acquires a target company. You and others at your company might assume this is good news. Now consider that you probably valued the target more than your competitors did and that there is lots of noise, or variation in value estimates, in this context. And as research by Daniel Kahneman and his colleagues, overviewed in the prior chapter, suggests, that noise is louder than most people expect.[6]

My research with Bill Samuelson also shows that when many bidders compete in an auction over a highly uncertain commodity, the winning bidder typically pays more than the commodity is worth. This partially

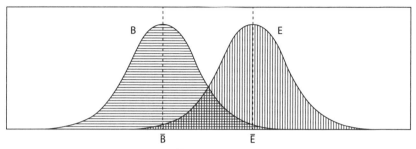

B = Bids   E = Estimates   B̄ = Average bid   Ē = Average estimate

FIGURE 10.1. The Winner's Curse in Auctions.

explains why it is so common for the acquiring firm in a merger to see their stock price fall upon the announcement of the acquisition.[7] The market for corporate takeovers provides evidence that acquiring companies often compete destructively against each other and pay too much for what they get. Many acquisitions prove to be failures, and any financial synergy created usually goes to the target, not the acquirer.

Figure 10.1 shows why the winner is so often cursed. Curve E is the distribution of bidders' estimates of the true value of a commodity, while curve B is the distribution of bids; each bidder is bidding less than they believe the commodity is worth to try to make a profit. Notice, this figure assumes that bidders are accurate, on average. But as Kahneman and colleagues' research suggests, considerable noise surrounds the most accurate estimate. Thus, the winning bidder is likely to have had one of the highest estimates and to have bid more than the actual value of the commodity. So, unless the bidder had reason to believe they had better information than the other bidders, the winner is likely to be cursed. The winner fails to draw a key inference: if they win the auction, they likely have estimated the value of the target as much higher than most or all the other bidders did. Thus, bidders for a noisy commodity should adjust their estimates of its true value downward and lower their bids accordingly.

The winner's curse is something for bidders to consider. But, bidders in an auction can also change the context that they are in. For example, consider an example my colleagues and I teach, "The Franklins." The case is based on a true story from a colleague who was a prospective buyer of a house on Martha's Vineyard. The Franklins, as we call them, primarily wanted to lure their children—and, more importantly, their grandchildren—to visit more often. The Franklins made an offer slightly above the asking price for a beautiful house. The response was that the seller had received another, slightly higher offer from another bidder also seeking a grandchild magnet. According to the seller's agent, it was the Franklins' turn to make the next bid in the auction. The Franklins could see where this was headed: two pairs of grandparents competing to see who loved their grandchildren the most. Instead of countering with a number, the Franklins announced they would not make another bid in the current game, but they offered a different game: they proposed that the seller ask both parties to submit their final offers by the next day at 10 a.m. The Franklins pointed out that if the seller did not accept their proposed game, they would only have the current offer on the table; if they accepted the Franklins' process, they could be assured of more. The seller agreed to the process. The Franklins slightly outbid the other bidder, and they now regularly lure their grandchildren to visit. I am not sure that the Franklins obtained a great price, but I am impressed by their ability to change the game and avoid being pulled into a disadvantageous bidding war.

Negotiating the Contract of the Book That You Are Reading

One final example of changing the game comes from the negotiation over the publication of this book with Princeton University Press. I had published my previous book with Princeton; without an agent, I had run a modified auction process with five publishers who were interested in that book, *Complicit*. After eliminating the two low bidders and getting second-round bids from the three bidders left in the auction, I thought this range gave me a pretty good idea of the advance I would get if I simply continued the auction. I also cared about other issues beyond the advance and was far more impressed with Princeton's publishing team than with the other publishers who were interested. So, after the second round of bidding, I told Princeton that I would accept an offer with a variety of terms, including an advance about 20 percent higher than their prior bid (and would agree to not take their response back to any other publisher). Princeton accepted, and we had a deal. I had changed the game from an auction to a negotiauction.

With *Complicit* in production, I started writing the book you're reading now. After I had drafted chapters 1–3 and a book proposal, I thought about whether to use an agent to sell the book and how to best create an auction. Then I took a look at my contract for *Complicit* and noticed, for the first time, clause 10:

> OPTION ON NEXT BOOK In consideration of the Press under-taking to publish the Work that is the subject of this Agreement, you hereby grant to the Press the first option to publish your next work, whether of similar nature or otherwise. You shall promptly submit the proposal or manuscript thereof, upon first availability, to the Press and shall not submit or offer the proposal or manuscript to third parties until the Press has notified you of its decision. If the Press fails to notify you within thirty (30) days of the date of its re-ceipt of your submission that it wishes to exercise its option to pub-lish, the Press shall be deemed to have refused the submission and you shall be free to submit the proposal or manuscript to third par-ties. If the Press notifies you within such period that it does wish to publish, the parties shall negotiate in good faith the terms of publica-tion. If the Press and you fail to reach agreement within a further thirty (30) days, you may submit the manuscript to third parties.

I thought I might have made a mistake in not negotiating to try to eliminate this provision from the contract, but it was too late to do any-thing about it. So, I contacted Princeton University Press and let them know about *Negotiation: The Game Has Changed*. I sent them the draft chapters and proposal, and started the sixty-day process specified in clause 10. Both sides understood that I could pass on Princeton's offers and then hire an agent to run an auction or run one on my own. Instead, we both negotiated in good faith, traded across issues, and reached an agreement that I perceive to have been satisfactory to both sides. With its clause, Princeton effectively turned my auction plans into a bilateral negotiation.

I changed the game on the *Complicit* contract, and Princeton changed the game on *Negotiation: The Game Has Changed* by adding clause 10 to the *Complicit* contract. Together, the stories highlight that we often have opportunities to define the rules of the game—yet often miss out on them.

The Final-Offer Arbitration Challenge

Insurance companies pay billions of dollars every year to settle claims, employing thousands of people to evaluate and negotiate hundreds of thousands of cases. Claims adjusters' decisions are not always optimal for their companies, resulting in overpayment on some claims and needlessly costly legal expenses on others. After the CEO of a large insurance company read Daniel Kahneman's book *Thinking, Fast and Slow*, the company hired a consulting firm with which Kahneman was affiliated to explore ways to improve the claims decisions made within the company. As the project shifted toward negotiation, Kahneman recruited me to lead their efforts in this area. The core of our project focused on helping the insurance company efficiently resolve claims and reach reasonable settlements, reduce costs, and improve its reputation for fairness. We helped devise a negotiation training program for thousands of claims adjusters in over 100 countries. These efforts significantly reduced the $3 billion a year the company was spending on external legal fees (in addition to internal legal costs), and we hope and expect it led to more satisfied claimants.

Employees liked the training course, and we trained the company's executives to deliver the course at its satellite offices around the world. Much of our training was built around ideas you have read about in this book. Kahneman and I generally argued for acting rationally and reasonably, but executives responsible for the largest claims repeatedly highlighted the challenges associated with unreasonable demands from claimants and their lawyers over very large claims. Many of these executives responded to unreasonable demands with equally unreasonable offers, as they admitted, and the legal fees grew as the dispute continued.

How else might a negotiator who wants to be fair deal with an unreasonable opponent? Our answer came from my early research on how different forms of arbitration in labor relations affect negotiator behavior.[8] The most common form of arbitration resembles an efficient judicial decision, where two parties make their cases to a neutral third party, who reaches a binding decision about what constitutes a fair resolution. In the 1960s, labor relations scholar Carl Stevens argued for settling disputes through final-offer arbitration—also known as "baseball arbitration" because of its use in Major League Baseball (MLB) salary disputes. The unusual feature of final-offer arbitration is that the arbitrator receives final offers from both parties and must pick one or the other, and not a compromise between the two. You might wonder why you would want to limit the arbitrator to selecting between two potentially unreasonable final offers. The benefit of final-offer arbitration is not that it improves the arbitrator's decision but that it changes the negotiators' behavior. In conventional arbitration, negotiators' offers often remain far apart because they expect the arbitrator will simply split the difference between them. If that is an accurate prediction of arbitrator decision making, then the more unreasonable one's offer is, the better one fares. Not allowing the arbitrator to split the difference between two offers neutralizes any incentive the disputants may have to be unreasonable, since the arbitrator is unlikely to choose the less reasonable offer.

In contrast, final-offer arbitration rewards parties for being more reasonable. Thus, each party competes to submit a more reasonable offer than the other side. The riskiness of the process drives the parties toward agreement, which dramatically raises settlement rates. Results from MLB arbitration support this logic. Teams and players often file to go through the formal final-offer arbitration process, then as the arbitration hearing approaches, the parties make reasonable concessions and usually settle before the arbitration hearing occurs. In 2022, for example, the New York Yankees and their superstar Aaron Judge filed for arbitration. As part of the arbitration process, Judge submitted a final offer of

$21 million for the 2022 season, while the Yankees submitted a final offer of $17 million. But, before an arbitration decision was made, the parties agreed to a $19 million contract that would allow Judge to earn two $250,000 bonuses, one for winning the American League Most Valuable Player award and the other for receiving the World Series Most Valuable Player Award.[9] He was the American League Most Valuable Player in 2022, but the Yankees did not make it to the World Series.

When arbitration does occur, the team's and the player's final offers are often not that far apart. The Atlanta Braves and their star pitcher Max Fried allowed an arbitrator to settle their dispute before the 2022 season. By the time the parties submitted their final offers, they were remarkably close; Fried asked for $6.85 million, while the Braves offered $6.6 million. Fried won the arbitration and received $6.85 million for his 2022 salary.[10]

Our understanding of final-offer arbitration led to the idea that Kahneman and I brought to the insurance company and described in a *Harvard Business Review* article about what we termed the *final-offer arbitration challenge*.[11] Here's how it works. If you believe you are acting reasonably and that the other side's behavior is far from reasonable, suggest a quick, efficient final-offer arbitration procedure in which both parties present their final offer to a professional arbitrator, who would have the authority to make a legally binding decision about which is more reasonable. If the other side truly believes in the merit of their offer, they will quickly accept, as this gives them the opportunity to benefit from the reasonableness of their position. If, by contrast, they have been anchoring on an unreasonable starting point, they will decline your challenge and are likely to make a more reasonable offer. If they refuse your challenge and still refuse to budge from their unreasonable position, you have good reason to believe that continuing to negotiate with them is unlikely to yield anything useful in the short term. In the insurance context, this may mean doing little to try to resolve the claim before a court hearing is upon you.

Soon after we introduced this process to the insurance company, one senior executive was facing a difficult negotiation with a man who had been injured while working in a factory. The insurance company was very willing to pay a fair amount to the injured party, but his lawyer was making an unreasonable demand—at least from the insurance company's perspective. The insurance company assessed the value of the claim to be between $1 million and $1.1 million, and made an offer of $850,000, leaving some room to move its offer up. The claimant's lawyer demanded $2.6 million—an amount he insisted was fair. The insurance company, confident that its position was far more reasonable, responded with our final-offer arbitration challenge, suggesting each side submit a final offer to a professional arbitrator, who would make a legally binding choice between the two. Recognizing the insurance company was confident in its position, the claimant's attorney dramatically reduced their demand, from $2.6 million to $1.25 million. This brought the negotiation into a reasonable range, and the case was settled for $1.05 million.[12] The challenge exposed the unreasonableness of the other side's position. It did not deliver the insurance company a low settlement, but it efficiently drove a fair settlement and lowered the legal costs of the case dramatically. Notably, the parties did not need to involve an arbitrator in this case to reach a reasonable settlement.

The final-offer arbitration challenge changes the game by signaling an honest belief in the fairness of your offer and potentially nudging an adversary out of their unreasonable position. This strategy comes with a few complications that should be noted. First, many opponents will be surprised by the idea, as they probably have never received such a proposal before. In addition, before making the challenge, you will need to be sure you aren't the more unreasonable party, since you would then likely lose the arbitration if one occurred. Margaret Neale and I had students engage in a labor-management simulation in which we told them that if they didn't reach agreement, each side would have to submit a final offer to an arbitrator, who would select one of the two offers.[13] Some participants still did not reach a negotiated agreement. When they submitted their final offers, we asked them to estimate the probability that the arbitrator would choose their offer over the other side's offer. The students systematically overestimated the probability that the arbitrator would accept their final offer: While the combined chance of the two parties in final-offer arbitration is 100 percent, the average negotiator believed their offer had a 68 percent, or 136 percent for the pair, chance of being accepted. Clearly, your overconfidence can be a hazard to proposing the final-offer arbitration challenge.

In negotiation, there are many ways in which the game can be changed. Examples of changing the game include thinking about whether you will negotiate dyadically, use an auction, or do something in between; whether you will be negotiating one-on-one or with teams of negotiators; whether you will be negotiating face-to-face, via Zoom, or by email; and whether an agreement has to go through legal review before a deal is closed. These are all decisions that may be more important than a 5 percent change in your offer. There is value in recognizing the potential to change the game, rather than simply playing the game as defined.

■ ■ ■

"We are about to put our house on the market. Our agent recommends that we list it on a Thursday, hold an open house on Sunday, and then not consider offers for three days, until Wednesday at noon. She argues this will increase the likelihood of having multiple offers to consider at the same time. She even recommends that we leave town so she can claim we aren't available to consider offers that might come in earlier. My spouse doesn't like the idea of waiting until Wednesday to consider offers, for fear we will lose a buyer who is unwilling to wait to get involved in what feels like an auction. Who is right, my spouse or our agent?"

"There is good logic to the process your agent outlined. As we saw with the opening story in this chapter and with the Franklins, interacting with two or more buyers at the same time can create some obvious advantages. But I also think your spouse raises a valid concern: some potential buyers might pass on joining a process that they feel is setting up a bidding war, particularly if they've already 'lost' a couple of such wars. In addition, some buyers may not want to be put on hold until Wednesday, which could keep them from making offers on another house. I think you should consider how hot the market is. The hotter the market, the more attractive the auction format. You also don't have to accept the agent's process as specified. An alternative could be to not show the house before Saturday or Sunday, have the open house on Sunday, and make it clear to prospective buyers that you will not be available until Monday at 6 p.m. to consider offers. This allows you to give all potential buyers the opportunity to make an offer without putting the process on hold for a lengthy time. You could then see what offers emerge before responding and defining the next steps in the game."

Chapter 11

Your Decisions
in Negotiation

"I follow the ideas you present in class, and the simulations have
been fun. But, to be honest, I have found some of your arguments
a bit insulting. You imply that we aren't great decision makers. Yet
I have been very successful in my career, which has included many
negotiations. Isn't my success evidence that my decisions in the
real world are better than you have suggested in this class?"

• • •

On February 24, 2022, Russia launched a large-scale invasion of Ukraine,
expecting to quickly conquer and control the country. Russian president
Vladimir Putin failed to anticipate the fierce resistance that ensued from
the Ukrainian government and its people. What followed was what ap-
pears to have been a disaster for Russia, as of 2024, a disaster caused by
Putin's overconfidence. Russia's underestimation of its perceived opponent is not unique. The decision of the U.S. government to invade Iraq in
2003, like Iraq's decision to invade Kuwait in 1990, displayed unwarranted
confidence. Ukraine was far from Russia's first overconfident invasion, as
it had unsuccessfully invaded Afghanistan in 1979. Similarly, despite some
early victories, Hitler's invasions of Poland and then much of Europe
during World War II didn't turn out well for him or for Germany.

Across all these devastating invasions and many others, the aggressors had unwarranted confidence in their military strength and failed to think about the broader context of their attack, including the predictable responses of the other side. Postwar agreements have rarely left aggressors with a better result than they could have achieved without invading. A better outcome was available to the countries involved without horrific loss of life and property. As of this writing, Russia is paying an enormous price for its Ukrainian invasion in troop loss, economic isolation and stagnation, and the destruction of its diplomatic reputation.

The hubris involved in invading another large country may seem unique to authoritarian leaders. But the same type of overconfidence is also evident in many corporate behaviors, including acquisitions, where acquirers typically receive little of the synergy created from deals. Or, as discussed in chapter 10, consider the overconfidence that leads insurance firms and claimants to spend too much on unnecessary legal fees rather than settling more quickly at a fair price. Both the claimants and the insurer would be better off with a less legalistic approach. But overconfidence, sometimes fueled by intermediaries (that is, lawyers), can fool negotiators into believing they will obtain a better result by waiting for the other side to make concessions.

People tend to be overconfident that a neutral party will view disputes they are involved in from a perspective that favors their side, as my research with Margaret Neale shows (see the prior chapter).[1] In his book *Perfectly Confident*, Don Moore highlights that overconfidence affects negotiators in three ways: (1) overestimation, or thinking you're better on some dimension than you actually are; (2) overplacement, or incorrectly thinking you rank higher than others on some dimension; and (3) overprecision, when you are too confident in your beliefs and knowledge (such as how much your product will help a customer).[2] As a result of overconfidence, negotiators invest too little in investigating and understanding the perspective, interests, constraints, and motives of the other side. According to Moore, negotiators can defend themselves from overconfidence by asking, "Why might I be wrong?" "What assumptions am I making that are misguided?" and "How can I better orient and calibrate my judgments?"

Knowledge of how to think more systematically and rationally in negotiation developed in parallel with the research field now called behavioral economics. Behavioral economics helps us understand the systematic mistakes psychologists have identified in typical business contexts, including negotiation. Overconfidence is one of many common and destructive cognitive biases that affects negotiators. In this chapter, we consider the threat our cognitive limitations pose to our negotiation success in various contexts, particularly competitive ones such as auctions and entrepreneurship. We begin with a brief history of behavioral economics, the field where these limitations were discovered, then focus on some of the biases most important in negotiation. Prior chapters detailed how to effectively deliberate in negotiation. We now add insight into what biases we need to watch out for in ourselves and in others. (A full overview of these topics is beyond the scope of this book but can be found in Daniel Kahneman's book *Thinking, Fast and Slow* and *Decision Leadership: Empowering Others to Make Better Choices*, by Don Moore and myself.)[3]

This chapter is about you; we will save your concerns about your counterparts' rationality for the next chapter.

An Overview of Behavioral Economics

Before the 1970s, traditional "neoclassical" models in economics were built on the assumption that humans are fully rational. To the extent that errors exist in our decision making, economic models considered them to be random and expected that people functioning within markets would learn to behave rationally over time or be eliminated from these markets.[4] While departures from rationality were considered in economics as far back as the 1700s, with Adam Smith's observation that human decisions are imperfect, such observations did not significantly influence the field of economics for much of the twentieth century.[5] In the 1950s, Herbert Simon coined the term "bounded rationality" to describe how, in his view, humans strive toward rationality but are limited by their cognitive capacity.[6] While Simon won the 1978 Nobel Prize in Economics, most economists of the time believed his work reflected a misdirection in the wise development of their field.

Paralleling the rationality assumption dominating economics, on the negotiation front, economists developed models based on game theory to describe the behavior of rational actors in competitive contexts. Howard Raiffa's 1982 book, *The Art and Science of Negotiation*, offered a critique of game theory's rationality assumption and a new way of thinking about negotiation.[7] Specifically, Raiffa focused on helping people make rational decisions in a world where rational behavior could not be expected from the other side—that is, he incorporated reasonable assumptions about the behavior of others.

If negotiator rationality wasn't a reasonable assumption, how could we learn to negotiate more rationally, and what could we expect from our counterparts? In 1974, Amos Tversky and Daniel Kahneman provided some early insights in their now-classic article in the journal *Science*, "Judgment under Uncertainty: Heuristics and Biases."[8] This work specified systematic and predictable biases in judgment that lead to departures from rational decision making, such as the anchoring phenomenon we discussed in chapter 2. Psychologists immediately took to this fascinating work. However, economists of the 1970s largely ignored Tversky and Kahneman's research. Others criticized their 1974 article for using student participants and for not incentivizing them. And some critics falsely concluded that the mistakes the pair identified would not be found in important real-world contexts.

It wasn't until Kahneman and Tversky published their article "Prospect Theory" in *Econometrica*, a leading economics journal, that the field of economics took notice.[9] Using the mathematical form comfortable to economists, the authors offered an alternative model to how humans make risky decisions. Prospect theory argues that humans treat losses very differently than they treat gains. For example, most of us would make the risk-averse decision to take $1,000 over a 50 percent chance of getting $2,000. But if forced to choose between the unattractive options of definitely losing $1,000 or taking a 50 percent chance of losing $2,000, most of us opt for the riskier option to try to avoid any loss at all. As in this problem, the same dilemma could be "framed" as a gain or a loss simply by changing the reference point.[10] When a problem is framed as a gain, we tend to be risk averse. When the same problem is contextualized as a loss, we tend to be risk seeking. Obviously, these preferences are inconsistent and can lead us to make choices that are incompatible with our true preferences—including in negotiation.

As an example, consider a union that demands a wage increase for employees from $20/hour to $25/hour. The union insists anything less than $25/hour represents an unacceptable loss, given recent changes in the economic environment. The company, meanwhile, insists any raise above $20/hour would impose unacceptable losses on the firm. Would the two parties settle for $22.50/hour (a certain settlement) rather than a strike, lockout, or binding arbitration (risky options)? If each party views the conflict in terms of what it stands to lose, prospect theory predicts they will each be risk seeking and therefore less willing to accept the certain settlement than if they viewed the settlement in terms of what they had gain. If the union sees any raise above $20/hour as a gain, and management views any wage under $25/hour as savings, they are more likely to be risk averse, and a negotiated settlement will be more likely. Negotiators with positive frames are significantly more likely to make concessions and to reach mutually beneficial outcomes than their negatively framed counterparts, my research with Margaret Neale shows.[11] Generally, you want the other side to look at a negotiation with a positive frame, and you should consider the negotiation from both frames.

By the end of the twentieth century, Kahneman and Tversky's influence had become prominent in many academic fields. Tversky passed away at age fifty-nine in 1996. Their work captured a broad audience in the new millennium. Kahneman won the Nobel Prize in 2002, his best-selling book *Thinking, Fast and Slow* was published in 2011, and Michael Lewis documented Kahneman and Tversky's fruitful partnership in his 2016 book *The Undoing Project*. All these milestones contributed to making behavioral economics visible to the world outside academia.[12]

Both Kahneman's Nobel Prize talk and *Thinking, Fast and Slow* highlighted a distinction, first made by psychologists Keith Stanovich and Richard West, between System 1 and System 2 thinking.[13] System 1 refers to our common fast, automatic, effortless, implicit, and emotional decision-making processes, which we use to make most of our decisions. System 2 refers to our more reasoned decision-making processes, which are slower, conscious, effortful, explicit, and logical.

We need our System 1 processes, as deliberating on each of the hundreds of decisions we make each day would simply take too much time. In addition, many people like the message from writers (such as Malcolm Gladwell in his book *Blink*) that they can trust their intuition.[14] As a result, we continue to trust in our System 1 processes despite overwhelming evidence that our deliberative thoughts outperform our intuition in important decision contexts, as deliberation is less biased and more ethical.[15] So, part of the solution for avoiding bias and making better decisions in your most important negotiations is to deliberate. And, deliberation tends to lead to more ethical decisions as well. But the busier and more distracted we are, and the more time constraints we face, the more we fall back on System 1 thinking to make decisions.[16] Because biased inputs can enter our deliberative processes, we need to be on the alert. Next, we explore some of the most important biases to look out for in negotiation.

The Mythical Fixed Pie

At parties, I often meet nice people who ask what I do for a living. When they hear that I teach negotiation, they frequently ask, "What are the most important things I need to know about negotiation?" Like other experts, I think that what I teach and write about is complex and requires a full course or about 75,000 words to explain in appropriate detail. But I have given their question some thought and developed a response— actually, two of them, one of which I will save for chapter 12. My first response is to encourage them to understand that the pie of resources isn't fixed in negotiation. If there is more than one issue at stake, and the parties do not weight the issues equally, trades are available that allow the parties to enlarge the pie, as I discussed in chapter 4.

If this advice seems obvious to you, you might find it hard to believe it is the best I can offer. Yet it is critically important, as ample evidence shows that most people approach negotiations with the assumption that the pie of value is fixed, or what Margaret Neale and I first described as a belief in a "mythical fixed pie."[17] When my colleagues and I teach executives, who are typically well into a successful career, we have them engage in negotiation simulations that involve multiple issues. The simulations are scorable, such that each side can see the estimated profit they created in any agreement they might have reached. By making wise trades, both sides can end up with more profit than they would have earned by simply compromising on each issue. As these simulations demonstrate, the size of the pie is not fixed! By following my guidance, found in chapter 4, my executive students (and you) can find trade-offs across issues in simulations and, I hope, in real life.

In the first simulation of this type that the executives face in our class, not only do they not find all the available trade-offs and end up with a suboptimal pie, but some are truly shocked to see the opportunities they and their counterpart squandered in their negotiation. Many openly admit that despite decades of experience in negotiations, which led them to believe they were pretty good negotiators, they never thought of trying to enlarge the pie. They spent years claiming pies that were too small due to the mythical fixed-pie assumption. Not only did they lack the tools we discussed in chapter 4 for creating a larger pie, but they never even knew they were supposed to try to enlarge the pie.

Eliminating the mythical fixed-pie mindset improves relationships. Leaders can emphasize the importance of creating greater value with work colleagues and the value of building strong relationships with external parties. In addition, leaders can hold negotiators accountable not only for their results but also for how they negotiate. This type of accountability leads people to think more about the other side and to broaden beyond a strictly competitive mindset, Carsten de Dreu and colleagues have found in their research.[18]

Busting the mythical fixed-pie mindset can also improve society. Psychologist Samuel Johnson and colleagues, who describe the mindset using the term "win-win denial," have found in their research that many people think all negotiations must have a winner and a loser.[19] Anecdotally, Ken Auletta's book *Hollywood Ending: Harvey Weinstein and the*

Culture of Silence, documents how Weinstein's sex crimes against power-less women lined up with his broader bullying behavior and his view that all interactions had a winner and loser.[20] And policy expert Heather McGhee argues in *The Sum of Us: What Racism Costs Everyone and How We Can Prosper Together* that most racial discrimination and racist gov-ernment policies spring from the false belief in a zero-sum paradigm, in which progress for some must come at the expense of others.[21] She argues that we routinely forego a "solidarity dividend"—gains we could achieve from working productively across racial boundaries to accom-plish what we can't do on our own. When we add collaborative moves to our negotiating repertoire, we are more likely to achieve gains for ourselves and for society.

Ignoring the Competition

I used to love eating dairy-based ice cream, but, having become a vegan, I don't eat dairy products any longer. Fortunately, a bunch of people are working to meet my desire for the taste of ice cream without consuming dairy, typically by creating products made from almonds, cashews, soy, and/or coconut. Eclipse, Wicked, Sunscoop, Revolution, NadaMoo! Booja, Happy Cow Limited, Over the Moo, Doozy Pots, SorBabes, JD's Vegan Dairy-Free Frozen Dessert, Daily Harvest, O'MY! Dairy Free Gelato, Double Rainbow Ice Cream, Alden's Organic, Van Leeuwen, Coolhaus, Enlightened, Perry's Ice Cream, Arctic Zero, Glace, and Cos-mic Bliss are just some of the new products in this category. I apologize if I didn't list your favorite non-dairy ice cream, but my failure to do so underscores my point: there are lots of new entrants in this market.

The global non-dairy ice cream market was about a half billion dol-lars in 2019 and is predicted to reach one billion dollars by about 2030.[22] I am happy to see so many non-dairy vegan products available, and I root for these companies' success. As a small investor in new plant-based products, I have spoken to a number of them. They typically have a fine product, are trying to mimic full-dairy products as effectively as possible, and have a mission consistent with the plant-based movement (creating healthier foods, protecting the environment, feeding the world's population, reducing animal suffering, and so on). Often, these companies have run taste tests against leading dairy ice creams, with some positive results.

Yet I worry about these companies. Their start-up costs are high. Manufacturing and distributing frozen products is complicated. Most importantly, they face enormous competition in their attempts to get into the stores of leading retailers. When I speak to these socially minded entrepreneurs, I typically find they have great enthusiasm for their product but have given very little thought to the competitive context surrounding them. The market for non-dairy ice cream may be growing fast, but perhaps not as fast as the number of new entrants. Not to mention, some prominent dairy ice cream producers that have branched into the non-dairy market (including Talenti, Ben and Jerry's, and Häagen-Dazs) have large advantages, including established distribution systems, relationships with retailers, a staff of food scientists, and experience in a very competitive landscape. Some of these new entrants will make it, but too many will fail. In a good number of cases, a more thorough assessment of the competitive landscape might have saved them a great deal of effort. As founders and investors are negotiating the creation of start-ups, they face the key challenge of thinking carefully about the competition.

In a parallel story, Don Moore and I document the quick rise and fall of bike-sharing companies in Cambridge, Massachusetts, in our book *Decision Leadership*. After the city announced its bike-friendly plans in 2019, Ofo, Ant, Spin, Zagster, Lime, and Bluebikes entered the bike-sharing market. By the end of 2019, the first four companies were gone, and in early 2020, Lime quit the bike-share business as well. These bike companies saw a need, like our ice cream makers, but failed to think about the limited market for bike sharing. Entrepreneurs need to realize that what they see as an opportunity may also seem like a good idea to many others and that every new market is limited. The competition we face matters.

Like non-dairy ice cream producers and bike-share entrepreneurs, we are too often insensitive to the quality of our competition, a phenomenon called *reference group neglect*.[23] Entrepreneurs focus more on themselves, their strengths, and their weaknesses than on the competition, Moore's research demonstrates.[24] He and Daylian Cain showed in a study that focusing on yourself, and not the competition, leads entrepreneurs to be too quick to enter markets, particularly those where entry is relatively easy.[25] The rate of entry into industries like restaurants, bars, hobby shops, liquor stores, and retail clothing is persistently excessive, Moore argues. Confident about their product or service, entrepreneurs and investors ignore many pertinent external factors, particularly the strength of the competition.

Escalation of Commitment

As of 2021, the ten largest airline carriers in North America, based on number of passengers per year, were as follows (in millions):[26]

1. American Airlines	165.68
2. United Airlines	104.08
3. Delta Air Lines	102.90
4. Southwest Airlines	99.11
5. SkyWest	36.61
6. Alaska Airlines	32.41
7. Spirit Airlines	30.77
8. JetBlue	30.09
9. Volaris	24.41
10. Frontier Airlines	20.65

Southwest was the largest of the so-called low-cost airlines—those that offer lower fares, with accompanying lesser service. Other low-cost airlines include the last four on this list (all U.S.-based, except for Mexico-based Volaris), with Spirit often being mocked by comedians for its low-quality service and low customer-satisfaction ratings.[27] I booked one flight on Spirit, but it was canceled with very little notice and without any assistance in finding a new way to travel to a relative's funeral—that was the end of my personal experience with Spirit. Frontier also receives more than an average amount of criticism for an airline.

According to a 2021 survey of 6,285 randomly selected customers by the American Customer Satisfaction Index, JetBlue had the highest level of customer satisfaction of any U.S.-based airline.[28] At the start of 2022, *Forbes* magazine and other reviewers had a similarly positive view of JetBlue.[29] Yet, by the end of the third quarter of 2022, JetBlue's reputation had collapsed, approaching the low customer-satisfaction levels of Frontier and Spirit.[30] More striking, while the U.S. stock market fell by about 25 percent in the first nine months of 2022, JetBlue's stock price fell by more than half (54.6 percent, to be precise). While many factors affected JetBlue's decline, an important one was its dysfunctional competition with Frontier in the two companies' attempts to acquire Spirit. JetBlue escalated its commitment to a course of action that was not in the best interest of its investors.

Spirit began 2022 with a stock price of $22.48, which fell by about 10 percent during the month of January. On February 7, 2022, Frontier and Spirit announced that Spirit had agreed to be acquired by Frontier for $25.83/share, a price that included a combination of cash and Frontier stock (the price was based on the stock price of Frontier on the day of the announcement). Such mergers take time to come to fruition. As the process unfolded, the stock market declined, and Frontier stock declined even faster, such that the value of Frontier's offer to Spirit fell as low as $20/share. However, all interested parties, including JetBlue, understood that the Frontier-Spirit merger would move Frontier into the number five spot, in terms of customer traffic, and make the combined company Southwest's main competitor in the low-cost market.

JetBlue clearly viewed the Frontier-Spirit combination as a threat to its competitive position. Rather than accept this competitive disadvantage, in terms of customer traffic, and focus on running a high-quality airline, JetBlue decided to focus on competing at the low end of the market and entered the auction for Spirit. JetBlue knew it was at a disadvantage in the bidding, since a JetBlue-Spirit combination would trigger more antitrust scrutiny, due to overlapping routes, than a Frontier-Spirit combination. Nonetheless, in April 2022, JetBlue offered Spirit shareholders $33/share. Spirit rejected JetBlue's offer, questioning whether regulators would approve such a merger. "Given this substantial completion risk, we believe JetBlue's economic offer is illusory," Spirit stated.[31]

In May, JetBlue escalated the competition by directly encouraging Spirit's shareholders to reject the Frontier deal and offering a hostile all-cash offer of $30 per share, which JetBlue referred to as a "60% premium to the value of the Frontier transaction."[32] JetBlue clarified it was willing to pay as much as its earlier offer of $33/share if the merger was conducted cooperatively with Spirit's management.

By June, Frontier responded by highlighting the lower regulatory risk it posed, as compared to JetBlue, by offering Spirit $250 million in break-up fees in the event the deal did not close because it was rejected by the government. JetBlue further escalated the battle by raising its offer to $31.50 per share in cash plus a $350 million break-up fee if the deal didn't close. As the battle for the low-cost, low-service market continued, and service across the airline industry deteriorated, Senators Elizabeth Warren and Alex Padilla urged Transportation Secretary Pete Buttigieg to "aggressively" use his authority to hold airlines accountable for surging prices, delays, and cancellations.[33] Spirit's management continued to issue public statements favoring the lower-risk deal with Frontier but finally relented and agreed to merge with JetBlue after JetBlue increased its offer to $33.50/share in late July.

Throughout this competition, JetBlue continued to increase its bids for Spirit even as the stock market fell significantly and Spirit's value deteriorated. JetBlue won the auction in the short term, but its stock lost over half of its value during the acquisition process due to the market firmly rejecting its strategy of overpaying to become a larger, lower-quality, airline. Then came a worse blow. On January 16, 2024, Judge William G. Young agreed with the U.S. Department of Justice that the JetBlue-Spirit combination would be anti-competitive and blocked the merger from happening. Spirit stock fell by over 50 percent that day. The same day, JetBlue stock went up, as investors were relieved the judge had kept JetBlue from consummating a terrible deal. Over the prior two years, JetBlue had lost its focus and suffered in the long term from its misdirected pursuit of Spirit.

JetBlue is one of many companies that developed a strategy based on a critical challenge (in this case, Frontier's offer for Spirit) and escalated its commitment to that strategy beyond any rationally justifiable level.

JetBlue's attempted acquisition of Spirit also confirms evidence from the literature on mergers and acquisitions that acquirers do not get the synergy created from their deal. Instead, the financial synergy tends to go to the firm being acquired. Acquirers fail to make a profit in large part because of their tendency to escalate their commitment to beating the competition—in this case, Frontier. They win the auction, but may not want the prize. Many of these unprofitable acquisitions are the result of failing to fully consider the competitive context that the acquirer is facing (and the failure to consider the winner's curse discussed earlier).

Many years ago, Martin Shubik introduced the dollar auction, in which he auctioned off a dollar bill to the highest bidder in an undergraduate classroom. The rules were that the highest bidder would receive the dollar for their bid, and the second-highest bidder would have to pay the amount they bid and get nothing in return.[34] Typically, students would bid up the price enthusiastically until the bidding approached $1. Then the amount of people bidding would drop to two individuals. Eventually, the 95-cent bidder was faced with a dilemma when the other bidder offered $1. Often, the two bidders escalated their commitment to the auction and ended up bidding far in excess of $1 to avoid coming in second.

I am known for improving the precision of Shubik's rules governing the auction and, given my access to executive classes, adjusting the prize from $1 to $100 for inflation and to sharpen the impact. I have earned lots of money running the $100 auction, with some of my auctions going as high as $1,000.[35] Deliberative thought could prompt my students, as it should have prompted JetBlue, to choose to not bid and avoid this escalatory trap.

Successful negotiators learn to identify and avoid such competitive traps. A strategy for identifying such traps is to try to consider the decision to make an offer from the perspective of one's competitors. In the Spirit story, this strategy would have highlighted Frontier's additional moves and the reluctance of Spirit management to entertain JetBlue's offers, which ended up pressuring JetBlue to pay an even more dysfunctional price. JetBlue clearly wanted to beat Frontier, regardless of cost. But someone at JetBlue should have considered that as the parties escalated commitment, the bidders would lose, and only the target would benefit.

Lots of conflicts escalate. Many of us know friends who had a small conflict in their condo association that got out of control, with parties incurring legal expenses that far exceeded the value of the dispute. Too many divorcing couples fight a costly legal battle rather than pursuing lower-cost mechanisms, such as mediation, to separate and divide their assets. The key to avoiding escalation is to deliberate rather than following your intuition, which includes thinking about the likely outcomes you will face on more and less escalatory paths.

Self-serving Views of What Is Fair

One of my favorite negotiation simulations, Viking Investments, written by Dartmouth professor Len Greenhalgh, vividly sets up a conflict between a condo developer and a fine wood contractor. While the developer was traveling and unavailable, the wood contractor had to decide whether to upgrade the wood used. There was a limited supply of the better wood, and the wood contractor was concerned, on behalf of the developer, that a competitor of the developer would buy the wood if the wood contractor did not. The wood contractor and the developer's assistant had a miscommunication about the nature of the change, and the wood contractor upgraded the wood. Unbeknownst to the wood contractor, the developer sold off the project during their travels and would not benefit from higher-quality wood. In the simulation, each party has information the other does not. The contractor was expecting a $700,000 invoice from the wood contractor and is shocked to receive an invoice for $950,000. The simulation involves the students trying to resolve this dispute.

The simulation is very well written, and MBA students and executive students often get genuinely angry at each other while enacting it. As discussed in chapter 7, conflict resolution tends to be a more emotional process than negotiating a new deal, and people are generally more emotional when negotiating who will eat losses than when negotiating who will get gains. After the students negotiate and return to class for a debrief, I overview all the information on both sides. I then ask all the students to write down what they currently view as a fair resolution of the conflict. The degree to which simulating the conflict affects their assessment of what is fair is shocking: over 80 percent of those playing the role of the wood contractor think a fair resolution would be a payment from the developer of over $800,000, while over 80 percent of the developers think the fair price would be under $800,000. They weren't the ones actually in conflict, but being in the simulated role for an hour, arguing their side, fundamentally alters—in a self-serving direction—their assessment of what would be fair.

Linda Babcock, George Loewenstein, Samuel Issacharoff, and Colin Camerer have systematically documented that negotiators interpret data in a self-serving manner. Individuals tend to first determine their preference for a certain outcome based on self-interest and then justify this preference based on a fairness rule that favors them.[36] Self-serving logic allows people to believe it is honestly fair for them to get more of a given resource than an independent advisor would allocate. The problem lies not in a desire to be unfair but in our failure to interpret information in an unbiased manner.[37]

In one experimental study, Babcock and colleagues provided participants with materials describing a lawsuit over a collision between an automobile and a motorcycle. Both sides received the exact same materials (depositions, medical and police reports, etc.). The parties agreed that the automobile hit the motorcycle but were at odds over how much the driver of the car should pay the motorcycle driver to settle the case. The participants acted as lawyers for the plaintiff (motorcyclist) or defendant (auto driver) and attempted to negotiate a settlement. They were told that if they were unable to reach agreement, they would each pay substantial penalties, and the payment would be determined by an impartial judge who had already made his decision based on the same case materials. After learning which role that they would play, but before negotiating, all participants were asked to predict the judge's ruling. Those in the role of plaintiff's lawyer predicted the judge would award substantially more than those in the role of the defendant's lawyer did. The larger the difference in these assessments within a specific pair of negotiators (plaintiff and defendant), the lower the likelihood they reached agreement. Wise negotiators think through the negotiation from the perspective of the other side.[38]

Decisions Matter!

I hope this chapter has conveyed the importance and fallibility of your decisions in negotiations and the need to fully consider the competitive context that you face. I have attempted to cover some of the most important biases that could derail your negotiations; you can refer to the sources mentioned earlier for a more complete understanding of your decision making. In the next chapter, we look at the decisions of those across the table from you.

. . .

> "I follow the ideas you present in class, and the simulations have been fun. But, to be honest, I have found some of your arguments a bit insulting. You imply that we aren't great decision makers. Yet I have been very successful in my career, which has included many negotiations. Isn't my success evidence that my decisions in the real world are better than you have suggested in this class?"

> "First, if I was offensive in any way, I apologize. That was not my intent. Rather, my goal was to highlight potential limitations in negotiator decision making that, research documents, affect even the most experienced and talented negotiators. A great deal of evidence suggests that successful people can still improve and find new opportunities in their negotiations by examining their current decision-making processes. And by understanding how you make decisions in your most common negotiation contexts, you are likely to be able to better explain your negotiation strategy to others, teach others, and adapt as the external context changes. Through this process, I believe you can move from being a very good, experienced negotiator to being an expert negotiator with a greater ability to generalize across negotiation contexts."

Chapter 12

Them

"Is it ethical to psychologically manipulate the other side's choices and behavior in negotiation?"

■ ■ ■

In the previous chapter, I provided one of my two answers to the common cocktail party question, "What are the most important things I need to know about negotiation?" As you'll recall, my first answer is that the pie of resources is not fixed in negotiation—that trade-offs are usually available to help you enlarge the pie. Now it's time for my second answer: you should spend far more time than your intuition would suggest thinking about the decisions of the other side. Most of us fail to learn as much as we could by taking the other party's perspective. In this book, I have repeatedly encouraged you to think about your counterpart's BATNA, reservation price, and what's important to them. Yet, it is rare for negotiators to take the perspective of the other side. This chapter is all about "them"—specifically, how you can be a more effective negotiator by thinking about your counterpart. It will also help you see how the specific context of your negotiations is affected by the person on the other side of the table.

Understanding Them

When a negotiation isn't going well, we rarely reflect on what we might be doing wrong. More commonly, we come up with what social psychologists call *external attributions*, or explanations for failures that lie outside of ourselves. One common category of external attributions consists of the actions of the other side. We often reach negative conclusions about them—including that they are insane—based on perceived irrational and frustrating behavior.

I have been in many classrooms and conversations where my empathic friend and coauthor, Deepak Malhotra, responded to such descriptions of the other party with the question, "So, do you think that *they* view their actions as crazy?" Once asked, the answer to this question is obvious: very few of us see our own actions as crazy, at least not in the moment. Deepak goes on to encourage the negotiator to try to understand why the other side would engage in the behavior they perceive as crazy. When we try to understand their "irrational" behavior, we gain insight that can put us on the path of a wise agreement. While the Soviet placement of nuclear weapons in Cuba felt irrational to many people on President Kennedy's team, it was far more useful for them to understand that the Soviets felt threatened by the presence of U.S. missiles in Turkey. These missiles contributed to the Soviets' seemingly irrational behavior. Understanding this was critical to the resolution to the crisis that I described in chapter 5.

In social psychology, a useful distinction is often made between individual determinants (such as intelligence, demographics, and personality traits) and structural determinants (such as the surrounding culture, the economic environment, and the sociopolitical environment) of outcomes. One important research result is that structure has a much greater effect on our outcomes than most of us realize. Social psychology would typically treat the people in a negotiation as individual determinants of our outcomes, and the economy, political system, and other broad factors of our environment as structural determinants of our outcomes. But, consistent with the categories I outlined in chapter 1, negotiators commonly see the people on the other side of the table as part of the context they face. Thus, for our purposes, a negotiator's context includes both structural elements of the negotiation, many of which we have discussed in previous chapters, and the uniqueness of the decision and behaviors of the people on the other side of the table.

In chapter 8, I described research arising from the "Acquiring a Company" problem, in which the target company in the acquisition negotiation knew its value, but the potential acquirer had far more ambiguous information. We used this problem, which I originally wrote with Bill Samuelson, to highlight how the mode of communication dramatically affects the outcomes of a negotiation. In the original version of the problem, where there was no discussion between the acquirer and the target, the acquirer had the opportunity to make a take-it-or-leave-it offer to the target, who would accept or reject the offer, at which point the game would end. As you probably recall, the arithmetic of the game led to all offers having a negative expected value to the acquirer. In this context, I argued, making no offer at all was the only rational response for the acquirer. Yet my research with Bill showed that those playing the role of the acquirer (including experienced financial executives) often chose to make an offer, which led them to lose money, on average. Why? Because they failed to think about the perspective of the other side!

Consider the following stories:

- While you're at a bar, you overhear a guy next to you talking to his friend about his need to sell his car to free up some cash. He mentions the year and model of the car, which happens to be the same type of used car you've been looking to buy. You know the average value of a car of this year and model, which is $14,850, and you happen to have that amount available. You interrupt the conversation and ask the owner if the car is in the parking lot. It is, and he's happy to show it to you. The car appears to be in good but not great condition. Should you offer the owner $1,000 less than what Edmund's suggestion is the value of the car?
- While visiting a bazaar in Turkey, you spot a very attractive rug and talk to the friendly merchant who is selling it. You have purchased a few nice rugs in your lifetime but are far from an

expert. After some pleasant discussion about Istanbul, should you make the merchant an offer that you believe to be on the low side?

- You just accepted a job in a city where you have spent little time, and you are in a hurry to buy a new condo. On a trip to finalize the job offer, you see a sign for an open house outside an attractive condo building. You stop and go inside. The condo looks great, and you like the idea of buying it and wrapping up your house search quickly. Back in your hotel room, you check the value of the condo on Zillow, which estimates the value of properties based on publicly available information. Should you make what you think is a reasonable but slightly low offer?

Imagine in each of these cases that you make the low offer you were considering, and the other side immediately accepts. Are you happy with your purchase? Probably not. Perhaps the seller's quick acceptance tells you that they knew something you did not know about the car, rug, or condo, something that makes you regret not trying to learn more about its value. Buyers often make the fundamental mistake of making an offer without considering that the other side knows more than they do about the value of what is being purchased. Economists refer to this problem as *asymmetric information*. To solve it, you need some expertise on your side.

In 2001, George Akerlof won the Nobel Prize in Economics for demonstrating that the selective acceptance of offers can lead to market distortions.[1] Why do used cars so often perform so poorly? As Akerlof noted, car owners tend to hang on to cars that run well, or they sell them to people they know. The lower the quality of the car, the more likely it is to enter the broader market of strangers. As the market adjusts to this result, the value of used cars goes down. Because customers are nervous about the quality of used cars, in part due to the selective availability of lower-quality cars, car dealerships can make money by charging more for cars they have inspected, improved, and warranted. They are solving the problem of selective availability.

This analysis shows the benefit of thinking about what the other side might know rather than relying on a simplified heuristic, such as the median value of a 2018 Honda CRV or Zillow's estimate of the value of a particular house. When you are at an information disadvantage, you may be able to reduce the information asymmetry by paying for independent expertise (such as a professional appraisal or a car inspection by your own mechanic). Margaret Neale and I documented that negotiators who have a greater tendency to think about the perspective of others are more successful.[2] Thinking about the other side's perspective allows you to predict your opponent's BATNA, their reservation price, and what they value in the negotiation beyond just getting a good price. Thinking about the other side helps you better understand the negotiation context that you face.

Influence in Negotiation

When I tell people that I teach negotiation, they typically assume that I instruct people on how to get others to do what they want them to do. In the negotiation and social psychology literature, we refer to this as "influence." As you have read, most of my treatment of negotiation does not focus on influence. Viewing negotiation only as a means of influencing others leaves out many of the strategic insights described earlier in this book, as well as how to understand the interests of the other side and develop your negotiation strategies accordingly. But influence is certainly a part of negotiation, and we turn to this topic here.

Strategies to influence the other side include issuing threats (which specify how the other party will be harmed if they do not do what you want them to do), providing incentives (how they will benefit by doing what you want them to do), reasoning (providing insight that will lead them to want to do what you want them to do), and deception (providing inaccurate information to encourage them to do what you want them to do). I am opposed to deception in negotiation, and I think you need to be very careful before making threats. Both of these negative actions can have long-term negative effects on the influencer and are more likely to destroy value than to help you create value. This section, however, is not about threats, incentives, argumentation, or deception. Rather, we will apply the social psychological research of Robert

Cialdini and the decision research described in chapter 11 to influencing the decisions of other parties in negotiation.[3]

The topic of influence can be thought about from the perspective of you influencing the other side or from the perspective of them trying to influence you. We will consider both, depending on the strategy, while also dealing with the ethical implications connected to the topic of influence. The strategies presented below are just a few of the ways in which you can influence others and be influenced by others (see Cialdini's book *Influence* and his coauthored book *Yes! 50 Scientifically Proven Ways to Be Persuasive* for extended treatments).[4] Everything we know about how humans make decisions has implications for how to influence others. The following influence strategies are particularly relevant to negotiation.

Influencing through the status quo. When finalizing a complicated agreement, you might offer to have your lawyers write up the formal contract. Why incur the added costs of legal fees? After all, the other party will have the chance to propose revisions to the legal language that your lawyer puts together. One reason to do so is that the negotiating party who creates the initial draft is likely to benefit from making dozens of choices about contractual elements to include or leave out, such as termination clauses, penalties for noncompliance, and contract renewal. The first draft is likely to be stickier than the parties would predict. In other words, the starting point—the default, or status quo—matters.

One of my favorite short teaching exercises is based on Eric Johnson and Daniel Goldstein's 2003 *Science* article "Do Defaults Save Lives?"[5] This paper compares organ-donation rates in European countries that have an "opt-in" system (that is, the default is non-donation) with those that have an "opt-out" system (the default is donation). I show my class the mean organ-donation rates for the four countries with opt-in policies, which range from 4 to 28 percent. I then ask the students to call out their estimates of the mean donation rates for the seven European countries that have opt-out processes. They know that the opt-out countries will have higher donation rates. I hear numbers like 50 percent, 60 percent, and sometimes even higher, like 80 percent. But students rarely offer estimates that are as high as the actual answers. Organ-donation rates in the opt-out countries range between 86 and 99 percent, with six of the seven over 98 percent. My students recognize that defaults matter, but they fail to appreciate how *much* they matter.

Just as sellers are better off anchoring on the high side of the zone of possible agreement, each party is better off starting with their own legal clauses in the contract. More broadly, most negotiators fail to appreciate how important creating the status quo will be. You can influence the other party in your preferred direction by taking steps to establish defaults or pushing back against their attempts to do so.

Separating gains and combining losses. Imagine you are a salesperson who is paid on commission. Which of the following two scenarios would make you happier?[6]

> *Scenario A:* You close a deal in which your company's goods or services are sold for $200,000.
> *Scenario B:* You close a deal in which your company's goods or services are sold for $100,000. The next day, you close another deal for $100,000.

Both scenarios would give you the same net result—your commission on $200,000 in sales. But when I present people with these choices, most say they would get more of a positive charge from the second scenario.

Now consider a different, less enjoyable pair of scenarios. Imagine that you are a salesperson who has four pending deals worth $100,000 each. You will only get your commission if a deal actually closes, and customers can choose to walk away from the agreement without penalty until it does. Which of these two situations would likely make you unhappier?

> *Scenario C:* You check your email to find that two of the pending sales, for a total of $200,000, have been canceled.
> *Scenario D:* You check your email to find that one of the pending sales for $100,000 has been cancelled. The next day, you get another email informing you that another $100,000 sale has been canceled.

Again, these scenarios have the same net effect on your earnings. However, most people believe that Scenario D would be more painful than Scenario C. This preference is consistent with a great deal of evidence from Richard Thaler and others that people prefer multiple gains over a single gain of the same size but prefer to suffer one loss at once rather than multiple losses spread across time.[7]

The implications of this research for negotiators are clear: doling out our concessions to the other side across time will increase the attractiveness of what we are offering, while aggregating their losses will lessen the likelihood that they will walk away from the negotiation. People have diminishing marginal utility associated with gains and diminishing marginal disutility associated with losses, which means that we (and they) do not receive "additional" gains as positively as an initial gain and do not receive "additional" losses as negatively as an initial loss.[8] This is something to keep in mind both when delivering and entertaining offers.

Framing in terms of losses or gains. Another important contribution of prospect theory to negotiation is the observation that losses loom larger than gains, as it suggests negotiators will be more motivated to avoid losses than to accrue gains. This implies that your negotiating counterpart will weigh information about potential losses more heavily than they weigh information about potential gains—even when the gains and losses are of equal magnitude. To see this in action, consider the famous study by Robert Cialdini in which representatives from the local power company went door-to-door offering free energy audits to homeowners.[9] Once an audit was completed, the representative would offer products and services to help the homeowner lower energy costs. One group of homeowners heard a closing pitch that included a customized version of "If you insulate your home, you will save X cents per day." (The actual value of X was determined by the audit.) Take a moment to think about how you might improve that pitch.

When I ask my students to improve the pitch, many recommend aggregating from cents per day to dollars per year—which I agree is a good idea. But Cialdini found that a better strategy was to close with the statement, "If you *fail* to insulate your home, you will *lose* X cents per day."

Although the objective content was the same, homeowners who were told how much they stood to *lose* were significantly more likely to purchase the extra products and services.

Another classic demonstration of losses looming larger than gains comes from research on the endowment effect.[10] In the original version of this now-classic experiment, mugs were placed in front of some participants. These participants were told that they now owned their mug and would have an opportunity to sell it. Other participants were told that they would be given a sum of money, which they could keep or use to buy a mug from another participant. The researchers then assessed the minimum price that the sellers would accept to sell their mugs and the maximum price the buyers would pay to obtain a mug. While sellers required a median value of $7.12 to sell the mug, buyers offered a median price of $2.87 for the mug. Ownership, or being endowed with the mug, made the mug much more valuable to the sellers. Overall, participants cared much more about losing a mug than about gaining a mug. The endowment effect has been replicated hundreds of times with many different commodities, and a roughly 2:1 differential in value between sellers and buyers is common.

Have you ever noticed in negotiations that people tend to think that their house, company, or piece of art is worth more than you estimate to be true? These high estimates can be explained by a combination of overconfidence and the endowment effect. In such negotiations, you need to try to move these sellers away from using their intuition to assess the value of the commodity by offering more objective, market-based information.

Escalating their commitment to you. Many consulting firms are well-known for selling prospective clients a small project for a low price, often a price that would make no sense if this was going to be the end of the story. The firm's strategy is to gain access to a new client, demonstrate its competence, and use the small project as an opportunity to scout for bigger projects to sell to the client. The consulting firm understands that once the client makes a commitment to the firm, they are more likely to escalate that commitment by contracting with the firm for additional work.

This common practice illustrates the well-known foot-in-the-door technique.[11] It refers to the salesperson's hope that the customer's willingness to go along with a modest request will increase their compliance with additional requests and eventually lead them to make a purchase. You may have similarly noticed ads in which car dealers offer a price quote without having to visit the dealership; typically, when you follow up by requesting a price via email, they will simply encourage you to visit their dealership. If you comply, expect your opposing negotiator to waste as much of your time as possible, the goal of which is to get you to escalate your commitment to the time you have spent traveling to and hanging out in the dealership by buying a car. A great deal of research shows that once we make a commitment to a course of action, we tend to escalate our commitment to that action.[12] Thus, be careful about making initial commitments, and be aware of how such commitments can affect you and the other side.

"One more thing." Imagine that after a long negotiation, you reach a tentative agreement, and the other side says they simply need to have it approved by senior management. Two days later, they tell you, "We have a deal, but we need to make one small change to what we outlined." You listen to their requested adjustment, which turns out not to be small at all. However, you are eager to get the deal done. Would you accept the change or not?

Consider a possible third option. Specifically, you could respond by saying, "We're actually relieved about your need to make a change to the contract, since we have a change to make as well." You could then outline your needed change, which would restore the overall attractiveness of the deal to where it was when you reached the tentative agreement. This would not only keep the positive momentum going by confirming that both sides are trying to finalize the agreement but take advantage of the commonly felt norm of reciprocity: since you are agreeing to their change, they are likely to feel a need to agree to your change. This move also highlights that unilateral concessions will not be common in your relationship.

We are often tempted in negotiations to make a small or medium-sized concession, or to pay a bit extra in the midst of a larger transaction. Common examples include the product warranties offered at car dealerships and big box stores. After you conclude negotiations to buy a new car, during which the salesperson emphasized the car's safety and reliability, you can expect them to try to sell you a multiyear extended warranty, saying, "For a small amount more, you'll never have to worry about repairs." Most new car buyers go for the pitch, and most are making a mistake.[13] Often, over half of the warranty price goes to the salesperson as a commission. Consumers would be better off turning down all extended warranties, putting the money saved in the bank, and using it to pay for necessary repairs. Across their life span, by saving all of the premiums, and occasionally paying for a loss not covered by insurance, most consumers will end up far better off financially.

Why are extended warranties so tempting? Because their price seems small in comparison to the huge amount we're about to spend on that new car or refrigerator. We feel the same incremental effect when the agent at the rental car counter encourages us to buy insurance on our rental, when the vast majority of the risk is already covered by our regular car insurance policies and the credit card we are using to rent the car. The percent of the insurance that is actually spent to cover damages is remarkably low. Yet, too many of us know little about our existing coverage, are scared by the vivid prospect of liability, and decide to pay the incremental cost for the insurance. If you don't trust me on the topic of insurance, consider the advice offered by Janet, a character on the TV show *The Good Place*. Janet has access to all knowledge across time. In the final episode, Michael, a mid-level manager in the afterlife, decides to return to Earth as a human. He has no experience with life on Earth, and Janet is preparing him for his new home. Her final piece of advice? She tells him not to buy insurance from car rental companies because "it's a scam."

When you're buying a car, paying an extra $1,000 for an extended warranty might feel like an incremental difference. But think of what else you might spend that $1,000 on: maybe a new computer or a vacation. When a negotiating counterpart tries to collect extra money from us based on it being "just one more thing," we need to avoid making this decision intuitively, as our intuition is susceptible to incrementalism. Right now might be a good time to step back and deliberate on how you would like to respond to incremental requests in the future.

Directing attention. In a prior book, *The Power of Noticing*, I described how cognitive limitations can prevent us from noticing important information that is available in our environment.[14] I devoted one chapter to those who want to keep us from noticing critical information. My favorite of the many occupations skilled at keeping us from noticing is that of magician. One key skill of magicians is to misdirect our attention, which allows them to make the "magic" happen. Con artists do the same. Think about a street hustler conning you into trying to keep track of the Ace of Spades among three cards that they are manipulating. This is a good time for their friend to steal your wallet, as your attention is directed toward the cards.

Advertisers are another group that tries to influence our attention by distracting us from important information. Often, they do so by exploiting our desire to compare multiple products across different dimensions in an organized manner. Have you ever seen print ads in which a chart compares the featured product to its competitors, with each of them rated on rows of attributes? These charts portray the advertised product as much more attractive on every dimension. A blog by tech journalist Adam Pash analyzed such a chart in a Microsoft ad that favorably compares the company's Internet Explorer browser to two competing browsers, Firefox and Chrome.[15] In the chart, Microsoft outperforms the competition on every dimension. If you were interested in choosing an internet browser, you might study the chart carefully while overlooking the fact that Microsoft paid for the ad, chose the dimensions for comparison, decided on the ratings, and had its employees or advertising agency write comments on the article. Such organized comparison charts misdirect consumers from a logical decision-making process that might lead them to a competitor's product. Like magicians and con artists, these advertisements misdirect our attention.

Similarly, skilled negotiators often try to influence which attributes you focus on as you compare their services to those offered by their competitors. Their aim is to define your context in ways that increase the likelihood that you will buy their product or service. To defend yourself, think about what attributes you value in a product or service *before* you show up at the negotiating table.

How Context Creates Process

I regularly negotiate the terms of my consulting and teaching services outside my professorial obligations at Harvard. Often, I'm being hired to advise on negotiations or teach negotiation. The initial call typically comes from an executive who is already familiar with my work, whether from one of my books or articles, from taking a class with me, or from encountering my work in a professional meeting. While executives are often nervous about negotiating negotiation services with a negotiation professor, the basic negotiation is typically quite straightforward, and we reach an informal agreement fairly quickly. Often, however, the executive works for a large organization that has a procurement division that is in charge of finalizing the agreement. When I hear this, I quickly inform the executive that many large organizations, perhaps including their organization, tend to send me a boilerplate contract that makes little sense in the context of a one-person consulting assignment and that has many clauses that I cannot and will not sign. As nicely as possible, I encourage them to make sure that any contract they draft is simple and that I can read and sign it in under thirty minutes; otherwise, I will need to renegotiate our agreement.

Why introduce this somewhat awkward discussion with someone who is simply trying to hire me to do some work for them? Because a number of large organizations have sent me very long contracts that would take me hours to read, require a lawyer to fully understand, require me to state that I have insurance policies that I do not have (and that would not make sense for the work that I do), and provide the client with ownership of materials I use in my teaching that are owned by other parties. Simply put, many boilerplate contracts would provide a very dysfunctional anchor in our attempt to find a mutually acceptable set of terms on factors unrelated to price. I find it far easier to nicely blow up that anchor before it ever gets set. My response typically causes a bit of work for the other party, but far less work for both of us than if I received the long contract and had to negotiate from that anchor.

To facilitate these agreements, I try to empathize with the other side. The executive who reached out to me has little interest in the terms in their company's boilerplate contract. Other people within their organization, however, have thought about the legal terms in their procurement process and created a procedure aimed at influencing their suppliers by stipulating a favorable set of terms in their default contract that are relevant to many of their negotiations. By understanding this, I can develop a strategy to preempt it and do my best to get the executive interested in hiring me to work to save us both lots of time. Yet, I have erred when I was busy, forgot to anticipate the issue, and only started to manage the contract process after receiving a twenty-two-page document.

My contracting management strategy is consistent with Cialdini's focus on defending oneself against the influence strategy of the other side.[16] While Cialdini's book on influence became a bestseller in the sales world, he originally wrote it to help all of us understand, anticipate, and defend ourselves against the influence attempts of our counterparts in negotiation and other contexts. Despite starting off with a good relationship with the executives who call me, I anticipate their organization's likely influence strategy and do my best to preempt it from entering my negotiation. This requires an awareness of likely influence strategies, a refusal to take the influence attempt personally, and an effort to reframe the dialogue as early as possible. If I execute this plan optimally, the executive will recognize that I am aiming to help both of us save time down the road.

Much of this book has emphasized the importance of preparation in negotiation, an emphasis that will continue in the next and final chapter. We are far less likely to be influenced in ways that work against our best interests in negotiation when we show up prepared. The more we know about our BATNA, reservation price, and the issues we care about, the less likely our intuitive processes are to be influenced by the other party's possible attempts at misinformation and misdirection.

■ ■ ■

"Is it ethical to psychologically manipulate the other side's choices and behavior in negotiation?"

"Thank you for thinking about this critical question about the ethics of influencing the other side. It is something we all need to think about if we want to negotiate with integrity and develop long-lasting, productive negotiation relationships. It also underscores the importance of working to create as much value as possible in negotiation.

Some aspects of your question are easy for me to answer. I do not endorse, excuse, or recommend lying or deception in negotiation (unless you have the opportunity to save the world; see the discussion of the Cuban Missile Crisis in chapter 5). Deceptive acts destroy relationships and value over the long run. For me, that makes them unethical.

If, however, you are in a context where you want to claim as much value as possible without lying or otherwise deceiving the other party, you already know that I think you should assess your BATNA and reservation value, their BATNA and reservation value, and the zone of possible agreement. Bringing logic to a negotiation makes sense, and the honest use of the psychology of influence is similarly appropriate. Cialdini agrees, employing the term 'triggers' to refer to influence tactics like those discussed in this chapter: 'The use of these triggers by practitioners is not necessarily exploitative. It only becomes so when the trigger is not a natural feature of the situation but is fabricated by the practitioner.'[17] It is also useful to realize that whenever we present information to the other side, we are framing the presentation of that information. Drawing on the psychology of influence simply involves selecting one of many possible honest frames to convey your ideas to the other side.

It is also important to consider that your counterpart can reject even good ideas that would benefit both of you. The effective and honest use of influence strategies to create value is not just OK with me; I think it is necessary to get your value-creating moves accepted—and thus to be as ethical as possible. Thus, I recommend that you don't question the integrity of influencing others in general but instead question the ethicality of any specific action that involves deception."

Chapter 13

Preparation in Context

Covid-19 descended on the world with surprising speed, leaving manufacturers and health-care systems scrambling to catch up. If you visited your local pharmacy in March 2020, they may not have had hand sanitizer and face masks in stock. If you ended up in an ICU with the disease, they may not have had a ventilator available for you. In the midst of providing medical care, some physicians were forced to negotiate the question of who should live and who should die, as we discussed in chapter 7. They never should have been in this situation.

Preparation *before* a crisis breaks out allows us to make wiser decisions. Similarly, preparing for our most important negotiations allows us to make wiser decisions at the negotiating table.

In this concluding chapter, we return to the overarching theme of the book, as introduced in chapter 1: the fact that, for our negotiations to go well, we need to adapt our strategies to the specific and unique context we are facing. It may seem unusual to conclude a negotiations book with a chapter on preparation. My reasoning is that we needed to establish what we are preparing for before exploring how to prepare. This chapter will highlight the importance of preparation when implementing the advice provided throughout the book, with an emphasis on how to prepare for the specific contexts in which you find yourself. I will integrate ideas about how understanding the context of a negotiation can help us generalize foundational concepts to our own unique world.

Meta-Preparation

The story in chapter 7 about the allocation of scarce ventilators in Italy during the Covid-19 crisis reminded me of a negotiation simulation called Liberty Hospital, written by Harvard Kennedy School philosopher Chris Robichaud.[1] The Liberty Hospital simulation asks students to imagine they sit on the ethics committee of a hospital confronted with a series of ethical decisions as the city in which it is located is hit by a terrorist attack. Netta Barak-Corren adapted Liberty Hospital to the Covid pandemic and, as a law professor at Hebrew University in Jerusalem, changed the setting to Mt. Scopus Hospital, a hospital serving the Jewish and Arab neighborhoods of northern and eastern Jerusalem. In the Mt. Scopus simulation, students are put into groups to play the role of the ethics committee that must allocate scarce, lifesaving resources during a Covid outbreak—before any Covid-19 vaccines had been invented—when there are not enough resources for all the patients in need.

When I run the Liberty Hospital and Mt. Scopus Hospital simulations, participants are confronted very quickly with the first crisis of the ethics committee. This crisis involves deciding who should get scarce respirators when more patients need the lifesaving equipment than are available. Emotions are strong as the parties confront this moral conflict. In the spirited discussions that follow, participants tend to express different views about the goal: Some argue for saving as many lives as possible and others for saving as many life years as possible. Some argue in favor of saving the weakest, while others favor respecting age by favoring the oldest patients. And others prefer allocating ventilators on a first-come, first-served basis. You can probably think of other bases for creating a set of procedures for allocating the scarce respirators. Many readers will not be surprised that I look at the problem by focusing on doing as much good as possible with the limited resource. For me, this leans toward trying to save as many quality-adjusted life years as possible. This is different than the number of lives saved, since saving a fifteen-year-old saves more expected life years than saving an eighty-year-old. It also means valuing *quality* years, rather than simply keeping people alive. But, for our current purposes, I am fine with you having a different view.

I have also modified these simulations to give the ethics committee time to discuss their strategies, goals, and ideas before the first crisis occurs. Adding conversation, in which issues are discussed in the abstract, significantly changes the subsequent discussions—for the good, I believe. The abstract discussion leads the group to make subsequent decisions that are more focused on an overarching objective and based more on reason than on emotion. The decisions also tend to create more value, or reduce more harm, consistent with the utilitarian logic discussed through this book. Preparing for a crisis negotiation before the crisis leads to more deliberation, less emotion, and less conflict.

The context of preparing for a terrorist attack or a pandemic may seem distant from your own work life. My broader goal is to encourage you to consider the negotiation contexts that will confront you and those around you, and to think about how you and your organization can be better equipped to deal with such negotiations when they arise. I often run into people involved in labor-management negotiations, and the stories they tell me tend to concern their poor relationship with the other side and the difficulty they have getting the other side to act reasonably. One contributor to these problems is the fact that these negotiators don't recognize the need to improve their ability to communicate with the other side until they are in the midst of a hostile negotiation in the context of a bad relationship. A far better approach would be to engage with the other side, perhaps in joint negotiation training, before active contract negotiations begin. In this less intense environment, the parties are likely to be better able to develop a positive relationship, appreciate the concerns of the other side, and create a better context when the actual contract negotiation comes along.

I also often hear managers complain about the contracts that their sales force brings back for approval. While such complaints are common, the details vary widely across different managers within the same firm. In chapter 9, I shared the conclusion of Daniel Kahneman and his colleagues that managers are very noisy when making decisions—that is, they reach very different conclusions when presented with the same information. Not only are their quantitative assessments noisy, but so are their assessments of what constitutes a good agreement in a negotiation. When I was reading an early draft of *Noise*, I told Kahneman about a teaching exercise that economist Linda Babcock shared with me, which she conducted with managers from the same company. The context was the task of negotiating contracts involving many issues beyond price. Linda gave all of the managers the task of rating the quality of a large number of contracts. She then ran an analysis for each manager to assess what they thought made a contract great. She found that the managers' models were noisy: that is, managers within the same firm had extremely different models of what constituted a good agreement. If the managers didn't agree about what factors should be rated most heavily, how could they expect the sales force to deliver the best agreement? Babcock's exercise is a useful demonstration of the need for management to identify and communicate what they hope their negotiators will try to achieve. Only by reaching consensus as to what constitutes a "great" agreement will they equip negotiators to actually reach one. This is an important structural element in leading good negotiation practices.

Planning to Create Value

In chapter 4, I mentioned the scoring systems that my colleagues and I often use in the negotiation simulations in our classes. These systems allocate points to various outcomes, or convert each issue to value on some common currency, such as dollars. When simulations are scorable, they can provide useful feedback to students, allowing them to compare their performance to that of other students who just experienced the same simulation. In addition, as I mentioned in chapter 4, such scoring systems also highlight to students the value of thinking through how important each issue is to them. By creating a way of aggregating value across issues, negotiators explicitly consider the value of different issues and are better positioned to make trade-offs at the negotiating table.

The description of Babcock's analyses of managers within the same firm also highlights the benefit of working with others in your firm to identify how important different issues are to the firm. This process might begin with allowing different members of your organization to independently specify the importance of different issues to them. Disagreement would signal the need not only to identify the importance you place on different issues but to learn from others why they value the various issues differently from you.

As I hope has been clear throughout this book, and particularly in chapter 12, determining how important various issues are to the other party is critical to finding wise trades. Similarly, thinking about what the other side's scoring system might look like is a useful exercise for identifying what they care about, which in turn can point to mutually beneficial trades. If an actual scoring system feels impractical, at least explicitly think about what issues are likely to be most important to the other side. If you are stumped, then you understand that you need to learn this critical information during the negotiation.

Preparing for the Questions
You Least Want to Answer

Having been a business school professor for many years, I often receive visits from former students seeking negotiation advice, which I am happy to provide. I appreciate that they value taking time to prepare for the upcoming negotiation and am happy to be part of their preparation process. I most often get these visits during the peak of the job market season. Typically, these students have a common challenge: they have received exactly one job offer and want to negotiate to make the offer better. Students who have gotten two or more offers tend to be very good at using their second-best offer as a BATNA to leverage their negotiations with their preferred organization. So, it is the one-offer students who most seek my advice.

After they explain the situation, I ask them what's wrong with the existing offer, and they commonly say that the salary could be higher. I then propose that we simulate the upcoming negotiation, like the simulations we conducted in class, with me playing the role of the manager

recruiting the student. After they agree, I ask them to pretend to call me, using our cell phones, and start the discussion. I allow them to awk-
· wardly start the conversation and to eventually raise the possibility of an adjustment to the starting salary. As the recruiting manager, I respond by saying something like, "We certainly want to be competitive with the market, and I would be surprised if our offer was below market. So, it would help me argue for a better salary for you internally if you could confirm the salaries of the other formal offers you have received." The student then responds that they would prefer that the recruiter not ask that question. I point out that the student has limited control over what the recruiting manager might ask and that my question would be an appropriate and common response. I also note that good negotiators prepare responses to the questions they least want the other side to ask. Most importantly, thinking through such a response could change how the student approaches the salary negotiation.

When it is clear to me that the student will definitely accept the offer they have received and that any attempt to negotiate a better salary offers more downside (such as losing the offer or annoying their future boss) than upside (getting a higher salary), I recommend changing the game from "negotiation" to "fairness." Specifically, I suggest that the student consider a very different strategy for their call to the recruiting manager, one more like this script:

> "I am delighted to have received your offer. Your firm is where I want to be working after graduation. So, I have already decided to accept your offer. However, I do have a request. It has to do with the starting salary. While I will accept your offer regardless of your response, and I understand that it may take a bit of time for you to respond, I would like to share with you some data on starting salaries for students in my school. I think you will see that your offer is on the low side, and I would simply like you to consider raising the starting salary."

When I stop talking, the student often questions whether it is wise to give up so much of their negotiating power by committing to accepting the offer even if the salary doesn't change. I respond by questioning whether they had any power to lose. I point out that it makes complete sense for the recruiting manager to ask about other offers and that once this happens, they are about to lose the game called "negotiation." If, by contrast, they put themselves on the recruiter's team, give them something they want (acceptance of the offer), and ask for a favor in return, norms of reciprocity and fairness are likely to kick in. This may be a more successful approach to getting a higher salary—and a fairer one, as well.

My broader advice here is to think about what the other side might do that you least want them to do. Think about your responses without the pressure of being in dialogue with the other side. And consider how being confronted with what you least want to happen might change how you initiate the negotiation.

Check Your Overconfidence

Throughout the book, I have provided lots of evidence that negotiators, and decision makers more broadly, tend to be overconfident. As a result, many negotiators are not well prepared when the negotiation doesn't unfold as they initially anticipated. This can easily lead to impasse, a negotiation with a poor outcome, or a deal that isn't sustainable over time. One strategy for checking your overconfidence and preparing for difficult shifts in the negotiation is to conduct a *negotiation premortem*. Imagining why an event might go wrong is an effective strategy for better anticipating possible future events, Deborah Mitchell, Jay Russo, and Nancy Pennington have found.[2] Gary Klein refers to this strategy as a premortem.[3]

Klein presents the idea of a premortem against the more common concept of a postmortem. After something goes wrong (the death of a patient, for example, in a medical context), a postmortem explores what happened. Clearly, a postmortem doesn't stop the bad event from happening. By contrast, a premortem allows a negotiator to anticipate what might go wrong and adjust their strategy accordingly.[4]

Imagine that you are the lead negotiator in an upcoming important negotiation. Bring together other relevant and informed people from your organization, perhaps adding a couple of the most cynical and difficult members. Overview the upcoming negotiation, and ask your colleagues to imagine that it ends with no agreement having been achieved or with an agreement that ultimately creates massive problems for your organization. Ask your colleagues to imagine why the poor outcome occurred, and encourage them not to constrain themselves by being too nice. Get all of their ideas on the table, then use these ideas to think through what actions on the front end might prevent these negative negotiation outcomes from occurring. Now you can adapt your negotiation plan so that you are ready for difficult situations you might encounter.

Contextualizing Your Preparation

I hope this book has been successful in convincing you that context matters in negotiation and that many of the core concepts we use in negotiation analyses remain critical across contexts. Expertise in negotiation includes the ability to assess the context of any specific negotiation and, within that context, identify how the context affects the interests and opportunities available to you and the other parties. When we are in stable environment, in a context that is comfortable, following the preparation advice offered will be easier. But when we are in unfamiliar contexts, either because of the uniqueness of the specific negotiation or due to a massive economic, political, or social change, we need to adapt our preparation to the specific context. The culture, economic conditions, political environment, relationships, and mode of communication matter—and we too easily overlook the importance of context.

You will be far better off in your future negotiations if you consider the interests, alternatives, and likely behaviors of the other side. This requires understanding the context. Understanding the norms of their culture, as well as whether that culture is based on their industry, region, or nationality, will help you assess why they might engage in behavior that is unfamiliar to you, why they may value things that you do not (creating the opportunity for trades), and what you need to learn to develop a value-creating relationship. Understanding the economic environment may help you identify the other party's BATNA and why you find their behavior to be difficult. Insight about the politics of their organization or nation may help you grasp why their behavior diverges from what you would expect if they were acting on their own.

Thinking about the importance of your long-term relationship with the other party may lead you to consider additional advantages of value-creating negotiation strategies. Thinking about the communication mechanisms you will use may affect what information you send to the other side in advance. And thinking a great deal about the likely decisions of those across the table can provide you with enormous insight.

Collectively, we can see a pattern emerging that eliminates the question of whether all negotiations are the same or are all different. They are all the same in that they are all different in their own unique way. Thinking about the contextual elements outlined in this book will help you implement basic negotiation strategies as an expert. I hope this book helps you on your journey to developing this expertise.

Gratitude

I signed an agreement to write this book with Princeton University Press in 2022, but I had been working on these ideas for decades. I have heard the contextual concerns of my executive students for as long as I have been teaching. And while I wrote this book without a coauthor, I developed the ideas in the process of researching, writing, and publishing a large number of conceptual and empirical papers on negotiation with colleagues. If I have a superpower (not a term I'm wild about), it is getting great people to work with me. My coauthors on papers and cases on negotiation include Sally Blount, Jeanne Brett, John Carroll, Eugene Caruso, Tina Diekmann, Nick Epley, Hank Farber, James Gillespie, Linda Ginzel, Andy Hoffman, Boaz Keysar, Roy Lewicki, George Loewenstein, Thomas Magliozzi, Deepak Malhotra, Beta Mannix, Kathleen McGinn, Don Moore, Maggie Neale, Katie Shonk, Lisa Shu, Harris Sondak, Ann Tenbrunsel, Leigh Thompson, Cathy Tinsley, Chia-Jung Tsay, Kimberly Wade-Benzoni, and Laurie Weingart, among others.

I previously published *Negotiating Rationally* with Maggie Neale and *Negotiation Genius* with Deepak Malhotra. Many of the concepts in this book were described in these prior works. And while I would describe both prior books as more basic and conceptual than contextual, my ongoing interactions with Deepak are at the core of my thoughts about contextualizing negotiation and thus central to this book.

I have been on the faculty of the Negotiation, Organizations & Markets unit of the Harvard Business School for the last couple of decades. Our unit takes the teaching of negotiation very seriously. We teach MBA and executive classes on negotiation, write articles and cases about negotiation, and get advice from each other about the negotiations of the day. We also watch each other teach negotiation, learn from each other, and offer feedback. Many of my colleagues have taken the contextualization of negotiations more seriously than I have for a longer time. This book has benefited from what I have learned informally and formally from these excellent colleagues. They include Livia Alfonsi, George Baker, John Beshears, Alison Wood Brooks, Alex Chan, Edward Chang, Katie Coffman, Ben Edelman, Christine Exley, Amit Goldenberg, Thomas Graeber, Jerry Green, Brian Hall, Lorraine Idson, Leslie John, Jillian Jordan, Nour Kteily, Michael Luca, Deepak Malhotra, Kevin Mohan, Kym Nelson, Mike Norton, Matthew Rabin, Al Roth, Josh Schwartzstein, Jim Sebenius, Guhan Subramanian, Andy Wasynczuk, Ashley Whillans, and Julian Zlatev. One final member of this group, Kathleen McGinn, has been my colleague for over thirty years and has always been more sensitive to context than I have been. I have learned so much from her insights.

My work on negotiation is also deeply informed by my work in the related fields of decision making and behavioral ethics. The work of my friends and colleagues in these areas, as well as my discussions with them, have influenced many aspects of this book. Important friends and colleagues in these areas include Modupe Akinola, Mahzarin Banaji, Iris Bohnet, Dolly Chugh, Josh Greene, Danny Kahneman, David Laibson, Katy Milkman, Don Moore, Todd Rogers, and Peter Singer.

I also received enormously helpful feedback on prior drafts of some or all of this book from Dolly Chugh, Marla Felcher, Laura Kray, Nour Kteily, Terri Kurtzberg, Katy Milkman, Barry Nalebuff, Todd Rogers, Maurice Schweitzer, and Ann Tenbrunsel. They provided numerous insights and saved readers from many of the limitations of my first draft. I also benefited from the insightful input of my repeat editor Joe Jackson of the Princeton University Press, Jenn Backer, and two anonymous reviewers.

I have improved my understanding of negotiation thanks to the participation, questions, and arguments of tens of thousands of MBA students and executives from around the world whom I have had the privilege of teaching. I trust that some of the most critical members of this group will see their questions asked in this book—and hopefully find some useful answers as well.

As always, my writing is better due to the amazing editing of Katie Shonk. She always improves my writing on a sentence-by-sentence basis but also by helping me think about the perspective of the reader. I am enormously grateful to have Katie as a trusted colleague. In addition, Elizabeth Sweeny is a careful and precise proofreader, error-checker, and reference expert, and I appreciate all that she added to this book.

Lots of things take a village, and that certainly includes my writing. With gratitude,

Max H. Bazerman

Notes

Chapter 1: The Game Has Changed

1. Simone Moran, Yoella Bereby-Meyer, and Max H. Bazerman, "Stretching the Effectiveness of Analogical Training in Negotiations: Teaching Diverse Principles for Creating Value," *Negotiation & Conflict Management Research* 1, no. 2 (2008): 99–134.

2. Max H. Bazerman and Margaret A. Neale, *Negotiating Rationally* (New York: Free Press, 1992); Deepak Malhotra and Max H. Bazerman, *Negotiation Genius: How to Overcome Obstacles and Achieve Brilliant Results at the Bargaining Table and Beyond* (New York: Bantam, 2007).

3. Max H. Bazerman and William F. Samuelson, "The Winner's Curse: An Empirical Investigation," in *Aspiration Levels in Bargaining and Economic Decision Making*, ed. Reinhard Tietz (New York: Springer-Verlag, 1983), 186–200.

4. Deepak Malhotra worked with me to improve the simulation and publish it with Harvard Business Publishing as "The Book Deal: Confidential Instructions for the PUBLISHER," HBS No. 908-050 (Boston: Harvard Business Publishing, 2008), https://store.hbr.org/product/the-book-deal-confidential-instructions-for-the-publisher/908050 and "The Book Deal: Confidential Instructions for the AGENT," HBS No. 908-051 (Boston: Harvard Business Publishing, 2008), https://store.hbr.org/product/the-book-deal-confidential-instructions-for-the-agent/908051.

5. Erin Meyer, "Getting to Si, Ja, Oui, *and* Da," *Harvard Business Review*, December 1, 2015.

6. Deepak Malhotra, "Hamilton Real Estate: Confidential Role Information for the CEO of Estate One (BUYER)," HBS No. 905-052 (Boston: Harvard Business Publishing, 2005); Deepak Malhotra, "Hamilton Real Estate: Confidential Role Information for the Executive VP of Pearl Investments (SELLER)," HBS No. 905-053 (Boston: Harvard Business Publishing, 2005).

Chapter 2: Extreme Anchors

1. I was reminded of this example by Barry Nalebuff.

2. Adam Galinsky and Maurice Schweitzer, *Friend or Foe: When to Cooperate, When to Compete, and How to Succeed at Both* (New York: Crown Business, 2015).

3. Galinsky and Schweitzer, *Friend or Foe*, 243.

4. "WHO Covid-19 Dashboard," World Health Organization," https://covid19.who.int/, accessed February 19, 2023.

5. Amos Tversky and Daniel Kahneman, *Judgment under Uncertainty: Heuristics and Biases* (Cambridge: Cambridge University Press, 1974).

6. Thomas Mussweiler and Fritz Strack, "Comparing Is Believing: A Selective Accessibility Model of Judgmental Anchoring," *European Review of Social Psychology* 10, no. 1 (1999): 135–67.

7. Tversky and Kahneman, *Judgment under Uncertainty.*

8. Don A. Moore and Max H. Bazerman, *Decision Leadership: Empowering Others to Make Better Choices* (New Haven: Yale University Press, 2022).

9. Max H. Bazerman, *Complicit: How We Enable the Unethical and How to Stop* (Princeton: Princeton University Press, 2022).

10. Edward J. Joyce and Gary C. Biddle, "Anchoring and Adjustment in Probabilistic Inference in Auditing," *Journal of Accounting Research* 19 (1981): 120–45.

11. Linda Babcock and Sara Laschever, *Women Don't Ask: Negotiation and the Gender Divide* (Princeton: Princeton University Press, 2003).

12. Laura J. Kray, Jessica A. Kennedy, and Margaret Lee, "Now, Women Do Ask: A Call to Update Beliefs about the Gender Pay Gap" (Working paper, University of California, Berkeley, 2023).

13. "Chapter 177 of the Acts of 2016: An Act to Establish Pay Equity," 2016, https://malegislature.gov/Laws/SessionLaws/Acts/2016/Chapter177.

14. "Salary History Bans," HR Dive, https://www.hrdive.com/news/salary-history-ban-states-list/516662/; Kray, Kennedy, and Lee, "Now, Women Do Ask."

15. Gregory B. Northcraft and Margaret A. Neale, "Experts, Amateurs, and Real Estate: An Anchoring-and-Adjustment Perspective on Property Pricing Decisions," *Organizational Behavior and Human Decision Processes* 39, no. 1 (1987): 84–97.

16. Moore and Bazerman, *Decision Leadership.*

17. Adam D. Galinsky and Thomas Mussweiler, "First Offers as Anchors: The Role of Perspective-taking and Negotiator Focus," *Journal of Personality and Social Psychology* 81, no. 4 (2001): 657–69, https://doi.org/10.1037/0022-3514.81.4.657.

18. Galinsky and Schweitzer, *Friend or Foe.*

19. Galinsky and Schweitzer, *Friend or Foe,* 244.

20. For an excellent treatment of the limits of evidence from laboratory experiments on negotiation, see Erica Boothby, Gus Cooney, and Maurice Schweitzer, "Embracing Complexity: A Review of Negotiation Research," *Annual Review of Psychology* 74, no. 1 (2023): 299–332, https://doi.org/10.1146/annurev-psych-033020-014116.

21. Max H. Bazerman, *Judgment in Managerial Decision Making,* 6th ed. (New York: Wiley, 2006), 158–59.

22. Amy K. Nelson, "Dream on a Shelf," ESPN.com, http://www.espn.com/espn/eticket/story?page=090423/harrington.

23. Nelson, "Dream on a Shelf."

24. Nelson, "Dream on a Shelf."

25. Roger Fisher and William Ury, *Getting to Yes: Negotiating Agreement without Giving In* (New York: Penguin, 1981).

26. Einav Hart and Maurice Schweitzer, "Getting to Less: When Negotiating Harms Post-agreement Performance," *Organizational Behavior and Human Decision Processes* 156 (2020): 155–75, https://doi.org/10.1016/j.obhdp.2019.09.005.

Chapter 3: 50-50 Splits

1. Chris Voss, *Never Split the Difference: Negotiating as If Your Life Depended on It* (New York: HarperCollins, 2016).

2. Barry Nalebuff, *Split the Pie: A Radical New Way to Negotiate* (New York: HarperCollins, 2022).

3. Barry Nalebuff and Adam Brandenburger, "Rethinking Negotiation: A Smarter Way to Split the Pie," *Harvard Business Review* 99, no. 6 (November–December 2021): 110.

4. Nalebuff and Brandenburger, "Rethinking Negotiation," 110.

5. D. M. Messick, "Equality as a Decision Heuristic," in *Psychological Issues in Distributive Justice*, ed. B. A. Mellers (New York: Cambridge University Press, 1991).

6. Kathleen L. McGinn, Margaret A. Neale, and Elizabeth A. Mannix, "Friends, Lovers, Colleagues, Strangers: The Effects of Relationships on the Process and Outcome of Dyadic Negotiations," in *Research on Negotiation in Organizations*, ed. Robert J. Bies, Roy J. Lewicki, and Blair H. Sheppard (Greenwich, CT: JAI Press, 1995).

7. Werner Güth, Rolf Schmittberger, and Bernd Schwarze, "An Experimental Analysis of Ultimatum Bargaining," *Journal of Economic Behavior & Organization* 3, no. 4 (1982): 367–88.

8. Charlotte Nickerson, "Understanding Collectivist Cultures," *Simply Psychology*, September 22, 2021, https://www.simplypsychology.org/what-are-collectivistic-cultures.html.

9. Nickerson, "Understanding Collectivist Cultures."

10. Ariel Eckblad, "In Pursuit of Fairness: Re-negotiating Embedded Norms & Re-imagining Interest-Based Negotiation," *Harvard Negotiation Law Review* 26, no. 1 (Fall 2020): 1–28.

Chapter 4: Value Creation as a Way of Life

1. "*Super Pumped* (TV series)," in *Wikipedia*, https://en.wikipedia.org/wiki/Super_Pumped_(TV_series); Amir Efrati, "How Kalanick-Gurley Tensions Shaped Uber of Today," *The Information*, https://www.theinformation.com/articles/how-kalanick-gurley-tensions-shaped-uber-of-today.

2. Efrati, "How Kalanick-Gurley Tensions Shaped Uber of Today."

3. Katie Benner, "In Silicon Valley, a Voice of Caution Guides a High-Flying Uber," *New York Times*, March 18, 2017, https://www.nytimes.com/2017/03/18/technology/bill-gurley-uber-travis-kalanick-silicon-valley.html.

4. Efrati, "How Kalanick-Gurley Tensions Shaped Uber of Today."

5. Efrati, "How Kalanick-Gurley Tensions Shaped Uber of Today."

6. Howard Raiffa, "Post-Settlement Settlements," *Negotiation Journal* 1, no. 11 (1985): 9–12.

Chapter 5: Negotiating Ethically

1. Robert F. Kennedy, *Thirteen Days: A Memoir of the Cuban Missile Crisis* (New York: W. W. Norton, 1969).

2. There can be lots of discussion of the appropriateness of allowing political concerns to drive our ability to resolve a nuclear crisis.

3. Immanuel Kant, *Groundwork of the Metaphysics of Morals*, trans. Mary Gregor and Jens Timmermann, 2nd ed., Cambridge Texts in the History of Philosophy (Cambridge: Cambridge University Press, 2012).

4. Many utilitarians are thinking about all humans, but others, like Peter Singer, consider the interests of all sentient beings.

5. While there is little doubt that Aristotle had enormous influence, some argue that we should question his perspective on virtue, since he failed to consider the virtue of all; see "Should We Cancel Aristotle?" *New York Times*, July 21, 2020, https://www.nytimes.com/2020 /07/21/opinion/should-we-cancel-aristotle.html.

6. Mahzarin R. Banaji, Max H. Bazerman, and Dolly Chugh, "How (Un)ethical Are You?" *Harvard Business Review* 81, no. 12 (December 2003): 56–64.

7. Upton Sinclair, "I, Candidate for Governor and How I Got Licked," *Oakland Tribune*, December 20, 1934.

8. Nicholas Epley, Eugene M. Caruso, and Max H. Bazerman, "When Perspective Taking Increases Taking: Reactive Egoism in Social Interaction," *Journal of Personality and Social Psychology* 91 (2006): 872–89.

9. Epley, Caruso, and Bazerman, "When Perspective Taking Increases Taking."

10. Michael Ross and Fiore Sicoly, "Egocentric Biases in Availability and Attribution," *Journal of Personality and Social Psychology* 37 (1979): 322–36.

11. Ilana Ritov and Jonathan Baron, "Reluctance to Vaccinate: Omission Bias and Ambiguity," *Journal of Behavioral Decision Making* 3 (1990): 263–77.

12. The structure of this game is often simplified so that only high- and low-price options exist, counter to the real-world situation where a continuous range of prices is often an option.

13. James J. Gillespie and Max H. Bazerman, "Parasitic Integration," *Negotiation Journal* 13 (1997): 271–82.

14. Jonathon Baron, Max H. Bazerman, and Katherine Shonk, "Enlarging the Societal Pie through Wise Legislation: A Psychological Perspective," *Perspectives on Psychological Science* 1, no. 2 (June 2006): 123–32.

15. Deepak Malhotra and Max H. Bazerman, *Negotiation Genius: How to Overcome Obstacles and Achieve Brilliant Results at the Bargaining Table and Beyond* (New York: Bantam, 2007).

16. Paul Ekman, *Telling Lies: Clues to Deceit in the Marketplace, Marriage, and Politics* (New York: W. W. Norton, 2002).

17. Todd Rogers and Michael I. Norton, "The Artful Dodger: Answering the Wrong Question the Right Way," *Journal of Experimental Psychology: Applied* 17, no. 2 (2011): 139–47.

18. Robert S. Adler, "Negotiating with Liars," *MIT Sloan Management Review* 48, no. 4 (Summer 2007): 69–74.

Chapter 6: Betting on the Future

1. Joel Corry, "Agent's Take: Inside the 2021 Performance Bonuses of 20 Notable Players, Including Tom Brady and Stefon Diggs," CBS Sports, December 22, 2021, https://www.cbssports .com/nfl/news/agents-take-inside-the-2021-performance-bonuses-of-20-notable-players -including-tom-brady-and-stefon-diggs/.

2. Brady Henderson, "Los Angeles Rams Left Tackle Andrew Whitworth Retires after 16 NFL Seasons, Goes Out on Top," ESPN, March 15, 2022, https://www.espn.com/nfl/story/_/id /33510042/los-angeles-rams-left-tackle-andrew-whitworth-retires-16-nfl-seasons.

3. The Bulls won three championships in a row, then Jordan became a baseball player, and they didn't win for two years in a row. Jordan then returned to basketball, and the Bulls won two more championships in a row.

4. Don A. Moore, *Perfectly Confident: How to Calibrate Your Decisions Wisely* (New York: Harper Business, 2020).

5. Shireen Mahdi, "Quality Contingent Contracts: Evidence from Tanzania's Coffee Market," World Bank Policy Research Working Paper No. 6171, August 1, 2012, https://papers.ssrn.com /sol3/papers.cfm?abstract_id=2129613.

6. Lisa D. Ordóñez, Maurice E. Schweitzer, Adam D. Galinsky, and Max H. Bazerman, "Goals Gone Wild: The Systematic Side Effects of Over-Prescribing Goal Setting," *Academy of Management Perspectives* 23, no. 1 (2009): 6–16.

7. Steven Kerr, "On the Folly of Rewarding A, While Hoping for B," *Academy of Management Executive* 9, no. 1 (1959): 7–9.

Chapter 7: The Context of Disputes

1. Much of my description of Project Restart is based on Nour Kteily and Deepak Malhotra, "Project Restart: Deciding the Future of English Football," HBS No. 921-050 (Boston: Harvard Business Publishing, 2021). I am grateful for all they taught me about this sport and this particular dispute.

2. William L. Ury, Jeanne M. Brett, and Stephen B. Goldberg, *Getting Disputes Resolved: Designing Systems to Cut the Costs of Conflict* (San Francisco: Jossey-Bass, 1988).

3. John Rawls, *A Theory of Justice* (Cambridge: Belknap Press, 1971).

4. Rawls, *A Theory of Justice*, 12.

5. Karen Huang, Joshua Greene, and Max H. Bazerman, "Veil-of-Ignorance Reasoning Favors the Greater Good," *Proceedings of the National Academy of Sciences* 116, no. 48 (2019): 23,989–95.

6. Don A. Moore and Max H. Bazerman, *Decision Leadership: Empowering Others to Make Better Choices* (New Haven: Yale University Press, 2022).

7. Mary C. Kern and Dolly Chugh, "Bounded Ethicality: The Perils of Loss Framing," *Psychological Science* 20, no. 3 (2009): 378–84.

8. "Inside Italy's Covid War," *Frontline*, May 19, 2020, season 2020, episode 19, https://www .pbs.org/wgbh/frontline/documentary/inside-italys-covid-war/.

9. Karen Huang, Regan Bernhard, Netta Barak-Corren, Max Bazerman, and Joshua D. Greene, "Veil-of-Ignorance Reasoning Favors Allocating Resources to Younger Patients during the COVID-19 Crisis," *Judgment and Decision Making* 16, no. 1 (January 2021): 1–19.

Chapter 8: Transacting Online

1. Dennis Schaal, "The Definitive History of Online Travel," Skift, https://skift.com/history -of-online-travel/.

2. I do not mean to favor Zoom over Google Meet, Microsoft Teams, or other competitors in the market. When I mention Zoom, I am referring to this entire class of communication services.

3. Kathleen L. Valley, Joseph Moag, and Max H. Bazerman, "A Matter of Trust: Effects of Communication on Efficiency and Distribution of Outcomes," *Journal of Economic Behavior and Organizations* 35 (1998): 211–38.

4. William F. Samuelson and Max H. Bazerman, "The Winner's Curse in Bilateral Negotiations," in *Research in Experimental Economics*, vol. 3, ed. V. Smith (Greenwich, CT: JAI Press, 1985).

5. Valley, Moag, and Bazerman, "A Matter of Trust."

6. Samuelson and Bazerman, "The Winner's Curse in Bilateral Negotiations."

7. Terri R. Kurtzberg, Sanghoon Kang, and Charles E. Naquin, "The Effect of Screen Size and E-Communication Richness on Negotiation Performance," *Group Decision and Negotiation* 17, no. 4 (2018): 573–92.

8. Don A. Moore, Terri Kurtzberg, Leigh Thompson, and Michael Morris, "Long and Short Routes to Success in Electronically Mediated Negotiations," *Organizational Behavior and Human Decision Processes* 77 (1999): 22–43.

9. Max H. Bazerman and Jeanne M. Brett, "El-Tek," Dispute Resolution Research Center (DRRC), Kellogg School of Management, Northwestern University.

10. Boaz Keysar, "The Illusory Transparency of Intention: Linguistic Perspective Taking in Text," *Cognitive Psychology* 26, no. 2 (April 1994): 165–208.

11. Justin Kruger, Nicholas Epley, Jason Parker, and Zhi-Wen Ng, "Egocentrism over E-mail: Can We Communicate as Well as We Think?" *Journal of Personality and Social Psychology* 89, no. 6 (2005): 925–36.

12. Kurtzberg, Kang, and Naquin, "The Effect of Screen Size and E-Communication Richness on Negotiation Performance."

13. Aparna Krishnan, Terri R. Kurtzberg, and Charles E. Naquin, "The Curse of the Smartphone," *Negotiation Journal* (April 2014): 191–208.

14. PON Staff, "Ask a Negotiation Expert: Zooming into the Future of Negotiation," Program on Negotiation, September 30, 2020, https://www.pon.harvard.edu/daily/negotiation-skills-daily/ask-a-negotiation-expert-zooming-into-the-future-of-negotiation-nb/.

15. Not me—Katie Shonk has edited my books for many, many years.

16. I have consulted for Slice.

17. Amit Goldenberg and Max Bazerman, "Slice Labs: Creating a Fraud-free Online Insurance Platform," Harvard Business School Teaching Plan No. 922-019 (Boston: Harvard Business Publishing, 2021).

18. Fiona Scott Morton, Florian Zettelmeyer, and Jorge Silva-Risso, "Customer Information and Discrimination: Does the Internet Affect the Pricing of New Cars to Women and Minorities?" *Quantitative Marketing and Economics* 1, no. 1 (2003): 65–92.

19. Benjamin Edelman, Michael Luca, and Dan Svirsky, "Racial Discrimination in the Sharing Economy: Evidence from a Field Experiment," *American Economic Journal: Applied Economics* 9, no. 2 (April 2017): 1–22, https://doi.org/10.1257/app.20160213.

Chapter 9: Beyond Two Negotiators

1. Edward Wilson, "Thank You Vasili Arkhipov, the Man Who Stopped Nuclear War," *The Guardian*, October 27, 2012, https://www.theguardian.com/commentisfree/2012/oct/27/vasili-arkhipov-stopped-nuclear-war.

2. Wilson, "Thank You Vasili Arkhipov."

3. Deborah Kamin, "Powerful Realtor Group Agrees to Slash Commissions to Settle Lawsuits," *New York Times*, March 15, 2024, https://www.nytimes.com/2024/03/15/realestate/national-association-realtors-commission-settlement.html.

4. Max H. Bazerman, Margaret A. Neale, Kathleen Valley, Edward Zajac, and Peter Kim, "The Effect of Agents and Mediators on Negotiation Outcomes," *Organizational Behavior and Human Decision Processes* 53 (1992): 55–73.

5. Deepak Malhotra and Max H. Bazerman, *Negotiation Genius: How to Overcome Obstacles and Achieve Brilliant Results at the Bargaining Table and Beyond* (New York: Bantam, 2007).

6. Don Moore, Daylian Cain, George Loewenstein, and Max H. Bazerman, *Conflicts of Interest: Problems and Solutions from Law, Medicine, and Organizational Settings* (London: Cambridge University Press, 2005).

7. Daylian Cain, George Loewenstein, and Don Moore, "The Dirt on Coming Clean: Perverse Effects of Disclosing Conflicts of Interest," *Journal of Legal Studies* 34 (2005): 1–25; Sunita Sah and George Loewenstein, "Conflicted Advice and Second Opinions: Benefits, but Unintended Consequences," *Organizational Behavior and Human Decision Processes* 130 (2015): 89–107.

8. Cain, Loewenstein, and Moore, "The Dirt on Coming Clean."

9. Kathleen L. Valley, Sally B. White, Margaret A. Neale, and Max H. Bazerman, "Agents as Information Brokers: The Effects of Information Disclosure on Negotiated Outcomes," *Organizational Behavior and Human Decision Processes* 51 (1992): 220–36.

10. Robyn M. Dawes, "Social Dilemmas," *Annual Review of Psychology* 31 (1980): 169–93, http://dx.doi.org/10.1146/annurev.ps.31.020180.001125.

11. Garrett Hardin, "The Tragedy of the Commons," *Science* 162, no. 3859 (1968): 1243–48.

12. Kimberly Wade-Benzoni, Ann Tenbrunsel, and Max H. Bazerman, "Egocentric Interpretations of Fairness in Asymmetric, Environmental Social Dilemmas: Explaining Harvesting Behavior and the Role of Communication," *Organizational Behavior and Human Decision Processes* 67 (1996): 111–26.

13. Don A. Moore and Max H. Bazerman, *Decision Leadership: Empowering Others to Make Better Choices* (New Haven: Yale University Press, 2022).

14. Daniel Kahneman, Oliver Sibony, and Cass Sunstein, *Noise: A Flaw in Human Judgment* (New York: Little Brown, 2021).

15. James Surowiecki, *The Wisdom of Crowds: Why the Many Are Smarter than the Few and How Collective Wisdom Shapes Business, Economies, Societies, and Nations* (London: Little, Brown, 2004).

16. Richard P. Larrick, Albert E. Mannes, and Jack B. Soll, "The Social Psychology of the Wisdom of Crowds," in *Frontiers in Social Psychology: Social Judgment and Decision Making*, ed. J. I. Krueger (New York: Psychology Press, 2012), 227–42.

17. *The Dialogues of Plato*, trans. Benjamin Jowett, vol. 1 (New York: Random House, 1937), 60.

18. Albert E. Mannes, Jack B. Soll, and Richard P. Larrick, "The Wisdom of Select Crowds," *Journal of Personality and Social Psychology* 107, no. 2 (2014): 276–99.

19. Mannes, Soll, and Larrick, "The Wisdom of Select Crowds."

20. Ken Auletta, *Greed and Glory on Wall Street: The Fall of the House of Lehman* (New York: Open Road Media, 1986).

21. Elizabeth A. Mannix, "Organizations as Resource Dilemmas: The Effects of Power Balance on Group Decision Making," *Organizational Behavior and Human Decision Processes* 55 (1993): 1–22.

Chapter 10: Changing the Game

1. Annie Zhao and Guhan Subramanian, "Go-Shops Revisited," *Harvard Law Review* 133, no. 4 (2020), https://harvardlawreview.org/2020/02/go-shops-revisited/.

2. Marco della Cava, "eBay's 20th Made Possible by Canadian Retiree," *USA Today*, September 11, 2015, https://www.usatoday.com/story/tech/2015/09/11/ebays-20th-made-possible-canadian-retiree/72074218/.

3. https://en.wikipedia.org/wiki/EBay.

4. Patrick Bajari, Robert McMillan, and Steven Tadelis, "Auctions versus Negotiations in Procurement: An Empirical Analysis," *Journal of Law, Economics and Organization* 25, no. 2 (2009): 372–99; Guhan Subramanian and Richard Zeckhauser, "For Sale, but How? Auctions versus Negotiations," *PON Negotiations Newsletter* 7 (October 2004): 7–9.

5. Guhan Subramanian, *Dealmaking: The New Strategy of Negotiauctions*, 2nd ed. (New York: W. W. Norton, 2020).

6. Daniel Kahneman, Oliver D. Sibony, and Cass O. Sunstein, *Noise: A Flaw in Human Judgment* (New York: Little Brown, 2021).

7. Max H. Bazerman and William F. Samuelson, "I Won the Auction but Don't Want the Prize," *Journal of Conflict Resolution* 27 (1983): 618–34.

8. Max H. Bazerman and Henry S. Farber, "Arbitrator Decision Making: When Are Final Offers Important?" *Industrial and Labor Relations Review* 39 (1985): 76–89; Max H. Bazerman and Henry S. Farber, "Analyzing the Decision-Making Processes of Third Parties," *Sloan Management Review* 27 (1985): 39–48; Max H. Bazerman, "Norms of Distributive Justice in Interest Arbitration," *Industrial and Labor Relations Review* 38 (1985): 558–70.

9. Joel Sherman, "Aaron Judge's Arbitration Showdown with Yankees Is Last," *New York Post*, May 11, 2022, https://nypost.com/2022/05/11/aaron-judges-arbitration-showdown-with-yankees-is-last/.

10. Associated Press, "Atlanta Braves' Max Fried Wins Arbitration Case, Gets $6.85 Million," ESPN.com, June 22, 2022, https://www.espn.com/mlb/story/_/id/34132444/atlanta-braves-max-fried-wins-arbitration-case-gets-685-million.

11. Max H. Bazerman and Daniel Kahneman, "How to Make the Other Side Play Fair: The Final-Offer Arbitration Challenge," *Harvard Business Review* 94, no. 9 (September 2016): 76–81.

12. Bazerman and Kahneman, "How to Make the Other Side Play Fair."

13. Max H. Bazerman and Margaret A. Neale, "Improving Negotiation Effectiveness under Final Offer Arbitration: The Role of Selection and Training," *Journal of Applied Psychology* 67 (1982): 543–48; Ralph Cassady Jr., *Auctions and Auctioneering* (Berkeley: University of California Press, 1967).

Chapter 11: Your Decisions in Negotiation

1. Margaret A. Neale and Max H. Bazerman, "The Role of Perspective-Taking Ability in Negotiating under Different Forms of Arbitration," *Industrial and Labor Relations Review* 36 (1983): 378–88; Max H. Bazerman and Margaret A. Neale, "Improving Negotiation Effectiveness under Final Offer Arbitration: The Role of Selection and Training," *Journal of Applied Psychology* 67 (1982): 543–48.

2. Don A. Moore, *Perfectly Confident: How to Calibrate Your Decisions Wisely* (New York: Harper Business, 2020).

3. Daniel Kahneman, *Thinking, Fast and Slow* (New York: Farrar, Straus and Giroux, 2011); Don A. Moore and Max H. Bazerman, *Decision Leadership: Empowering Others to Make Better Choices* (New Haven: Yale University Press, 2022).

4. Vernon L. Smith, "An Experimental Study of Competitive Market Behavior," *Journal of Political Economy* 70, no. 2 (1962): 111–37.

5. Adam Smith, *The Theory of Moral Sentiments*, ed. D. D. Raphael and A. L. Macfie (Indianapolis: Liberty Fund, 1982).

6. Herbert A. Simon, *Models of Man* (New York: John Wiley, 1957), 98.

7. Howard Raiffa, *The Art and Science of Negotiation* (Cambridge, MA: Belknap, 1982).

8. Amos Tversky and Daniel Kahneman, "Judgment under Uncertainty: Heuristics and Biases," *Science* 185 (1974): 1124–31.

9. Daniel Kahneman and Amos Tversky, "Prospect Theory: An Analysis of Decision under Risk," *Econometrica* 47, no. 2 (1979): 263–91; Jodi Beggs, "What Is Behavioral Economics?" ThoughtCo, August 27, 2020, thoughtco.com/intro-to-behavioral-economics-1146878.

10. Amos Tversky and Daniel Kahneman, "The Framing of Decisions and the Psychology of Choice," *Science* 211, no. 4481 (1981): 453–58.

11. Margaret A. Neale and Max H. Bazerman, "The Effects of Framing and Negotiator Overconfidence on Bargaining Behaviors and Outcomes," *Academy of Management Journal* 28, no. 1 (1985): 34–49.

12. Kahneman, *Thinking, Fast and Slow*; Michael Lewis, *The Undoing Project: A Friendship That Changed the World* (New York: Penguin, 2016).

13. Keith E. Stanovich and Richard F. West, "Individual Differences in Reasoning: Implications for the Rationality Debate," *Behavioral & Brain Sciences* 23 (2000): 645–65; https://www.nobelprize.org/prizes/economic-sciences/2002/kahneman/lecture/.

14. Malcolm Gladwell, *Blink: The Power of Thinking without Thinking* (New York: Little, Brown, 2005).

15. Moore and Bazerman, *Decision Leadership*.

16. Dolly Chugh, "Societal and Managerial Implications of Implicit Social Cognition: Why Milliseconds Matter," *Social Justice Research* 17, no. 2 (2004): 203–22.

17. Max H. Bazerman, "Negotiator Judgment: A Critical Look at the Rationality Assumption," *American Behavioral Scientist* 27 (1983): 618–34; Max H. Bazerman and Margaret A. Neale, "Heuristics in Negotiation: Limitations to Effective Dispute Resolution," in *Negotiating in Organizations*, ed. Max H. Bazerman and Roy J. Lewicki (Thousand Oaks, CA: Sage Publications, 1983).

18. Carsten K. W. De Dreu, Sander L. Koole, and Wolfgang Steinel, "Unfixing the Fixed Pie: A Motivated Information-Processing Approach to Integrative Negotiation," *Journal of Personality and Social Psychology* 79, no. 6 (2000): 975–87.

19. Samuel G. B. Johnson, Jiwen Zhang, and Frank C. Keil, "Win-Win Denial: The Psychological Underpinnings of Zero-Sum Thinking," *Journal of Experimental Psychology: General* 151, no. 2 (2022): 455–74, https://doi.org/10.1037/xge0001083.

20. Ken Auletta, *Hollywood Ending: Harvey Weinstein and the Culture of Silence* (New York: Penguin Press, 2022).

21. Heather McGhee, *The Sum of Us: What Racism Costs Everyone and How We Can Prosper Together* (New York: One World, 2021).

22. Global Market Insights, "Non-Dairy Ice Cream Market Size by Source (Coconut Milk, Almond Milk, Cashew Milk, Soy Milk), by Flavor (Vanilla, Chocolate, Butter Pecan, Strawberry, Neapolitan, Cookies & Cream, Mint Choco Chip, Caramel), by Product (Impulse, Artisanal, Take Home), by Form (Singles, Blends), by Distribution Channel (Supermarkets, Convenience Stores, Food & Drink Specialists, Restaurants, Online Stores), Industry Analysis Report, Regional Outlook, Growth Potential, Price Trend, Competitive Market Share & Forecast, 2020–2026," August 2020, https://www.gminsights.com/industry-analysis/non-dairy-ice-cream-market.

23. Colin F. Camerer and Dan Lovallo, "Overconfidence and Excess Entry: An Experimental Approach," *American Economic Review* 89, no. 1 (1999): 306–18.

24. Don A. Moore, John M. Oesch, and Charlene Zietsma, "What Competition? Myopic Self-Focus in Market-Entry Decisions," *Organization Science* 18, no. 3 (2007): 440–54.

25. Don A. Moore and Daylian M. Cain, "Overconfidence and Underconfidence: When and Why People Underestimate (and Overestimate) the Competition," *Organizational Behavior & Human Decision Processes* 103 (2007): 197–213.

26. "Number of Passengers Carried by Selected Airline Groups in North America in 2021," https://www.statista.com/statistics/1109993/largest-airlines-north-america-passengers/.

27. Nick Ewen, "Special Report: TPG's Best US Airlines of 2022," The Points Guy, August 17, 2022, https://thepointsguy.com/news/tpg-best-us-airlines-2022/; Linnea Ahlgren, "JetBlue Knocks Delta & Southwest from Top Spot on American Customer Satisfaction Index," Simple Flying, April 26, 2022, https://simpleflying.com/jetblue-top-airline-american-customer-satisfaction-index/.

28. Ahlgren, "JetBlue Knocks Delta & Southwest from Top Spot on American Customer Satisfaction Index."

29. Laura Begley Bloom, "Ranked: The Best Airlines in America in 2022, According to J. D. Power Report," *Forbes*, May 11, 2022, https://www.forbes.com/sites/laurabegleybloom/2022/05/11/ranked-the-best-airlines-in-america-in-2022-according-to-jd-power-report/?sh=528c1a3d7407.

30. Ewen, "Special Report: TPG's Best US Airlines of 2022."

31. Chris Isidore, "Spirit Rejects JetBlue's Offer, Saying It Wants Less Lucrative Deal with Frontier," CNN Business, May 2, 2022, https://www.cnn.com/2022/05/02/investing/spirit-rejects-jetblue-offer/index.html.

32. Isidore, "Spirit Rejects JetBlue's Offer."

33. Matt Egan, "First on CNN: Elizabeth Warren Demands Airline Crackdown amid Travel Chaos," CNN Politics, July 26, 2022, https://www.cnn.com/2022/07/26/politics/airline -crackdown-travel-warren-padilla-buttigieg-letter/index.html.

34. Martin Shubik, "The Dollar Auction Game: A Paradox in Noncooperative Behavior and Escalation," *Journal of Conflict Resolution* 15, no. 1 (1971): 109–11.

35. Max H. Bazerman and Don A. Moore, *Judgment in Managerial Decision Making*, 8th ed. (Hoboken, NJ: Wiley, 2014). I donate the profits to charity or have the two highest bidders pay their losses in food and/or drinks for the class.

36. Linda Babcock, George Loewenstein, Samuel Issacharoff, and Colin F. Camerer, "Biased Judgments of Fairness in Bargaining," *American Economic Review* 85, no. 5 (1995): 1337–43.

37. Kristina A. Diekmann, Ann E. Tenbrunsel, Pri Pradhan Shah, Holly A. Schroth, and Max H. Bazerman, "The Descriptive and Prescriptive Use of Previous Purchase Price in Negotiations," *Organizational Behavior and Human Decision Processes* 66, no. 2 (1996): 179–91.

38. Babcock et al., "Biased Judgments of Fairness in Bargaining."

Chapter 12: Them

1. George A. Akerlof, "The Market for Lemons: Quality Uncertainty and the Market Mechanism," *Quarterly Journal of Economics* 89 (1970): 488–500.

2. Margaret A. Neale and Max H. Bazerman, "The Role of Perspective-Taking Ability in Negotiating under Different Forms of Arbitration," *Industrial and Labor Relations Review* 36 (1983): 378–88; Max H. Bazerman and Margaret A. Neale, "Improving Negotiation Effectiveness under Final Offer Arbitration: The Role of Selection and Training," *Journal of Applied Psychology* 67 (1982): 543–48.

3. Robert B. Cialdini, *Influence: Science and Practice*, 3rd ed. (New York: HarperCollins College Publishers, 1993).

4. Cialdini, *Influence: Science and Practice*; Noah J. Goldstein, Robert B. Cialdini, and Steve J. Martin, *Yes! 50 Scientifically Proven Ways to Be Persuasive* (New York Free Press, 2008).

5. Eric J. Johnson and Daniel Goldstein, "Do Defaults Save Lives?" *Science* 302 (2003): 1338–39.

6. Adapted from Richard H. Thaler, "Mental Accounting and Consumer Choice," *Marketing Science* 4 (1985): 199–214; and Richard H. Thaler, "Mental Accounting Matters," *Journal of Behavioral Decision Making* 12 (1999): 183–206.

7. Thaler, "Mental Accounting Matters."

8. Daniel Kahneman and Amos Tversky, "Prospect Theory: An Analysis of Decision under Risk," *Econometrica* 47 no. 2 (1979): 263–91.

9. Cialdini, *Influence: Science and Practice*.

10. Daniel Kahneman, Jack L. Knetsch, and Richard H. Thaler, "Experimental Tests of the Endowment Effect and the Coase Theorem," *Journal of Political Economy* 98, no. 6 (1990): 1325–48.

11. Jonathan L. Freedman and Scott C. Fraser, "Compliance without Pressure: The Foot-in-the-Door Technique," *Journal of Personality and Social Psychology* 4 (1966): 195–202.

12. Annie Duke, *Quit* (New York: Penguin Random House, 2022).

13. PMC Staff, "What Percentage of People Are Interested in Extended Auto Warranties?" Protect My Car, https://blog.protectmycar.com/what-percentage-of-people-are-interested-in -extended-auto-warranties.

14. Max H. Bazerman, *The Power of Noticing: What the Best Leaders See* (New York: Simon & Schuster, 2014).

15. Adam Pash, "Microsoft's Browser Comparison Chart Offends Anyone Who's Ever Used Another Browser," Lifehacker, June 19, 2009, https://lifehacker.com/microsofts-browser -comparison-chart-offends-anyone-whos-5296936.

16. Cialdini, *Influence: Science and Practice.*

17. Cialdini, *Influence: Science and Practice,* 229.

Chapter 13: Preparation in Context

1. Chris Robichaud, "Simulating the Demands of Ethical Decision-Making: A Simulation on Allocating Scarce Resources at Liberty Hospital," https://www.hks.harvard.edu/more /about/leadership-administration/academic-deans-office/slate/chris-robichaud-innovations -award.

2. Deborah J. Mitchell, J. Edward Russo, and Nancy Pennington, "Back to the Future: Temporal Perspective in the Explanation of Events," *Journal of Behavioral Decision Making* 2 (1989): 25–38, doi:10.1002 / bdm.3960020103

3. Gary Klein, "Performing a Project Premortem," *Harvard Business Review* 85, no. 9 (2007): 18–19, https://hbr.org/2007/09/performing-a-project-premortem.

4. Klein, "Performing a Project Premortem," 18–19.

Index

psychological factors: in ethics, 73–78; in extreme offers, 16–19; in 50–50 splits, 39–42; gains vs. losses, 164–65, 183–85. *See also* behavioral economics; social psychology

Putin, Vladimir, 161

quality of products/services, 89

question asking, 60, 81–82

Raiffa, Howard, 63, 164

USS *Randolf*, 127

rationality: assumption of, in game-theoretic and classical economics models, 2, 41–42, 115–17, 163–64; bounded, 163; in dispute resolution, 109–10; final-offer arbitration and, 156–58; incomplete, in behavioral situations, 2, 163–64; perspective taking on the other party's, 178. *See also* cognitive limitations

Rawls, John, 106–7, 109–10, 133

reciprocity, 60–61, 80–81, 186, 198

Redfin, 120, 128–29

reference group neglect, 169–70

relationships: channel richness and, 117–18; collectivist cultures' emphasis on, 42–43; as context, 9; extreme offers and, 25, 29–32; 50–50 splits and, 39–41, 43–44; political polarization as factor in, 12; pre-negotiation building of, 194

reservation price/value: BATNA as basis for, 26; concealing one's own, 61, 131; as core concept, 3, 6; as means of establishing the ZOPA, 27–28; of the other party, 26, 30, 141, 177, 181, 191; strategic value of, 5, 30, 36, 38, 141, 181, 190–91

reverse auctions, 149

rights: in dispute resolution, 103; interests in relation to, 105, 108; power in relation to, 104–5

risk reduction, 92–93, 164–65

risk-sharing. *See* contingent contracts

Robichaud, Chris, 193

Rodman, Dennis, 87

Rogers, Todd, 81

Ross, Michael, 76

Russia, 161–62

Russo, Jay, 198

SabbaticalHomes, 124

Samuelson, Bill, 115–16, 151, 179

Savitsky, Valentin, 127, 134

Schweitzer, Maurice, 16, 21, 30–31

scoring systems, 56, 195–96

select-crowd strategy, 136

self-interest, 75–77. *See also* conflicts of interest

self-serving bias, 74–77, 130, 133, 174–75

Shubik, Martin, 173

Sicoly, Fiore, 76

Silva-Risso, Jorge, 122

Simon, Herbert, 163

Sinclair, Upton, 74

Sinema, Kyrsten, 139–40

Singer, Peter, 208n4

Slice Insurance, 121

social heuristics, 40

social psychology, 178, 181–82. *See also* behavioral economics

Socrates, 135

Soviet Union, and Cold War nuclear threats, 68–70, 126–28, 134, 178

special-interest groups, 80

Spirit Airlines, 170–73

Stanovich, Keith, 165

status quo, 182–83

stereotypes, 10–11

Stevens, Carl, 156–59

Subramanian, Guhan, 145, 150–51

Super Pumped (miniseries), 51

Surowiecki, James, 135

Svirsky, Dan, 122

System 1 thinking, 165–66

System 2 thinking, 165–66

Tanzer, Tommy, 23, 24

Taskrabbit, 120

27–30, 46–50, 53–56, 60–62; as obstacle
to value creation, 53
Viking Investments, 174
virtue ethics, 72–73
Voss, Chris, 34
Vrbo, 113

Wall Street Journal (newspaper), 135, 136
warranties, 186–87
Warren, Elizabeth, 172
Weinstein, Harvey, 167–68
West, Richard, 165
Whitworth, Andrew, 85–86
Wilson, Edward, 127
winner's curse, 116–17, 151–52
"win-win" principle, 34, 82–83, 167
wisdom of crowds, 135–37
women, salaries of, 19

World Health Organization, 16–17
World War II, 161

Zeckhauser, Richard, 150
zero-sum paradigm, 37, 50, 52, 167–68
Zettelmeyer, Florian, 122
Zillow, 129
zone of possible agreement (ZOPA): initial
offers and, 27–29, 31–32, 38, 183; strategic
value of, 191; value creation and, 49–50,
53–54
Zoom: attitudes toward, 114; as communication platform, 9–10, 114–15, 117–19,
209n2; negotiating on, 1, 113–20, 123–24;
preparations for appearance on, 119–20;
teaching on, 9–10, 97
ZOPA. *See* zone of possible agreement
(ZOPA)